Windows 2000 Clustering and Load Balancing Handbook

ISBN 0-13-065199-0

90000

9 780130 651990

PRENTICE HALL PTR MICROSOFT® TECHNOLOGIES SERIES

BACKOFFICE

- Microsoft Exchange 2000: Programming Collaborative Web Applications
Ammann

- Microsoft SQL Server 2000 Optimization Guide
Fields

- BizTalk: Implementing Business-To-Business E-Commerce
Kobielus

- Designing Enterprise Solutions with Microsoft Technologies
Kemp, Kemp, Goncalves

- Microsoft Site Server 3.0 Commerce Edition
Libertone, Scoppa

- Building Microsoft SQL Server 7 Web Sites
Byrne

- Optimizing SQL Server 7
Schneider, Goncalves

ADMINISTRATION

- Samba Essentials for Windows Administrators
Wilson

- Tuning and Sizing Windows 2000 for Maximum Performance
Aubley

- Windows 2000 Cluster Server Guidebook
Libertone

- Windows 2000 Hardware and Disk Management
Simmons

- Windows 2000 Server: Management and Control, Third Edition
Spencer, Goncalves

- Creating Active Directory Infrastructures
Simmons

- Windows 2000 Registry
Sanna

- Configuring Windows 2000 Server
Simmons

- Supporting Windows NT and 2000 Workstation and Server
Mohr

- Zero Administration Kit for Windows
McInerney

- Windows NT 4.0 Server Security Guide
Goncalves

- Windows NT Security
McInerney

CERTIFICATION

- Core MCSE: Windows 2000 Edition
Dell

- Core MCSE: Designing a Windows 2000 Directory Services Infrastructure
Simmons

- MCSE: Implementing and Supporting Windows 98
Dell

- Core MCSE
Dell

- Core MCSE: Networking Essentials
Keogh

- MCSE: Administering Microsoft SQL Server 7
Byrne

- MCSE: Implementing and Supporting Microsoft Exchange Server 5.5
Goncalves

- MCSE: Internetworking with Microsoft TCP/IP
Ryvkin, Houde, Hoffman

- MCSE: Implementing and Supporting Microsoft Proxy Server 2.0
Ryvkin, Hoffman

- MCSE: Implementing and Supporting Microsoft SNA Server 4.0
Mariscal

- MCSE: Implementing and Supporting Microsoft Internet Information Server 4
Dell

- MCSE: Implementing and Supporting Web Sites Using Microsoft Site Server 3
Goncalves

- MCSE: Microsoft System Management Server 2
Jewett

- MCSE: Implementing and Supporting Internet Explorer 5
Dell

- Core MCSD: Designing and Implementing Desktop Applications with Microsoft Visual Basic 6
Holzner

- MCSD: Planning and Implementing SQL Server 7
Vacca

- MCSD: Designing and Implementing Web Sites with Microsoft FrontPage 98
Karlins

Windows 2000 Clustering and Load Balancing Handbook

JOSEPH M. LAMB

PH
PTR

Prentice Hall PTR
Upper Saddle River, NJ 07458
www.phptr.com

Library of Congress Cataloging-in-Publication Data

Lamb, Joseph.
    Windows 2000 clustering and load balancing handbook/Joseph Lamb.
      p.   cm.
    Includes bibliographical references and index.
    ISBN 0-13-065199-0
    1. Microsoft Windows (Computer file) 2. Operating systems (Computers) I. title.

    QA76.76.)63 L3547 2001
    005.4'4769—dc21   2001045920

Editorial/production supervision: Jan Schwartz
Acquisitions editor: Jill Harry
Marketing manager: Dan DePasquale
Manufacturing manager: Alexis R. Heydt-Long
Buyer: Maura Zaldivar
Editorial assistant: Justin Somma
Cover design director: Jerry Votta
Cover designer: Talar Boorujy
Art director: Gail Cocker-Bogusz
Interior design: Meg VanArsdale
Composition: Laurel Road Publishing Services

 © 2002 Prentice Hall PTR
Prentice-Hall, Inc.
Upper Saddle River, NJ 07458

Prentice Hall books are widely used by corporations and government agencies
for training, marketing, and resale.

The publisher offers discounts on this book when ordered in bulk quantities.
For more information, contact: Corporate Sales Department, Phone: 800-382-3419;
Fax: 201-236-7141; E-mail: corpsales@prenhall.com; or write: Prentice Hall PTR,
Corp. Sales Dept., One Lake Street, Upper Saddle River, NJ 07458.

All products or services mentioned in this book are the trademarks or service marks of their
respective companies or organizations.

Screen shot(s) reprinted by permission of Microsoft Corporation.

Printed in the United States of America

10 9 8 7 6 5 4 3 2 1

ISBN 0-13-065199-0

Pearson Education LTD.
Pearson Education Australia PTY, Limited
Pearson Education Singapore, Pte. Ltd.
Pearson Education North Asia Ltd.
Pearson Education Canada, Ltd.
Pearson Educación de Mexico, S.A. de C.V.
Pearson Education—Japan
Pearson Education Malaysia, Pte. Ltd.
Pearson Education, Upper Saddle River, New Jersey

CONTENTS

PREFACE

So, it is 11:30 a.m., time for lunch. You close the spreadsheet you are working on, lock your workstation, grab your keys, and hit the door. You think that life could not be any better. Short hours, great job as a senior systems administrator, and all the respect in the world from vice presidents who don't have a clue what you do for a living. Ten minutes into lunch, your pager beeps, catching you off guard. Knowing that your pager has not gone off in the three months that you have been at this company compels you to quickly view the message. You look down at your alphanumeric pager to see the message, "Web site is down again...where are you?" Knowing that you are in charge of the Web site, you quickly wolf down your lunch, grab your barely opened soda, and scoot back to the office. Upon entering the office, your boss screams from his office, "Johnson, get in here!" For the next 30 minutes, you receive a thorough thrashing from your superior. It seems that prior to your employment, three other systems administrators had been fired because they could not keep the Web site, the company's main source of income, online. You inform your boss that the problems with the Web site are due to the shabby work your predecessor engineered (an excuse you will be able to use only once) and promise him that it will never happen again. He believes your barrage of techy jargon and says that if you value your job, you had better make sure the Web site is re-engineered in a more reliable fashion. You leave his office a bit distraught, because you don't have a clue how to keep the Web server from crashing again.

This is a typical scenario. Although maybe a bit more dramatic than most, the story is a common one. The rise of dotcoms through the 1990s introduced the world to the joys of electronic commerce. Buying and selling goods online just might be the future of all commerce. However, just as brick-and-mortar businesses cannot survive if they keep sporadic operating hours, companies that build their business around an e-commerce model, but fail to engineer fault-tolerant and reliable applications, are bound to fail. Downtime for an e-commerce business means lost revenue. Downtime for any company is intolerable, but for an e-commerce company, downtime can mean bankruptcy.

How do you build a server that will provide 100 percent uptime? How do you engineer a system that will deliver high performance and high availability? How do you provide data to users in a way that is consistent and reliable? Many innovators have attempted to build computers that employ fault tolerance in every area, including hard disks, memory, power, and networking, but these machines still fall short of the goal. Other attempts have been made to provide redundancy within different types of architectures (such as VAX and mainframe environments), but they have been limited in nature and not a strong fit for e-commerce client/server computing.

Clustering to the rescue! Clustering is a concept that was developed to provide a fault-tolerant design to client/server environments. A cluster is a group of computers that cooperate as one unit to serve a particular application or service. Clustering rescues system administrators and designers by providing the ability to join several machines together to provide the same service. Clusters employ a concept known as *failover* to ensure that if one server within a group fails, another server within the group will take over the client load.

The early clustering deployments used hardware devices as a mechanism to forward requests for the same IP address to multiple machines, but these solutions were difficult to implement and cost inhibitive. As the clustering technologies have grown, we have seen the clustering market explode. Companies are now deploying fault-tolerant SAN (storage area networks) to host applications and services that used to be hosted on single servers. Clients can now transparently connect to clusters of servers and reliably run applications.

Not long ago, Microsoft decided to join the party by releasing Microsoft Clustering Services (MSCS) for Windows NT 4.0 Enterprise edition. This began Microsoft's journey into the world of clustering. Microsoft now has a suite of products designed to allow administrators the tools and services necessary to deploy high availability Web sites, databases, and applications in a way that distances itself from prior service deployment methods. Through the use of MSCS, servers can be clustered together to provide high availability and reliability. The Microsoft Network Load Balancing (NLB) service allows administrators to build large server farms—clusters of servers that operate together to perform a single function, distributing load across the cluster and providing failover for server failures. Application Center 2000 enhances the abilities of the NLB service by granting administrators the power of a single console where NLB clusters can be created and managed.

These tools, in conjunction with other Microsoft technologies such as Active Directory, Distributed file system, and Internet Information Server, provide a solid foundation for the deployment of applications and services that outperform any system to date. Performance, high availability, and reliability that were once only a distant vision can now be obtained and utilized to deploy mission-critical applications and services.

What Does This Book Include?

This book seeks to guide you through the development and deployment of clustered server solutions. The object is not to teach every possible configuration option associated with each technology (for that would be a very large book), but to guide you through the implementation of several different clustering technologies. This book can be used as a handbook for the step-by-step construction of a clustered solution. It discusses not only the functionality of each product, but wise design goals that should be the focus of your implementation. With this book, you will learn

- The problems with current networking solutions that are solved by cluster server implementations.
- How to design and document a cluster server solution for any type of application or service.
- The hardware and software necessary to construct a cluster server solution.
- How to implement a failover cluster using MSCS.
- How to implement Microsoft Exchange Server on a cluster server.
- How to implement Microsoft SQL Server on a cluster server.
- How to implement file and print shares on a cluster server.
- How to implement Web servers and FTP servers on a cluster server.
- How to implement Microsoft NLB on multiple machines to form a Web server cluster.
- How to design and configure an NLB solution using Microsoft Application Center 2000.

You can read this book from beginning to end, or you can use it as a guide for the deployment of a particular cluster server solution. If you choose to use it as a guide, make sure to read chapter 1 through 3 as a preface to your implementation so that you will have the design skills necessary to implement your solution.

Who Should Read This Book?

The intended audience of this book is anyone who wants to learn clustering concepts, design, and implementation skills. This can be the system administrator who has never built a server cluster or the technology student who wishes to augment his or her networking knowledge. Vendors who implement solutions on clustered servers may also benefit from the work, for the implementation of CRM, ERP, and e-commerce applications on Microsoft-based clusters is becoming more common. And finally, vendors who currently market clustering products and services may also wish to read this book to increase their knowledge of Microsoft's clustering and load-balancing technology products.

What Do I Need to Use This Book?

If you are a student learning to construct a cluster server or you work within an organization that has a problem with your building a Microsoft cluster server on production hardware, you are going to need a few things to complete the lessons.
If you want to build a failover cluster, you will need the following items:

- Two Pentium class computers equipped with two hard drive controllers (each machine must contain at least one SCSI controller) and two network cards (each)
- An external drive array with a minimum of three hard drives
- Two 8-port hubs/switches
- Four CAT5 patch cables
- Windows 2000 Advanced Server or Datacenter Server software
- Microsoft Exchange Server 2000 software (if applicable)
- Microsoft SQL Server 2000 software (if applicable)

If you want to build a network load-balanced cluster, you will need the following items:

- Two Pentium class computers equipped with a single IDE or SCSI hard drive (in each) and two network cards per machine
- Two 8-port hubs/switches
- Four CAT5 patch cables
- Windows 2000 Server, Advanced Server, or Datacenter Server software
- Application Center 2000 software (if applicable)

Conventions

Throughout this book, you will find helpful information in the form of notes and warnings.

Note

This is a note box, and you will find many of them in each chapter. Note boxes are used to give you details that are important to "note." These notes address issues that you will encounter during your implementation.

Warning

The warning text box should not be ignored. A warning text box will alert you to issues of a critical nature pertaining to the topic at hand. You would do well to carefully read each warning message.

Feedback

If you would like more information about clustering, need help with your clustering solution, or just want to submit feedback, feel free to submit your responses to *jlamb@qsourcenetworks.com* or visit the Web site of Qsource Networks at *www.qsourcenetworks.com.*

ACKNOWLEDGMENTS

The writing of a book, regardless of the type, is a long and arduous journey. It takes not only the knowledge and desire, but also a team of people who are dedicated to the book's success. The following acknowledgments include a list of people, all of whom I would say are part of my "team." I would like to thank:

- First of all, Prentice Hall, for granting me the opportunity to complete this work.
- Jill Harry, Jim Markham, Jan Schwartz and all of the people at Prentice Hall for their efforts in the editing of the manuscript.
- Microsoft, for creating a suite of products worth studying.
- My partner and friend, Kim Y. Tan, for all of the resources he provided for me during the long writing process.
- My mentor, Dr. Ricky Cotton, at Southeastern College, for teaching me to love words.
- My loving and supportive wife Jenny and my three wonderful children, for allowing me to dedicate time to the writing and encouraging me through the process.

Chapter 1

CLIMBING THE MOUNTAIN: 24/7 DATA ACCESS

Technology is, in many ways, more an art than a science. It is driven more by innovative minds than by textbook models. Much in the same way our drive to invent products for the future is often hindered by a lack of engineering ability, the development of products for the Internet generation has often times placed a distance between what the developer envisioned and the final product. After years of developing products under such constricting realities, it is easy to see how the integration of those products could be challenging. For example, the idea and development of tools to produce media-rich Web content was created many years before the telecommunications industry could provide the necessary bandwidth to make those products a reality. So, for many years, companies tried to integrate media-filled Web content with their own products and ideas, causing them to be challenged by the integration of products and the limitation of bandwidth.

Amidst the mass of connectivity now flowing through our homes and telephone lines, rarely a day goes by that we do not have an "imperfect" experience on the Internet. We all have left shopping cart Web sites due to badly written programs or slow response times. Even on our best day, we often cannot connect to our favorite site or online store. Most people don't give thought to why they cannot access a site; they just accept it as commonplace, for the Internet has always been known as an unreliable, public medium.

A chief executive from one of the largest software companies in the world once criticized the automobile industry, stating, "If the automobile industry had grown the way the technology industry has grown, we would all be driving hover crafts." In retort, a chief executive from a leading automobile maker said that although the automobile industry could have grown that fast, the result would have been unreliable automobiles that stopped for no reason, consistently failed to start, and required constant maintenance to keep on the road.

Although the automobile executive responded in jest, his point rings clear. People who purchase automobiles expect them to be reliable. They expect them to operate when the key is turned, to go when the accelerator is pressed, and to stop when the brake is applied. Unreliability and component failure is not acceptable.

In the technology arena, users accept intermittent failures as commonplace, viewing it as a price paid for innovation. The demand for bulletproof hardware and software has not been great because the personal computer, from the date of its inception, has always been riddled with a lack of *fault tolerance*—the ability to recover from a single point of failure (SPOF). As the computing environment in companies began to move from internal data processing to a model that was more accessible by their clients, it made sense to replace the large mainframe environment with a lower cost client/server architecture that is accessible by a World Wide Web browser—giving birth to the era of e-commerce.

Unfortunately, as the systems in use changed from large, reliable mainframe systems to low-cost client/server solutions, companies sacrificed fault tolerance for cost and the ease of integration with existing systems. Systems and applications became less reliable, even though they were more functional and easier to use. The sacrifice of fault tolerance was unavoidable due to a lack of client/server technologies that could provide the reliability and performance of a mainframe. But things are now changing.

Today, systems and services are being designed for high availability. Applications such as ERP (Enterprise Resource Planning) databases, business-to-business (B2B) e-commerce storefronts, and Web portals are in high demand. Along with that demand comes a need for servers that can provide data to users in a reliable fashion. Similarly to how mainframes were often used for data center environments that demanded 24/7 access, groups of servers, known as *clusters*, are now being deployed within data centers to rival, if not equal, the reliability and stability of the mainframe. A cluster, loosely defined, is a group of computers that work together to create a virtual server that can provide seamless services to a client or group of clients.

To acquire a better understanding of why a cluster is needed and how it provides the same reliability as a mainframe environment, several areas of concern must be addressed: fault tolerance, performance, scalability, and reliability.

1.1 Fault Tolerance

Fault tolerance is the ability of a system to respond to failure in a way that does not hinder the service offering provided by the server. This is often referred to as "graceful" response because it eliminates the failure gracefully, without interrupting service to users. Fault tolerance theory was applied to several other industries before it was ever used within a technology setting.

Consider the airline industry. If an airline did not have fault tolerance built into its airplanes, one small failure could bring a plane crashing to the ground. To avoid such catastrophe, airlines have eliminated every SPOF that they can. Most commercial airplanes have not one engine, but several, all of which are capable of keeping the plane in the air if one or more engines should stop working.

The average home computer user does not have fault tolerance built into his or her system. What happens if the power supply—the component that provides power to the machine—fails? The machine does not function anymore. What if the hard drive stops working? The user will likely lose not only the ability to run his or her computer, but also the data resident on the hard drive. Computers built for the consumer market have several SPOFs and typically do not provide fault tolerance. This is because of cost and the uptime factor. The machine you run at home does not provide services to other machines that may need to 24/7 access it, and therefore the cost of the fault tolerance is outweighed by the home user's need for inexpensive computing.

Many people run backup software to eliminate the risk of losing data, which is good practice, but backup software is a disaster recovery option, not a substitute for fault tolerance. Disaster recovery is a means of restoring your computer and all your data in the event of a failure, but it does not prevent the failure or assist the computer in functioning in spite of the failure.

In a corporate environment, fault tolerance is a bit more important, not necessarily for the workstations in use by the company's employees, but for the servers that contain the company's data. In most companies today, business cannot operate without the data stored on the server. How many times have you called a merchant to hear, "I would love to help you with that, but our systems are down right now." Companies have developed a dependence upon technology to the point that they cannot operate without the "system."

To ensure that downtime is minimized, network engineers apply fault tolerance theory to their systems and applications. They ask the question, If *blank* were to fail, would my system still run and provide service to users? That blank could be anything that assists in providing an application or service to the company's users. For instance, if the power were to fail, would the system

3

still run and provide service to users? Unless your system is battery-powered or protected by an uninterruptible power supply (UPS) system, then the answer is no, and power becomes an SPOF for your system.

Fault tolerance theory should be applied not only to the environmental issues such as power and cabling, but also to the machine or server itself. Within the server, you have several points of failure: the power supply, the hard drive(s), the network card, the motherboard, the memory, and so on. A failure in any one of those areas can cause your system not to function. Hardware manufacturers have begun to provide fault tolerance within their architectures, often building redundancy in the power supply or network card, and systems such as *RAID* (Redundant Array of Inexpensive Disks) have been developed to provide fault tolerance to as many parts of the machine as possible. However, even in the most advanced systems built today, redundancy for all of the components is not available. If your server has redundant power supplies, redundant network cards, redundant hard disks, and redundant processors, and the machine experiences a motherboard failure, the system still goes down.

So, although every machine you run that provides business-critical functionality should have every form of redundancy available, even the most advanced hardware/software combinations don't offer complete redundancy and fault tolerance within a single machine.

1.2 Performance

Within any system, performance is always important. The performance of your personal computer in some ways dictates how fast you can get your work done. Servers are not any different, with the exception of user quantity. Personal computers typically have only one person to support, whereas servers have to support thousands, sometimes millions, of users. The ability of a machine to respond to a request within a certain period of time is greatly affected by the performance of the machine. Many different items make up the quality of performance.

1.2.1 CPU

The CPU—central processing unit—has often been referred to as the "brain" of the computer, and rightly so, for all information that is processed on a computer is controlled by the CPU. On a mainframe system, the CPU would often span several circuit boards, but in personal computers and servers, the CPU is housed within a small chip on the motherboard, called a *microprocessor*.

The CPU consists of two components: the arithmetic logical unit (ALU) and the control unit. The ALU is responsible for arithmetic and all logical operations performed on the machine, while the control unit is responsible for the extraction, decoding, and execution of instructions stored in memory as well as for calling on the ALU when necessary for computation.

Note

Remember, even though we use the decimal system and text to communicate, the computer uses only binary—a system of language that uses only 0's and 1's to communicate. The CPU plays a vital role in coding and decoding the 0's and 1's into a language that users can understand.

Within any computer, the CPU is what dictates how fast the machine can process information. The CPU must process all information that is sent to the screen (as well as a lot that is not). A slow processor will be evident to the user. Even more so, a computer that serves users on the Internet or within a large organization will suffer performance loss due to a slow processor.

Most of the servers that are manufactured today can now be equipped with dual processors: two processors within the same machine sharing the processing load. Some hardware manufacturers are producing machines that run between 4 and 64 processors within the same machine. As these types of machines, as they become more affordable, will assist systems administrators in eliminating the processor as a possible bottleneck within a system.

1.2.2 Memory

The memory within a machine, also called RAM (random access memory), is responsible for short-term storage for programs and applications. A computer uses RAM to cache working data. In the same way that a human brain has a short-term memory and long-term memory, a computer has RAM, which stores data temporarily, and a hard drive, which stores data for extensive periods. While a hard drive is nonvolatile memory, meaning that it retains data regardless of the power state; RAM is volatile memory, for it loses all data stored when a machine is powered off.

The importance of memory cannot be underestimated. When a PC or server loads a program or operating system, the files needed to run that application are loaded into memory. If there is not enough memory to load the applications and files being used, the system will be forced to store the excess data

5

on the hard drive, where access will be significantly slower. To ensure optimal performance, assess the memory needs of your application prior to purchasing hardware and ensure that you have adequate memory not only for the application you want to run, but for the operating system and services as well.

1.2.2.1 Memory Types

There are two basic types of RAM, SRAM (static RAM), and DRAM (dynamic RAM). SRAM is memory that remembers its content, while DRAM needs to be refreshed every few milliseconds. While SRAM is more efficient, it is also more expensive and tends to be used for L2 cache rather than for system memory.

Because SRAM is much more difficult to produce, the industry has standardized with DRAM. DRAM comes in many flavors:

- FPM—fast page mode
- ECC—error-correcting code
- EDO—extended data output
- SDRAM—synchronous dynamic RAM

FPM RAM was the first type of RAM introduced to Pentium computing and came in SIMM modules that had to be loaded in pairs. The transfer type was 70ns and 60ns. Shortly after its introduction, FPM RAM was replaced with EDO RAM, a faster (60ns or 50ns), more reliable memory architecture. Because of the demand for fault tolerance, ECC RAM was created. ECC RAM provides error correcting within the RAM itself. ECC was much more reliable than its predecessors and became the standard for PC-based servers due to its parity-based error checking and recovery. Recently, SDRAM has become the most common memory in use due to the fast response times of 8ns to 12ns. SDRAM also integrates the error-checking technology of ECC RAM, making it the smartest choice for PCs and servers alike.

1.2.2.2 Virtual Memory

Although a PC or server may have a significant amount of RAM, there will always be times when the machine needs more memory than it has. To overcome this limitation in some of the first personal computers ever developed, engineers designed the operating system to use what is called virtual memory. By using virtual memory, an operating system sets aside a small portion of the hard drive to be used like RAM, so that if the machine needs to work with more information than can be stored in RAM, it will use the hard drive space as a "virtual" memory space. This type of process is often referred to as paging or accessing the page file, for the space used for virtual memory is actually a file stored on the computer's hard drive.

Virtual memory allows for computers that have a memory limitation to run programs they may otherwise not be able to run; however, there is a drawback. Reading and writing data to the hard drive is a much slower process than reading and writing data to RAM and is therefore a performance hindrance in many cases.

For most servers, a performance monitor program will detail the amount of paging taking place on a server. Paging should be minimal. If paging is consistently high, it is typically indicative of a lack of RAM within the machine.

1.2.3 Disks

The function of the hard disk should be central to any discussion of performance. If the CPU in a computer is the brain, and the RAM is the short-term memory, then the hard disk is the long-term memory. The ability to recall information that may not have been accessed for a long period of time is core to any computer system.

A hard disk—or hard drive—is a magnetic stack of flat metal platters that store information in contiguous sectors. A small arm, or spindle, moves back and forth across the disk to read and write information to the disk. As mentioned before, the hard disk, unlike RAM, does not lose its data when the computer is powered off. The data that is stored is permanent until it is deleted or overwritten.

The performance of the disk is related to the ability of the access arm to move back and forth across the disk and obtain information. There are two types of hard disks that are common in the PC market: SCSI disks and IDE disks. IDE stands for Integrated Device Electronics and is the standard mass-storage device interface for PCs. IDE allows for two devices to be connected to each interface, typically configured in a master/slave role. The transfer speeds used to be limited to 16 mbps (megabits per second), but recently have been enhanced to provide 33 mbps (ATA/33) in most machines and up to 100 mbps (ATA/100) in new models.

SCSI stands for Small Computer System Interface. SCSI, pronounced *skuzzy*, is a mass-storage device interface that is widely used within high-end computing environments. This architecture provides up to 160 mbps transfer rates. SCSI is unique because, unlike IDE, SCSI supports up to seven devices on one interface. Devices attached to a SCSI bus are daisy chained, using a special cable so they can all be controlled and maintained by the same controller. Because they are on the same controller, multiple disks can be written to and read from simultaneously. This makes SCSI a faster platform than IDE and more suitable to the server market. The difference, however, is in the cost. SCSI devices tend to be more expensive that IDE devices.

As you can see, the type of hard drive you use for a system can greatly impact the performance.

1.2.4 Network

Among all of the items that allow a computer to send and receive information, the network connectivity is the most important. The fastest computer in the world is of no value if it cannot serve its clients. It is vital that the speed of the network that a computer is connected to be fast enough to allow the processing within a machine to operate freely, without hindrance. Too often, individuals invest significant amounts of money into hardware and then use second-rate network standards to connect it to the network.

One of the very first LAN standards was called Token-Ring and ran at 4 mbps. This technology, pioneered by IBM, was on the forefront of networking and dictated that traffic flowing through a network should follow a ring pattern. This technology implemented a virtual ring that was passed from computer to computer on the network. When a computer had the token, it could transmit and receive all messages destined for other computers on the network. When the computer did not have the token, it remained silent. This created a highly fault-tolerant networking platform. Later, the Token-Ring specification was redesigned to operate at 16 mbps, which offered high-speed, fault-tolerant data transmission and a vast improvement over the 4 mbps standard. Unfortunately, strict patenting laws, driven by IBM, made the technology expensive to implement.

Shortly after the development of Token-Ring networking, another standard called Ethernet was being developed. Ethernet was a joint effort by Xerox, Digital Equipment Corporation, and Intel. Ethernet uses a bus or star topology and supports data transfer rates from 10 mbps to 1000 mbps. Unlike Token-Ring's token-passing technology, Ethernet provides a network where all machines can broadcast their information at any time. When more than one machine speaks at once, it causes a collision, which in turn causes all the machines on the network to "timeout" for a specific period of time before retransmitting. This technology, on the surface, may seem inferior to token-passing technologies because of the constant collisions, but Ethernet, due to its inexpensive cost and nonproprietary development, has far surpassed the installed base of Token-Ring networks.

From a performance standpoint, network speed should never be the bottleneck in the deployment of any system. Fast-changing technology horizons have ensured that high bandwidth remain inexpensive and easy to maintain. Technologies such as ATM, Gigabit Ethernet, and FDDI are all examples of high-speed networking options that can provide a system with high connection speeds and thus improved performance.

1.3 Scalability

Scalability is the ability of a system or service to adapt to increased demand. Scalability is essential to any system or service that may need to grow to meet the needs of a particular client base.

To understand scalability, a simple analogy is helpful. If you were to purchase a three–bedroom, two-bath home, and the following year you added one new family member, you would need a house that is scalable—meaning that you need a house that can be easily modified to meet the needs of a larger family. Adding a bedroom to the home would "scale" the house to meet the increased need. If you could not add a bedroom due to zoning restrictions or architectural issues, your home would be unable to scale. The only solution then would be to sell your home and buy another one that is larger.

In a networking environment, the same rings true. A network manager does not want to replace all of the networking equipment in the company to meet the needs of an additional fifty employees. It is more desirable to add the necessary equipment to the existing network so that the network will scale to meet the needs of the additional employees. Scalability is essential, not only for the cost savings, but for the ability to add additional capacity while minimizing downtime.

Consider the personal computer. When a person buys a personal computer from a computer store, they typically ask the question, Is it upgradeable? What they are actually asking is whether the computer will scale to meet their future needs. Most systems that you purchase will allow you to upgrade the memory, upgrade the video card, and in some cases, upgrade the processor. But some machines are built to reduce cost, not provide scalability. These machines usually have constraints that don't allow you to upgrade the memory or processor. These machines are cost effective, but can only be useful for about one to two years, whereas a machine that is scalable can be useful for about three to five years.

Systems that are designed for use as Internet servers or intranet servers have the same scalability issues, but also the added issue of what is often referred to as dynamic scalability. Dynamic scalability is the ability of a system or service to adapt to an increased demand within a short span of time. This span of time can be day-to-day, hour-to-hour, or minute-to-minute.

Many companies use Internet servers as a way to survey public opinion. Consider a company that decides to advertise a new Web site for the first time during a commercial break on Super Bowl Sunday. Once the commercial is aired, there will be literally millions of people hitting the site in response to the advertising. And seeing that the commercial most likely cost several million dollars, the owner of the site does not want to lose a single connection to the site. This scenario demands that the Internet server scale from a zero amount of traffic to one million plus hits worth of traffic within a matter of minutes. The ability for this system to handle the traffic is the system's dynamic scalability.

1.4 Reliability

Reliability is the ability of a system to provide a service without interruption. Although related to fault tolerance, performance, and scalability, reliability is the ability to provide continual service without regard to the amount of use or failure within the system. Reliability is related closely to availability, for the availability of a system proves its reliability.

Using the earlier example of the automobile, the reliability of a new automobile is expected. When the key is turned, the engine should turn over. A racecar driver knows the necessity of reliability. Mechanics go through the racecar in detail before the driver is allowed to race. The failure of one part within the vehicle could cause the driver to lose the race—or to lose his or her life.

Similarly, to ensure reliability, a systems designer must inspect every part of the system. A failure within any part of the system could cause the application or service to be unavailable to requests, proving its unreliability. To build reliability into a system, the designer must analyze all of the points previously discussed:

- Fault tolerance of the system
- Performance of the system
- Scalability of the system

Failure within a hard drive or network card could cause the server to quit servicing clients. Too many users could cause the system to respond slowly to requests, or to quit responding all together. If the application cannot scale to meet the needs of the clients as those needs change from day to day, the system could experience hours or even days of downtime caused by frequent hardware upgrades or replacements.

1.5 Designing Reliable Data Access

Throughout the corporate world, systems and services provide a communications and data storage channel that assists companies in generating revenue. The loss of productivity due to systems failures numbers in the billions of dollars per year. Client/server systems of the past have been powerless to reduce downtime, but things are changing. Now, more than ever, there are products and services available to keep systems up and running in spite of component failure, power failures, or user error, and although no software or hardware product can guarantee a zero percent failure rate, today's technologies can "virtually" eliminate hardware and software failures.

There are two scenarios that cause a system or service to be unavailable.

1. A component that is part of the system, or a dependency of the system, malfunctions, leaving the application or service (or path to the application or service) in an unusable or unavailable state.
2. The network load on an application or service is so great that the server cannot respond to client requests in a timely fashion.

To (virtually) eliminate these two events from taking place, a systems engineer or designer must seek to design systems that apply the following methodology:

1. Downtime due to failures within components of the system or components that the system is dependent upon does not affect the operation of the application or service being provided.
2. The application or service must respond in a timely manner to all requests, regardless of network load or requests being processed.

Note

It is important to note that no system can guarantee 100 percent uptime. There are many products and services on the market that tout figures such as 99.9995 percent uptime, but these are statistics typically taken from a controlled environment with minimal load on the server(s). Realistically, an engineer should never hope to achieve 100 percent uptime, but should strive to minimize unnecessary downtime due to component failures or software upgrades. The focus should always be the quality and reliability of service provided to the client, not the amount of uptime.

Let's take a brief look at how a designer might approach the construction of a reliable data access solution. To approach the design correctly, the designer must seek to provide the following:

- Fault tolerance
- High performance
- Scalability
- Reliability

The questions a designer must ask include, What are the needs of my application? Does the application need to operate 24 hours a day, 7 days a week? Where will the server physically be placed, and how will clients access it? Does the application need to be accessed by clients on the Internet? These questions help the designer discern what connectivity must be engineered to allow clients to access the application.

The designer continues the planning by envisioning the completed system and systematically tracing the connectivity from the client to the server, listing each component that is encountered as a client might access the system. Assuming this is an Internet application, let's start with the typical Internet client.

The client machine itself has many points of failure, but because they are beyond the control of the systems designer, they are ignored for the moment. The client machine is connected to the Internet through a dial-up line or a network connection of some sort. This is a critical point of failure, but again, beyond the control of the designer. The client makes a request for our application through an ISP (Internet service provider). The request travels across the Internet (through many routers and data lines) until it reaches the designer's Internet connection. At that point the request will most likely hit a Channel Service Unit/Data Service Unit (CSU/DSU), then a router, which will pass the request to a firewall. The firewall will pass the request through a cable to a switch or hub, which will pass the request on to the server, which is also connected with a network cable. The server will access the application by reading data from the hard drive or memory and send the desired information back to the client through the same route.

If you count all of the devices between the client and the server, you will easily see that there are many points of failure that could prevent the application from being accessible. Some of these items are not within the control of the designer, but many of them are. Take a look at the items that are within the control of the designer:

- The Internet circuit
- The DSU/CSU
- The router
- The firewall
- The switch or hub
- The server network card
- The server power supply
- The server hard drive
- The server memory
- All cables used to attach all network devices

All of the items listed can be controlled by the designer and must be evaluated to determine optimal fault tolerance. The failure of any one of these items will cause the application or service to be unavailable. Some of the items typically cannot be made fault-tolerant without great expense, but each item should be scrutinized to see what can be done to boost the reliability of the system. Table 1-1 lists each item and some of the fault tolerance options that are typically used.

Beyond fault tolerance, a designer must also consider the performance and scalability of the system. Hardware and software must be chosen that will provide high performance. The performance of a system is determined by usage. If you are in a controlled environment where the number of users is constant, it can be easy to determine performance requirements, but if you are building an Internet application, determining the performance requirements can be a bit tricky. A good plan is to always overestimate your need. If you believe the servers within your system need 256 MB of RAM to operate efficiently, buy 512 MB of RAM for each server. Always leave plenty of room. Don't just meet the requirements—exceed them. This will allow room for future growth.

Table 1-1   Fault Tolerance Options

Device/Item	Fault Tolerance Options
Internet Circuit	A secondary, low-bandwidth circuit could be installed to direct traffic through the event of a failure on the primary circuit.
DSU/CSU	DSU/CSU can be purchased with redundant power supplies. It is also a good idea to keep one DSU/CSU on the shelf in case you need to swap them.
Router	Routers can be purchased with redundant power supplies. Just as with the DSU/CSU, it is a good idea to have an extra router, configured exactly like the one you are using, just in case you need to swap it.
Firewall	There are different types of firewalls, so make sure your firewall is reliable and can handle the traffic. Many firewalls also have redundant power supplies and failover functionality.
Switch/Hub	Switches and hubs can be purchased to provide redundant power supplies and service.
Server Network Card	Within the server, you can use two network cards or you can build server clusters.
Power Supply	Most devices can be purchased with redundant power supplies. Also, make sure all power supplies use UPS.
Hard Drive	RAID 5 controllers can be purchased to make hard disks more fault-tolerant.
Memory	Clustering is the only answer to memory failure.
Cabling	Make sure all cabling in use is certified for the data that will travel on it.

1.6 Summary

As part of any enterprise application implementation, a systems designer must provide the applications and services in a way that is fault-tolerant and reliable. As computing has moved from mainframe-based systems to client/server systems, applications have suffered large blows to performance and reliability. The introduction of the cluster server seeks to change that. Already, cluster server software vendors are providing low-cost software options that allow systems engineers to rival mainframe reliability with client/server architectures.

As you will see, clustered and load balanced solutions meet the needs of fault tolerance by providing failover for systems and services that are critical to the enterprise. They meet the needs of performance and scalability by providing a system that can grow as needed, without having to replace hardware. They meet the needs of reliability and availability by providing a platform that can be upgraded, modified, and maintained without an interruption of service.

Chapter 2

What is a Cluster?

Business today is built on data—the ability to access data, manipulate data, transfer data, and analyze data. Large financial institutions and data processing firms lose billions of dollars a year due to data loss caused by system failure. In the data processing world of the past, mainframes ruled the arena. Today, many companies are trading in the mainframe for client/server-based applications and services that are more user-friendly and easier to integrate into their e-commerce implementation plans. Until recently, building a fault-tolerant, scalable, and reliable client/server system was a difficult task that included several months of planning, a room full of consulting companies, and several hundred thousand dollars. But the landscape is changing. Today, building a high-performance, reliable client/server system is easy to do—and more cost effective than ever.

Before diving into the Microsoft product offering, let's take a look at some of the clustering concepts and models that Microsoft and other companies are using to build their clustering and load-balancing software and hardware solutions.

2.1 Cluster History

The American Heritage Dictionary of the English Language defines a cluster as a group of the same or similar elements gathered or occurring closely together; a bunch. To *cluster* a group of computers is to use two or more independent computer systems to create one virtual server that provides seamless access to an application or service. The idea of clustering may be odd to someone new to the computing world, but clustering computers is not a new idea. Clustering theory dates back to as early as 1970. IBM was the first company to implement the clustering theory into its design, producing fault-tolerant mainframe computing products. At that point, however, clustering was a niche technology that, due to the reliability of the mainframe, was not in demand.

In the mid-1980s, Digital Equipment Corporation released the VAXcluster, a cluster of minicomputers that was supposed to solve the fault-tolerance dilemma of systems and services of the day by removing all single points of failure (SPOF) within a system. The VAXcluster was an attempt to duplicate every component that could fail within a system and run those components simultaneously (see Figure 2-1). This cluster produced a computing environment in which two computers could provide simultaneous service to users. This was not the jewel of the system, however. The greatest value was from the failover ability. If one part of the system were to quit functioning due to a failure, the other computer would begin servicing all of the clients.

The VAXcluster was the first "proof of concept" for the idea of clustering, but had many issues that needed to be resolved through later iterations. Later revisions of the technology were developed for the Reduced Instruction Set Computing (RISC) platform and relied solely upon the UNIX operating system. As the Intel architecture became more popular, the same methodology that was used to create the VAXcluster was applied to the Intel based client/server market.

As more and more companies began to rely on Microsoft networking products, the need for clustering and load-balancing technologies grew. Every step that Microsoft and other vendors have taken towards the development of a Windows-based clustering technology has brought excitement to the industry. For years, UNIX-based networking environments have had the ability to cluster servers in a way that rivals the reliability of the mainframe, while Windows administrators were left with minimal options in the clustering arena. However, the Wintel (Windows-based Intel architecture) platform is becoming more prevalent, offering new options for Windows-based clustering.

In 1995, Microsoft was delighted to announce the development of "wolfpack," the code name for the Microsoft Cluster Server (MSCS) software

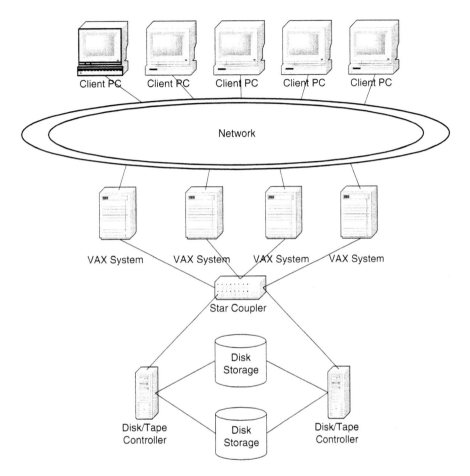

Figure 2-1
VAXcluster configuration.

package developed for the Windows NT 4.0 Enterprise server platform. This software was developed, in a collaboration between Digital Equipment Corporation and Tandem Computers, to allow two Windows NT 4.0 Enterprise servers to share a hard disk, providing automatic failover in the event of a failure within one of the servers. This would have been a triumph for Microsoft, for the cluster server functionality was beginning to be in high demand. Unfortunately, the software was not as solid and reliable as enterprise customers needed it to be, and third party products that offered more advanced functionality and reliability overshadowed the MSCS software.

There were many patches and upgrades to the MSCS software, and slowly the software began to take on the appearance of an enterprise-level product. In 2000, Microsoft released Windows 2000, along with a version of their server product called Windows 2000 Advanced Server. This server offered the reliability and stability of an enterprise-class operating system, as well as the tools and applications needed to build high availability cluster servers.

Along with Windows 2000 Advanced Server, Microsoft has released Windows 2000 Datacenter Server, a robust operating system positioned to displace the remaining mainframe hold on the market. Datacenter Server contains the same tools and applications as Windows 2000 Advanced Server, with the added support for higher amounts of memory, processor capacity, and greater clustering capabilities. Both Windows 2000 Advanced Server and Windows 2000 Datacenter Server offer a clustering and Network Load Balancing (NLB) services that are sure to become the industry standard for clustering Windows 2000-based applications and services.

In addition to greater operating system support for clusters, Microsoft has also released Application Center 2000, a software product that helps systems administrators to group Windows 2000 Servers into clusters, seamlessly manage Web site content and applications across multiple nodes, and maintain high levels of availability by managing processor load and site deployment.

All of these products, along with products such as Microsoft Internet Information Server and Microsoft SQL Server, allow administrators to deploy high-availability, fault-tolerant, scalable, client/server-based applications and solutions to meet the needs of small businesses and corporate enterprise customers alike.

2.2 Clustering for Fault Tolerance

As stated earlier, fault tolerance is the ability of a system to respond to failure in a way that does not hinder the service offering provided by the server. Clustering and load-balancing technologies provide fault tolerance by replicating the actions of a server. Before the appearance of affordable clustering software, many administrators would build a server and place it into production, and then create an exact duplicate of the server to keep as a "hot spare." This server would sit unused (and in many cases powered off) until it was needed. Once a failure occurred, the administrator would turn the production box off and turn the spare on. This provided some degree of manual fault tolerance, but lacked the high availability and reliability necessary to support mission-critical applications.

Clusters simplify this process. Instead of having a hot spare that is not running, clustering software actually groups two or more computers together to act as one virtual machine. In this case, the "hot swap" is automated. If a server fails, the other servers in the cluster are notified and all traffic destined for that server is distributed across all of the remaining servers. This is ideal for Web servers and database servers alike. Figure 2-2 shows a typically load balanced cluster configuration.

The virtual server is not a physical server, but a server created using a network address that all of the servers in the cluster share. All servers within the cluster have a virtual connection to the server and can respond to requests. If one of these machines were to quit functioning, the remaining servers would respond by eliminating that machine from the cluster and redistributing the load across the remaining servers within the cluster. If the server were to come back online, the clustered servers would recognize the server and dynamically allow it to join the cluster once again.

This is an example of only one type of cluster, but you can see how a clustered server design virtually eliminates the possibility for downtime. It is important to note that the cluster does not prevent failure, but allows the server(s) to continue to respond to requests in spite of a failure that may occur.

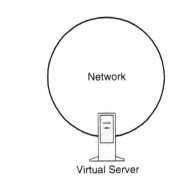

Virtual Server

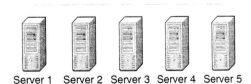

Server 1   Server 2   Server 3   Server 4   Server 5

Figure 2-2
Fault-tolerant, load-balanced servers.

21

Note

Clusters allow a service or application to continue responding to requests in spite of a system failure, but this does not preclude the need for fault tolerance within each individual system. Redundant power supplies, RAID disk array systems, and reliable hardware should always be used within each server in the cluster. This increases the reliability of each machine and minimizes the possibility of a downtime caused by multiple simultaneous failures.

2.3 Cluster Types

There are many types of clusters in use today. Some of them, like the early VAXcluster systems, share information and resources, while others act independently. There are different types of clusters because applications have different needs. One application may demand scalability, while another places higher priority on fault tolerance. In many cases, system designers use different types of clusters operating within the same system to provide the maximum amount of fault tolerance, scalability, and reliability.

2.3.1 Distributed Systems Clusters

A distributed systems cluster is a group of machines that are virtually or geographically separated and that work together to provide the same service or application to clients. It is possible that many of the services you run in your network today are part of a distributed systems cluster.

Consider a typical Windows 2000 network. Within that network there are many services that must be running in order for a client to access data on the servers, send email, access the Internet, and perform many other tasks. *Domain Naming System* (DNS), *Windows Internet Naming Service* (WINS), and Active Directory are all examples of services that are distributed yet provide a service to users.

If your network contains four geographically dispersed locations, it is likely that you have connectivity to those sites through a low bandwidth *wide area network* (WAN) connection. As a designer, you must provide network services to clients in those remote locations in a way that is fast, efficient, and reliable. To do so, you would most likely place a server in your main location, and then one server in each of the remote locations to answer requests made by clients in those remote sites. Each server would act as an Active Directory domain controller, a DNS server, and a WINS server (see Figure 2-3).

For the Active Directory, DNS, and WINS servers to operate properly and provide a benefit to the clients they serve, they must be able to exchange information about their environment and their actions with the other servers on the network. Fortunately, this is what these services are designed to do. The Active Directory Service, DNS, and WINS servers will exchange data with one another (if configured to do so) and provide a seamless service to the entire network.

So what makes it a cluster? It is defined as a cluster because the servers are fault-tolerant, and they provide seamless access to a service. Even though each server provides a service to the clients that are on the local network, any server within the network can respond to requests. For instance, if the Houston server were to become unavailable due to a hardware failure, clients within the Houston network that needed to query the Active Directory, DNS, or WINS databases would still be able to do so by accessing another server on the network. And because the servers exchange information regularly, the information obtained from any one of the other servers would be accurate.

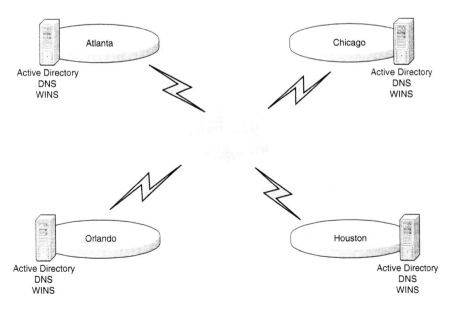

Figure 2-3
Typical Windows 2000 network.

This is further defined as a cluster because

- There is no single point of failure (SPOF).
- The design provides scalability.
- The data is shared between all machines.
- The design is reliable.

The distributed systems cluster eliminates the SPOF by providing redundancy in the data access. No SPOF will cause the service(s) to be unavailable. It provides scalability because more servers can be added to each location to field client requests, and new sites can be added to the WAN without necessitating an upgrade of existing systems. The data is shared between all machines, making the data accurate to clients that request it. Overall, the system is reliable and provides service seamlessly as one virtual server, even though many servers are involved.

Other applications can also be considered distributed systems clusters, including most SNA gateway products and network operating systems, such as Microsoft Windows NT and Novell Netware, which provide directory services. Network services such as Dynamic Host Configuration Protocol (DHCP) and Simple Mail Transfer Protocol (SMTP) relays, if configured correctly, can also be considered distributed systems clusters.

Distributed systems clusters work well in corporate LANs and WANs, but they don't fit every need. For Internet applications, connectivity takes place through one connection—an Internet connection—and therefore is not the best solution for systems where the Internet contains the client base. For other applications, where the data transfer is minimal or the protocol is lightweight, a centralized system may be more desirable.

2.3.2 Failover Clusters

The most popular cluster type is called a failover cluster. A failover cluster is typically built with one to four machines, physically configured to share disk storage. Like the other cluster types, all servers within the cluster work together to form one virtual server that provides an application or service to clients.

Although a failover cluster can contain one to four nodes, most implementations utilize only two nodes for the cluster, due to the lack of support for four-node clustering in most software. These two nodes are both attached to an external storage unit, which provides shared disk storage for the cluster server (see Figure 2-4).

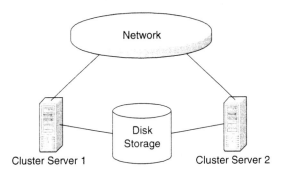

Figure 2-4
Failover cluster.

The failover cluster, like the other cluster types, has a specific purpose. The main purpose of the failover cluster is to provide uninterrupted service in the event of a failure within the cluster. Even though it is possible to configure a failover cluster to provide a small performance boost by changing certain settings, a failover cluster is not as scalable as other types of clusters. A failover cluster is a good fit for databases, file storage, and applications that have dynamic content, or data that changes often.

In a failover cluster, the nodes within the cluster share disk storage. The applications and data used on the cluster are stored on the shared disk so that each server can access the data in the event of a failure; however, data on the external storage array can never be accessed by both machines at the same time. There must be one owner for each physical disk used within the array. As you will see later, configuration of the cluster software entails assigning ownership of all applications on the cluster to one machine.

For example, if you chose to run SQL Server on your cluster, your SQL installation would be located on one of the disks within the external disk array. You would need to select an owner for that application and assign all of the resources necessary to run that application to that one server. Let's assume Cluster Server 1 (see Figure 2-4) is the owner of the SQL Server application. This means that Cluster Server 1 would respond to all SQL requests, while the other server sits idle. While Cluster Server 1 has ownership of the application, Cluster Server 2 would not be involved in the transactions and would not be able to access the drive that the data is stored on. If you were to open Disk Administrator or Windows Explorer to view your drives on Cluster Server 2, you would see that the disk does not even appear to exist!

In the event of a failure on Cluster Server 1, all resources for the application would failover to Cluster Server 2, and it would become the new owner of the application. Once Cluster Server 2 had been granted the ownership of the application, it would be able to see the disk and access the data. Once Cluster Server 1 comes back online, the application ownership would *fail back* to the previous owner, and Cluster Server 1 would begin servicing requests once again.

Failover clusters share disk storage, and therefore are best suited for applications that contain dynamic content, such as databases, file storage, and mail server applications. If you want to cluster an application and the application requires changing content or transaction processing, it must be run on a failover cluster, for a failover cluster is the only cluster model that allows all nodes to share information concerning transactions and changing content.

2.3.2.1 Single-Node Failover Clusters

A single-node failover cluster is a cluster that is designed as a failover cluster, but has only one node and, strangely enough, does not provide failover for applications (see Figure 2-5). This design provides one server that, like the two-node cluster, creates a virtual server whereby clients can access applications and services resident on that one machine. That may sound strange, but there are reasons why you might want to build a single-node failover cluster:

- Easier administration
- Easier network management
- Cost effectiveness
- Simplified testing

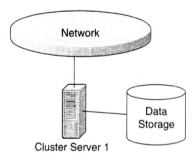

Figure 2-5
Single-node cluster.

Many organizations implement single-node clusters because of the advantages of administration. Once the clustering software is installed, all aspects of the server or application can be managed through the Microsoft Cluster Management snap-in. This can simplify administration and provide enhanced capabilities to remote personnel.

Another reason that an organization might implement a single-node cluster is for the network management capabilities. Many network-monitoring products on the market today have sophisticated cluster-monitoring capabilities that may give a company greater control and more granular monitoring than a traditional application agent that they might otherwise install.

Some organizations plan to implement a clustered server system but cannot justify the cost all at once. A single-node cluster gives them the ability to acquire one server and set it up within the cluster before ever purchasing the second server. This also helps the learning curve that some administrators experience when installing a cluster for the first time. Working with only one server gives them time to become comfortable with the system before adding additional servers. Most organizations don't throw applications into production without a long testing period. A single-node cluster allows developers and program designers to work within a real clustered environment to test their application before adding the second server and rolling it out to the masses.

A quality assurance lab or development group may choose to build a single-node cluster in order to test their applications. Applications must be designed to run on a cluster, due to the information that all the nodes within the cluster share. Building a single-node cluster for that purpose allows the quality assurance lab or development group to experiment with a cluster system without affecting the production cluster. This will not only give them more flexibility in their testing, but will ensure that the application runs well on the production cluster.

2.3.2.2 Dedicated Secondary Node Failover Clusters

The dedicated secondary node cluster is the most common form of the failover cluster. In the dedicated secondary node cluster, two machines are added to the cluster with an external storage device. One server runs all of the applications and services, while the other server sits idle (see Figure 2-6). When a failure occurs within the first server, all of the resources and data necessary to run that application are (virtually) transferred to the other server (see Figure 2-7).

This model provides for failover, but does not make full use of the hardware that is available within the cluster. It is not cost effective to allow one machine to sit idle, but many organizations nevertheless implement dedicated secondary node failover clusters in the following situations:

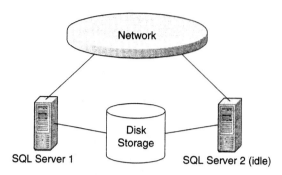

Figure 2-6
Dedicated secondary node cluster.

- Only one mission-critical application needs to be deployed.
- The two servers used for the cluster are significantly different with regard to power and processing speed.
- Rolling upgrades can be performed without downtime.

In many cases, an organization will implement a database or application that works in conjunction with other servers outside the cluster, and fault tolerance is only required for a single application, but there is another advantage to running a dedicated secondary node cluster. If the organization purchased identical servers for the cluster, failover to the secondary cluster node will not cause a change in the performance of the application. This is a design goal in many cases.

On some occasions, however, cost is a more important factor than consistent performance during a failure. When that is the case, an organization can purchase two vastly different sets of hardware, one server with a fast processor and plenty of memory to maintain preferred ownership of the application, and a second server that is a lower end cost-effective workgroup server. This will allow the higher cost server to respond to all requests and allow the workgroup server to step in only during an emergency. Although there would be a performance drop in the application, the application would continue to function despite the failure.

Another advantage of the dedicated secondary node cluster is that upgrades to the system do not require that the system be taken offline. Remember, any host within the cluster can own the application and respond to requests. If an administrator needs to upgrade a component or apply a service pack, he or she can, in many cases, apply the update without interrupting the service that the system is providing. To do this, an update would be applied to the secondary—

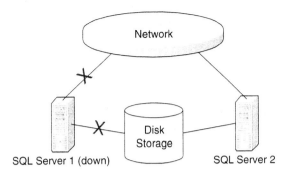

Figure 2-7
Dedicated secondary node cluster failure.

or idle—node. Once complete, ownership of the application would be transferred to the secondary node. Updates would then be applied to the primary node. Once complete, the ownership would be transferred back to the original owner. This is an efficient way to apply updates to a server cluster without affecting the service being offered by the system.

Note

Rolling upgrades can be performed only when the component that you are updating is not a part of the application running on the cluster. For instance, if you are running SQL Server on your cluster, you can use the rolling upgrade method to apply service packs to the operating system or updates to some other application, but you cannot apply the SQL Server service pack or update to an idle server because it will not own the resource (disk) that contains the SQL data files. In this case you would need to apply the service pack to the server that currently has ownership of the SQL Service, then transfer the ownership to the other server and apply the service pack to the second server.

2.3.2.3 Distributed Failover Clusters

A distributed failover cluster employs a method that is an extension of the dedicated secondary node cluster. Like the dedicated secondary node cluster, the distributed failover cluster has two (or more) nodes that create a virtual server that offers a service or services to clients. The unique difference in the distributed failover cluster is that each server can run the same application or different applications simultaneously (see Figure 2-8).

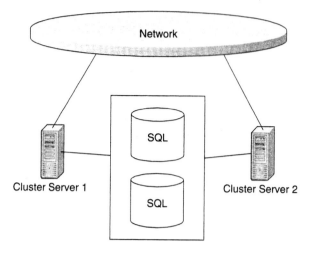

Figure 2-8
Distributed failover cluster.

Note

Do not confuse the distributed failover cluster with the distributed systems cluster discussed earlier, for they are separate types of clusters. Servers within a distributed systems cluster are typically geographically separated, and they do not share disk storage, whereas a distributed failover cluster is a two-node to four-node cluster that must be in close proximity and must share disk storage.

Within a distributed failover cluster, each node runs a clustered application and depends upon the other node for failover in the event that one node should fail. This allows organizations the following flexibility:

• Better use of available hardware.
• Ability to scale applications slightly while providing fault tolerance.
• Ability to run separate applications that are managed through one console.

Because both nodes within the cluster are servicing requests, none of the hardware remains idle. Administrators can take advantage of the secondary node by running applications that may complement their system, such as file shares, IIS Virtual Servers, or SQL Server databases. This is a better use of the hardware purchased for the system.

The distributed failover cluster allows an administrator to scale the application or service being offered by running the same or complementary applications on the other node within the cluster. In many cases, the application being run on the cluster can be separated into two installations. For example, if you have a large database that you want to run on a distributed failover cluster, you can separate certain tables within the database and move them to the other installation as a different database. Tables used for authentication and user data may be placed in one database, while product and pricing information can be placed in another. This splits the processing of the database application between two servers, instantly cutting your processing in half.

Note

Keep in mind that although you can separate your applications to span across two servers in the cluster, both nodes in the cluster must have the power and processing speed to run both applications simultaneously in the event of a failure, so make sure to plan your hardware requirements accordingly.

The distributed failover cluster also allows an administrator to run completely separate applications on the nodes within the cluster (see Figure 2-9). For example, if you have an application that requires an SQL Server database and mass amounts of file storage, you can configure one node in the cluster to service SQL Server requests, while the other node in the cluster provides file-sharing capabilities. Each machine performs a vital function while also providing failover for the corresponding application.

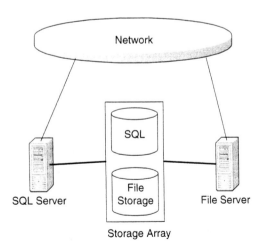

Figure 2-9
Two-application distributed failover cluster.

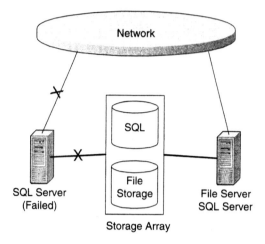

Figure 2-10
Application failure within distributed failover cluster.

In Figure 2-9 two servers are clustered together to provide both SQL Server and file sharing on the network. If these machines were not clustered, you would simply have two machines providing two separate services. If one machine were to fail, that service would also fail. In a cluster environment, both machines have the ability to run both applications. If one server were to fail, the responsibility of running the failed server's application would fall on the other server, and it would immediately begin processing requests for that application (see Figure 2-10).

The distributed failover cluster is the most efficient form of clustering to provide failover for mission-critical applications. It allows reliability, performance, and fault tolerance to an application or set of applications while fully utilizing an IT department's investment in hardware.

2.3.3 Load-Balanced Clusters

Load balancing is the ability to distribute processing or communications across multiple nodes to minimize the possibility of overworking one machine. This is often referred to as a server cluster, server farm, or Web farm. Most companies that deploy high-traffic Internet sites utilize the load-balanced cluster in one form or another.

Load-balanced clusters differ from failover clusters in that they provide not only fault tolerance and reliability, but also scalability and performance. Load-balanced clusters are not limited to a handful of machines that co-operate as a virtual server; machines can be added as needed to increase performance and the system can scale to meet the needs of any application it is providing.

Deploying an application utilizing a load-balanced cluster server model has the following benefits:

- Load balancing of incoming requests.
- High availability and automated recovery from single machine failures.
- The ability to add machines to the cluster as needed for scalability and performance.

Unlike the failover cluster, which must have an "owner" for each application, the load-balanced cluster distributes the load of the application requests across multiple machines simultaneously (see Figure 2-11). This allows administrators to configure multiple machines to provide the same application. Like other clusters, the nodes within a load-balanced cluster create a virtual server that responds to all requests. This virtual server distributes the client requests across all of the machines within the cluster.

Servers within a load-balanced cluster are configured to operate as a group of servers providing the same service or application. In the past, load balancing required expensive hardware to route requests to the appropriate server, and the servers within the cluster did not communicate with each other, for the clustering logic was maintained within the hardware. Microsoft has eliminated

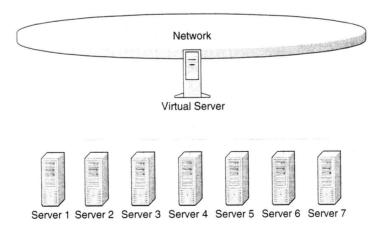

Figure 2-11
Load-balanced cluster.

the need for hardware solutions by providing an NLB service within the Windows 2000 Advanced Server operating system.

Load-balanced clusters provide high performance due to the number of servers that can be added to the cluster to provide a service or application. They provide scalability through the addition of nodes to the cluster, and they provide fault tolerance by dynamically removing from the cluster machines that fail, so that those machines do not receive client requests.

Although it may sound as if the load-balanced cluster has all of the benefits of the failover cluster and more, there is one drawback to consider. Load-balanced clusters do not share disk storage, so data or applications that they provide to clients have to be static and must be the same on every machine in the cluster. Because the nodes within the cluster do not share information with one another, transaction-tracking and programs that require dynamic content, such as databases, are not possible.

Load balancing, in recent years, has been used mostly for Web servers, due to its robust performance and scalability. But load balancing can be used for any application or service that does not have dynamically changing content. Most companies use a combination of load-balanced clusters and failover clusters to provide applications to clients. The failover cluster is typically used for database hosting or file storage, while the load-balanced clusters are used for the front-end Web application.

2.4 Cluster Models

Based upon clustering theory, there are only two types of clusters: a *shared-resource* cluster and a *share-nothing* cluster. These are more academic labels than actual systems, but understanding the differences between the separate models will help to clarify the actions that take place within a clustered server system.

2.4.1 Shared-Resource Cluster Model

A shared-resource cluster is a group of machines that share simultaneous access to a resource. This resource is typically a file or object that needs to be manipulated by the system. Because all nodes within the model have the ability to read and write to files and objects that are shared between the systems, applications that utilize dynamic content, such as database applications and file-sharing applications, can be distributed across multiple machines, providing load balancing for incoming requests.

This design model presents a robust and scalable system that can be used for just about any application. It offers the greatest amount of flexibility, providing performance, scalability, and fault tolerance within the same model; however, it also presents an overly complex software design requirement and a large overhead of processing that must take place for the system to work properly.

Note

It is important to understand that based upon the architecture and programming standards in common use in all applications today, a file or object cannot be accessed and edited by more than one process at once. A process that accesses a file must open the file, edit the file, and then close the file again to allow another process or application to access the file. If two processes access the file simultaneously, data corruption occurs.

Take, for example, a file. Suppose you have a two-node cluster that shares disk storage. The disk storage is known as the D: drive. Both nodes within the cluster need access to the D: drive and must be able to read and write to the drive to provide simultaneous access to the application or service on either machine. Once a node accesses the file, it must write into memory that the file is open and place a "lock" on the file that dictates to other processes that the file is being edited by the system and cannot be opened. This warning, or lock, is not written to the memory on machine 2, but only on machine 1. Therefore, if machine 2 tries to access the file, it will open a file that is already being edited by machine 1, thus causing data corruption within the file.

Designers have come up with ways to get around this flaw within the model, one of which is called the *DLM* (distributed lock manager). The DLM interfaces between the two machines and communicates to each machine a list of files that are locked and a list of files that are available. This virtually eliminates the possibility of one machine accessing a file that is open by another machine. Problems arise; however, when you consider the possibility of failure within one of the nodes. The DLM is a transaction-based system and must read the activity of a machine and translate it to the other machine. If one machine in the cluster crashes, it is possible that some actions taken by the node before it crashed were executed, but not recorded in the DLM. Because of this variable, designers have to build sophisticated error checking and fault tolerance within the DLM itself. This presents two problems. First, disk access is the most time-consuming process for a machine to perform. The use of a DLM increases disk access significantly, slowing the overall processing of a machine. Second, the DLM halts the service of the cluster during a failure so that it may process all of the remaining locks within the system and reassign the blocks

35

based upon the remaining members of the cluster. This process can take several minutes, depending on the size of the cluster and the amount of files being accessed, causing the system to be offline during the process.

In theory, the shared-resource cluster model is highly functional, scalable, and more flexible than other models, but most cluster software and hardware have not embraced the methodology because of the high overhead, development complexity, and the long convergence times during failures.

2.4.2 Share-Nothing Cluster Model

The share-nothing cluster model, in contrast to the shared-resource model, is based upon the premise that all nodes within a cluster own the resources that they are responsible for managing. While a resource is being owned, it does not allow other nodes to access the resource in any way.

The most applicable resource, the hard disk, can be a part of a shared-storage system, such as an external disk array connected to two machines, and still have the methodology applied. In this case, two machines would have "physical" access to the disk array, but only one server would actually own the disk and be able to read and write from it at any given point in time.

The idea of resource ownership allows clusters to be built without questioning who can access what files within a system. The only concern becomes who currently owns the resource (disk). This is a much easier table to maintain than the DLM and minimizes the overhead required to run the system.

The disadvantage to the share-nothing cluster model is the inability to load balance single applications across multiple machines. Because only one node can access the data at a time, only one node can run any given application. The only way to load balance the application is to manually install different portions or subsets of an application on different nodes and configure them to run as separate applications. This requires greater administration and provides a more complex system.

Another disadvantage to this model is related to hardware requirements. Because a node within a cluster "owns" an application, it must own all resources associated with that application while it is servicing client requests. This includes the disk itself. So when designing a share-nothing cluster model system, the designer must ensure there is a separate disk for each application that needs to be run on the system.

Just like the shared-resource cluster model, the share-nothing cluster model has its advantages and disadvantages, but due to the large overhead and development complexity needed to build shared-resource cluster systems, most vendors have standardized upon the share-nothing cluster model.

2.5 Windows 2000 Clustering

Clustering products have been around for many years, but only recently has Microsoft joined the party. As it has done in the development of many of its service offerings, Microsoft partnered with several companies, including DEC (Digital Equipment Corporation) and Tandem Computers, to develop its clustering products. The development of wolfpack, the application that eventually became the MSCS for Windows NT 4.0 Enterprise Server, was an exciting addition to the Windows NT Server platform, and although the service was a large step in the right direction, it lacked many of the necessary tools and functionality it needed to gain market share in the cluster server market.

In late 2000, Microsoft released Windows 2000 Advanced Server. A short time later, Microsoft released Windows 2000 Datacenter Server. Both products contained two services related to clustering: MSCS and the Microsoft NLB service. These services were a part of the four-year development project that brought Windows 2000 to the market. They provide a solid infrastructure for the design and deployment of clustered servers.

2.5.1 Microsoft Product Summary

The clustering and load-balancing products included with Windows 2000 are the most significant contribution Microsoft has made to the cluster server community to date. By utilizing these tools, enterprises can now implement systems and services that rival the reliability of the mainframe and the stability of past Unix platforms. Products such as Microsoft SQL Server, Microsoft Exchange Server, and File and Print Services can now be clustered at a lower cost and greater speed than ever before.

2.5.1.1 Microsoft Cluster Service

Included with Microsoft Windows 2000 Advanced Server and Microsoft Windows 2000 Datacenter Server, the MSCS enables the easy construction and management of failover clusters, providing high levels of service and availability. There are a variety of applications that can benefit from the MSCS, including:

- **Web-Based Applications**—Internet Web sites and portals, intranet Web programs and services, and extranet business-to-business commerce engines.

37

- **Enterprise Database Applications**—Customer resource management, enterprise resource management, and manufacturing systems.

- **File and Print Services**—File storage, data warehousing, and enterprise-level print services.

- **Communication Services**—Email systems, streaming video, virtual private networking, fax servers.

In addition to application support, MSCS provides developers with the programming interfaces and tools to design their own "cluster-aware" applications and services. Also included is the Cluster Administrator, a Microsoft Management Console snap-in that allows easy administration of MSCS servers locally and remotely.

The MSCS is installed through the Add/Remove Programs interface found in the Windows Control Panel. The Windows 2000 Advanced Server version supports up to two-node failover clusters, while the Windows 2000 Datacenter Server supports up to four-node failover clusters.

2.5.1.2 Microsoft NLB Service

The Microsoft NLB service is included with both the Windows 2000 Advanced Server and Windows 2000 Datacenter Server operating systems. Using NLB, companies can deploy high-performance, scalable applications to meet the needs of today's Internet-driven business. NLB can be used to deploy any of the following applications and services:

- **Web Based Applications**—Internet Web sites, intranet Web applications, and extranet e-commerce applications.

- **Communication Services**—Streaming media, virtual private networking, and fax gateways.

- **Terminal Services**—Thin-client access to high-performance, scalable terminal services.

The Microsoft NLB service is installed by default and need only be enabled and configured for proper operation. Configuration of the NLB service can be done through the Network Properties icon located in the Control Panel.

The Windows 2000 Advanced Server and the Windows 2000 Datacenter Server both support up to 32 hosts within the load-balanced cluster and require no proprietary hardware for implementation. This provides a large amount of scalability when building Web server farms or enterprise services that need to scale for thousands of users.

2.5.1.3 Microsoft Application Center

As part of its increasing desire to innovate the software market, Microsoft released a concept known as .NET. .NET is a development methodology that allows organizations to create distributed client/server applications and services that operate across the Internet. The .NET concept has given rise to a suite of products that will help businesses to easily integrate existing client/server systems and services into the Web-based world of e-commerce. The following applications are part of the first-generation .NET product offering:

* Internet Security and Acceleration Server
* Application Center 2000
* Commerce Server 2000
* BizTalk Server 2000
* SQL Server 2000
* Exchange Server 2000
* Host Integration Server 2000

The vision for the .NET methodology is rooted in system integration. Microsoft has endeavored to make the art of integration between .NET applications a painless process, constructing all the applications using open Web standards such as XML (Extensible Markup Language). Through this vision, Microsoft seeks to allow system administrators of small and large companies the ability to offer comprehensive Web-based applications and services as one system, rather than through the implementation of individual modules.

As part of the .NET application offering, Microsoft has included Microsoft Application Center 2000. AppCenter 2000 is Microsoft's cluster server deployment and management tool that allows administrators to synchronize Web content across multiple servers while monitoring the health and performance of the cluster itself. AppCenter 2000 provides the following benefits:

* Synchronize Web content across multiple servers within a network load-balanced cluster.
* Deploy COM+ applications across multiple servers within a network load-balanced cluster.
* CLB (Component Load Balancing) service to allow business logic processing to be load balanced separately from front-end and back-end applications.
* Cluster health monitoring and notification services.

AppCenter 2000 works with the Microsoft NLB service to provide a high-availability, scalable cluster solution that can be easily managed, monitored, and expanded. Using AppCenter, organizations can deploy front-end Web content to multiple servers without having to visit each server. This makes deployment of new Web content easy and reliable, ensuring that all content on each server is identical.

One of the frustrations systems administrators experienced with the Windows 2000 Advanced Server NLB service was the overhead of duplicating efforts for each change made to a machine. Because the NLB service employs a share-nothing architecture, information between each server is not shared by default. This means that administrators must duplicate every change made to one server to all servers within the cluster. This may be manageable with two or three servers, but when a cluster reaches 20 or more machines, this duplication of effort becomes too time consuming.

AppCenter seeks to change that by providing not only Web-content deployment automation but the deployment of COM+ applications as well. COM+ applications used in the past had to be registered manually on each server within a cluster. Now, administrators can deploy COM+ components and applications through one console to all machines within the cluster.

For high-traffic applications, AppCenter allows the COM+ applications to be offloaded to a group of servers that are clustered together to create a "second tier" within the application. By offloading the processing of COM+ applications, typically used for business logic, systems designers can speed the performance of their overall system. Through the use of the CLB cluster, designers can dynamically balance the workload of the application by building business logic into COM+ applications and building a separate set of clustered servers to handle incoming requests for COM+ objects (see Figure 2-12).

AppCenter 2000 also simplifies management by allowing all servers within a cluster to be managed from one console. Using the AppCenter 2000 console, administrators can track a cluster's health, performance, and availability. In conjunction with performance monitor, AppCenter provides a single console for viewing performance statistics on all servers within the cluster.

2.5.2 Windows 2000 Clustering Architecture

As a preface to any technical study, it is important to understand the architecture of the technology and how it interoperates with network services and applications. Both the MSCS and the Microsoft NLB service are included with the Windows 2000 Advanced Server and Windows 2000 Datacenter Server operating systems. These services integrate with many of the other

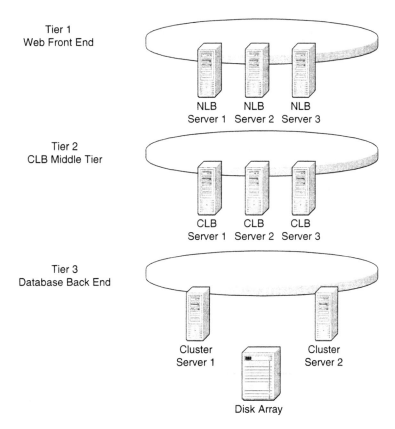

Tier 1
Web Front End

NLB   NLB   NLB
Server 1 Server 2 Server 3

Tier 2
CLB Middle Tier

CLB   CLB   CLB
Server 1 Server 2 Server 3

Tier 3
Database Back End

Cluster   Cluster
Server 1   Server 2

Disk Array

Figure 2-12
Component load balancing.

features resident in the operating systems, and when used in conjunction with services such as the Internet Information Server or File and Print Services, can provide high availability and scalability for applications and services.

2.5.2.1 Microsoft Cluster Service Architecture

The MSCS enables the construction of high-availability failover clustering and allows administrators to solve reliability issues easily and inexpensively. As discussed before, a failover cluster is a group of one to four computers connected to a shared disk storage system, seamlessly providing an application or service to clients as a virtual server.

MSCS software uses the concept of resource ownership to make configuring and administering a cluster server easy for administrators. Each application that is configured to run on a cluster has a set of resources that are interdependent upon each other and must all be functioning for the application to service clients. The resources can include the following items:

- Network (NetBIOS) name
- TCP/IP address
- Physical disk storage
- Secondary application (dependency)

For each application running on the cluster, a network name, IP address, and physical disk is assigned. These resources are collected into a group and treated as one entity, or virtual server. One node within the cluster owns the application and controls all of the resources of that application as long as the server can respond to clients. Once a failure occurs, the server that owns the application transfers ownership of the application to the surviving node. The secondary node then owns the application and responds to client requests.

Resources are implemented as dynamic-link libraries (DLLs) and run as a service within privileged mode under the system account. Resources expose interfaces and properties to the cluster service. Certain resources may have dependencies; that is, they rely upon the existence of another service before they can function properly.

The MSCS contains six components that work together to provide the cluster server functionality:

- Node manager
- Configuration database manager
- Resource manager/failover manager
- Event processor
- Communications manager
- Global update manager

The node manager is responsible for maintaining cluster membership. It does so by sending periodic messages to other servers within the cluster. These messages are called "heartbeat" messages, and allow each member of the cluster to keep track of the state of the other nodes within the cluster. When a node fails to send the heartbeat messages to the other nodes, one node will remove the failed node from the cluster membership table and inform all other nodes in the cluster to do likewise. This keeps the cluster membership consistent among all nodes within the cluster.

The configuration database manager is responsible for maintaining the cluster configuration database. The configuration database contains all information related to the cluster, including cluster systems, groups, and resource types. It is vital to the operation of the cluster that all nodes within the cluster contain the same database configuration. The configuration database manager ensures that the database is consistent from node to node.

The resource manager/failover manager is responsible for the management of resources within the cluster. It maintains the resource group ownership, failover status, and group dependencies. This component receives information from the resource monitor and the node manager. It uses this information to make decisions regarding group ownership, configuration, and status. The resource manager manages the ownership of each resource, while the failover manager determines what to do with failed resources or dependencies of failed resources.

The event processor is the interface between applications and the cluster service. It is responsible for all event management and notification, as well as for the initialization of the cluster. When the cluster service is started manually or automatically, the event processor is the component that starts the service and then passes control to the node manager to determine cluster status and form or join the cluster.

The communications manager is the component that is responsible for providing communications between all nodes in the cluster. This component is used by all other components in the system to deliver messages to the corresponding components in other nodes within the cluster.

The global update manager is the component that is responsible for distributing information changes to the nodes within the cluster. Any changes made to the cluster configuration, node configuration, or resource configuration are distributed to all servers within the cluster by the global update manager.

Another valuable part of the cluster software is the resource monitor. The resource monitor is a component separate from the cluster service that communicates with the cluster service via *RPC* (remote procedure calls). Like the other cluster components, the resource monitor sits between the resource (physical disk, IP address, etc.) and the cluster service, handling communications between the two entities. Resource monitors are processes inherent in the operating system, but are spawned by the cluster service as each resource is brought online. Several resources can run within a resource monitor, or they can be configured to run in separate resource monitors. The job of the resource monitor is to verify the availability and functionality of resources that are running on the cluster server. In the event that a resource cannot be verified, a message is sent to the resource manager, which then decides to restart the resource or transfer the resource group to another server within the cluster.

2.5.2.2 Microsoft NLB Service Architecture

The Microsoft NLB service is a small service compared to the MSCS, yet it is powerful in its application. NLB does not install as an independent service, but is resident in any default installation of Windows 2000 Advanced Server or Windows 2000 Datacenter Server. To use the service, an administrator simply has to activate and configure the properties associated with the service.

2.5.2.2.1 NLB Components

There are three components used by the NLB service:

- WLBS.SYS
- WLBS.EXE
- WLBS.CHM

The core of the NLB service is the WLBS.SYS driver. This driver includes a statistical mapping algorithm that all hosts within a cluster use to determine which host responds to each incoming request. Once the driver is activated and configured, it creates a virtual IP address that is shared by all hosts within a cluster. This IP address is not bound to one machine at a time, but bound to all machines at the same time. All incoming requests to the virtual IP address are sent to all servers within the cluster, and using the WLBS.SYS driver, the statistical mapping algorithm (based upon settings the administrator provides) determines which host is to handle the incoming request. Once the receiving host is determined, all other hosts drop the network request.

WLBS.EXE is a command-line network load-balancing control program and can be used to start, stop, or configure the NLB service. Although there is a GUI interface that can be accessed through the network control panel to configure NLB, WLBS.EXE is often used to determine the status of the cluster or for scripting the modification of cluster configurations.

WLBS.CHM is a help file that is loaded as a part of the NLB service, and provides context-sensitive help for settings within the NLB configuration.

2.5.2.2.2 NLB Operation

To operate correctly, the cluster must act as one entity and therefore must be aware of which nodes are functioning and which nodes are not functioning. The state of the cluster is determined collectively by all hosts. Using the exchange of heartbeat messages, all hosts communicate their status with each other. This allows the cluster membership to be shared by all hosts and therefore prevents requests from being dropped due to failed servers within the cluster. If one host within the cluster fails or does not send a heartbeat message to the other servers within a preset period of time (about five seconds), a process known as convergence takes place on the cluster. Convergence is where all machines determine the active membership of the cluster and modify their cluster information based upon these results. In the same way, machines that are added to the cluster (or powered off and then on again) trigger convergence on the cluster so that all hosts within the cluster can list the new server as a part of the cluster group.

2.6 Summary

The clustering concept originated in the early 1970s as IBM searched for ways to make its mainframe computing environments more fault-tolerant. And although the idea did not catch on until the PC revolution of the 1980s, the technology industry has made great strides in the development of the technology for the client/server market. From the time of the earliest VAXcluster to today, the needs of e-commerce and industry have continued growing—demanding more fault-tolerant, high-performance, and reliable systems and services.

Microsoft, in the late 1990s, began developing software that would enable the systems administrator to deploy high-performance, reliable applications easily and cost effectively. The result of its efforts, the MSCS and the NLB service, have enabled engineers to look at network design and construction a little differently—opening a vast resource of options that were not available before. Through the clustering applications and the .NET initiative, Microsoft is bringing products to market that provide reliability never before realized in the client/server software industry.

Chapter 3

CLUSTERING DESIGN ISSUES

Before diving into the construction of a cluster server solution, it is important to plan the project accordingly. Fitting the system to the needs of the application is essential, for there are many good cluster solutions, yet not all are a good fit for every application. There are many benefits to running an application or service on a cluster server, but it must make sense to do so. Not only must you choose the type of cluster your application needs, but you must also consider the different hardware options that are available for the type of cluster you are creating. How many machines do you need? What types of processors should you use? How much memory is required? How should your disks be formatted? All of these are valid questions, and the choices you make will affect the performance and usability of your cluster solution.

In many cases, design is three parts experience and one part skill. Most designers stick with hardware and software combinations that are comfortable for them or with systems that they have had experience installing. Although there is nothing wrong with implementing systems that are "tried and true," don't limit your design to familiar hardware. If you are new to clustering, then many of the items discussed throughout this book will be new to you, and trying a variety of different platforms will be helpful. If you are familiar with clustering and have built cluster server solutions in the past, take the time to review the other hardware and software options that are available, for they may become useful in your next cluster server implementation.

3.1 Cluster Server Planning

Any valuable information technology project starts with a plan. Clustering is no exception. If you are thinking you can skip this chapter and go right to the cluster installation chapter (like many enthusiastic engineers do), you are mistaken. Although you could attempt to build a cluster server solution without taking the time to carefully plan your hardware and software solution, it is risky business. The result would most likely be high cost equipment and software that have to be returned to the vendor because they are not compatible with the Microsoft clustering software suite.

Planning a cluster server solution is not difficult and should be done prior to any hardware or software purchase. A carefully thought-out plan will save you many hours of wasted phone calls and RMA processing.

Following the proper procedure, obtaining the hardware and software for a cluster server solution is relatively straightforward and similar to any other purchase. Here are the steps you must take before beginning your project:

- Identify the needs of your application.
- Determine which clustering technology to use for the application.
- Determine the necessary clustering model to use for the application.
- Determine which network services you will need to implement to support your application.
- Determine the necessary hardware that is required for your application.
- Diagram your desired network configuration.
- Determine how your application will integrate with existing systems.
- Create a plan to implement your cluster server solution.
- Create a contingency plan.

By following these steps, you can build a complete project plan and network configuration before ordering any hardware or software. The planning process is essential to the success of any cluster server solution.

3.1.1 Identify the Needs of the Application

The first step in a good cluster server design plan is to identify the needs of the application (or applications) that will be running on the cluster server.

Consider the needs of the application based upon user requirements and vendor requirements. The user requirements to consider may be:

- How many users need to access the system simultaneously?
- What is the availability requirement of the users?
- At what times do users need to access the application, and will traffic to the system be higher during specific periods of the day?

The vendor requirements to consider may be:

- What are the licensing requirements for the application when running on a cluster server?
- Can the software run on a cluster server?
- Does the software require specific hardware?
- Does the software have software dependencies?
- What is the data storage required for the application?

How many users a system has will assist a designer in determining the bandwidth requirements for the application. This may make the difference between running the cluster server on a 100mbps connection or a 1000mbps connection. A cluster with multiple simultaneous users also requires fast processing of the server system as well as large amounts of memory. All these things should be taken into consideration. There is no real formula for determining how much memory or how many processors are required, because all applications have different needs, but examining the number of users that require simultaneous access will give a designer a better guess at the hardware requirements.

The availability requirement is determined by when the application must be accessible. Is the application accessed from 9 a.m. to 5 p.m., or does it need to be available 24/7? Using this information, designers can plan for downtime, schedule maintenance hours, or in 24/7 networks, determine a plan for upgrades without system downtime.

The time of day that users access the data may not seem significant, but it is important. Maintenance of servers' system backups needs to be scheduled during low usage times. Understanding the peak usage times will help a designer to plan these maintenance tasks accordingly.

In addition to the practical requirements that users may have, the vendor of the software may have their own requirements. Designers must consider the licensing restrictions of the software they are using. Many companies have different software license requirements for software installed on a cluster server as opposed to software installed in a single-server environment. Most companies will require you to purchase a copy of the software for each server in a cluster, but will only require you to purchase one client access license for each client that accesses the cluster, regardless of which server they connect to. However, some companies require you to purchase more than one client access license for the clients that are connecting to the cluster server system. Be sure to check with your software vendor to find out the specific requirements.

Probably the most important question is, Can the software run on the cluster? Applications must be specifically written for the cluster to operate properly. Applications that are written specifically for clustering are usually termed cluster-aware. This means that they have the ability to interface with the cluster API (application programming interface) and that resource ownership of the application can be transferred between different servers. If an application is not written to be cluster-aware, it will most likely not failover correctly and should not be clustered.

Note

Determining if a piece of software is cluster aware is more important to building a failover cluster than to building a load-balanced cluster. The load-balancing operation takes place at the network level and is application-independent. The load-balanced cluster also does not share data or application ownership. For this reason, most applications can be load-balanced, and specific programming is not required for correct operation.

Another design concern should be the specific hardware requirements of the application. Certain applications have hardware requirements that exceed the requirements of the operating system, and these additional requirements must be considered during the planning stages. For instance, many communications programs, such as fax server software, require the purchase of a line card that is used to interface with an incoming PRI (Primary Rate Interface) or BRI (Basic Rate Interface) circuit. These types of circuits are ISDN-based connections typically used for voice communications. If you were planning a load-balanced fax server solution, you would have to be mindful of this requirement and be sure not only to order a card for each server, but also to arrange multiple circuits so that you would have one interface for each server.

Related to the hardware requirements, some software actually requires the existence of other software for proper functionality. This may be as simple as the need for a RADIUS server or as complex as the need for a particular type of switch or firewall. Be sure you know the dependencies of your application so that you can include them into your design document.

Data storage is also an important requirement. Does your application need large amounts of space for the install? Does it create log files that grow over time? Are there files that the application creates that may need to be pruned over time? All of these questions will help to determine the hard disk space necessary to store the application and the data it controls.

3.1.2 Determine Cluster Technology

Prior to planning a cluster install, you must decide which cluster technology fits with your application's needs. The two primary cluster types you may consider are failover clustering and load-balanced clustering. Table 3-1 provides examples of typical application clusters and will help you to decide which cluster technology to choose. Keep in mind that you are not limited to only one. Many systems require both load balancing and failover, and incorporate both technologies into the design.

Table 3-1   Which Cluster Do I Use?

I need to cluster...	You should use...
An SQL server database that provides data storage for an e-commerce site.	A failover cluster.
A static web site with no dynamic content.	A load-balanced cluster.
A dynamic web site that stores data in a database.	A failover cluster for the database and a load-balanced cluster for the web site.
An exchange server.	A failover cluster.
A file share.	Either a failover cluster or a load-balanced cluster. Both will work; however the failover cluster will provide only fault tolerance for the file share, not load balancing. The load-balanced cluster will provide load balancing, but will not replicate content to other machines in the cluster automatically.

3.1.3 Determine a Clustering Model

If you decide to use a load-balancing cluster for your application, then you can skip this step. Determining the appropriate cluster model applies to the construction of a failover cluster only. There are three different failover cluster models:

- Single-node failover cluster
- Dedicated secondary node failover cluster
- Distributed failover cluster

As stated in Chapter 2, "What Is a Cluster?," a single-node failover cluster is one server configured as the first node within a failover cluster. This model is ideal for organizations that wish to build a cluster, but have a limited budget or need to produce a cluster application-testing environment. If you are building a test application or your budget is limited, you may choose the single-node failover cluster for your system.

The dedicated secondary node failover cluster is for organizations that wish to provide only one fault-tolerant application on their cluster. This is an ideal cluster model for exchange servers, SQL servers, file shares, and other types of applications that provide dynamic content. The difference between this cluster model and the distributed failover cluster model is that it provides only one application to the clients. If you have multiple application, or multiple instances of the same application, you would want to choose the distributed failover cluster so that your applications can be load balanced between the two (or more) nodes in the cluster.

3.1.4 Determine Required Network Services

Once you have decided on a cluster model, you will need to list all network services that your application is dependent upon so that you will know what additional hardware you may need. These services could include one or more of the following:

- DNS (Domain Naming Service)
- WINS (Windows Internet Naming Service)
- DHCP (Dynamic Host Configuration Protocol)

- Domain authentication
- Firewall services
- Routing

A dependent network service is any service that is not provided by the cluster and that your cluster is dependent upon to function properly. Naming services such as WINS and DNS are obvious dependencies to most cluster implementations, but some may overlook the not-so-obvious services such as domain authentication or static routes from a router to the local subnet. All of these dependencies will depend upon your particular network, so don't hesitate to investigate every requirement. If your network has an individual dedicated to WAN, be sure to ask for his or her advice or concerns. It may save you some troubleshooting in the future.

Many of the services you will need are already on your network, but you will need to list them so they can be included in your network diagram. This will ensure that the persons responsible for those services understand their roles in the project and provide the needed support.

3.1.5 Determine Hardware Requirements

As discussed previously, there are many types of clusters, and based on the cluster technology and model you choose for your application, you will have to carefully plan which hardware to purchase so that your cluster project is not hindered. Be sure to also plan for the hardware necessary to implement the network services that your application is dependent upon. Although it is not possible to make a list of hardware required for every application or cluster type, Table 3-2 will give you a good understanding of the hardware necessary to implement your project.

Table 3-2 does not provide strict rules, but a general guide. Your network may need more or less hardware, depending on the services present and the requirements of your application.

3.1.6 Diagram the Network

Once you have compiled all the data you need, it is time to diagram your network. This is where you will get the greatest visual picture of your project. Many engineers today overlook the need for adequate documentation—to their detriment. Building a cluster server system is a complex task that should be documented and diagramed prior to ordering the first piece of hardware.

Table 3-2   Hardware Requirements

Cluster Type	Cluster Model	Hardware Needed
Network Load Balanced	N/A	• Two or more servers equipped with two network interface cards per server • One network hub • One network switch (layer 2)
Failover	Single Node	• One server equipped with two network interface cards per server • One server to serve as Domain Controller, DNS, and/or WINS server • External SCSI disk array • One network hub • One network switch (layer 2)
Failover	Dedicated Secondary Node	• Two servers equipped with two network interface cards per server • External SCSI disk array • One server to serve as Domain Controller, DNS, and/or WINS server • One network hub • One network switch (layer 2)
Failover	Distributed Systems	• Two servers equipped with two network interface cards per server • External SCSI disk array • One server to serve as Domain Controller, DNS, and/or WINS server • One network hub • One network switch (layer 2)

There are many diagramming software programs on the market that will assist you with your diagram. The type of software is not as important as the accuracy of your diagram. Here are some of the things you should include in your diagram:

- All Servers and their connectivity to each other
- All network hardware that will be implemented
- IP subnetting design, including IP addresses for your servers, cluster resources, virtual servers, routers, firewalls, and other devices
- Server names
- Applications in use

Take a look at the diagram in Figure 3-1. Your diagram should be similar in design.

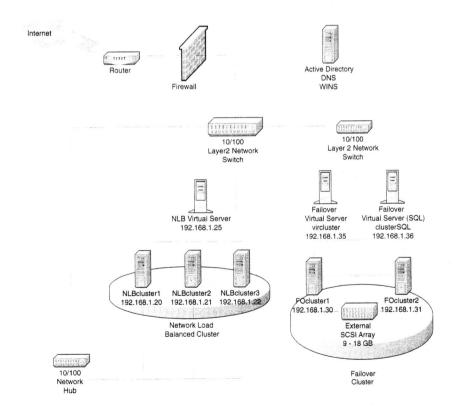

Figure 3-1
Sample cluster system diagram.

3.1.7 Determine Integration Strategy

Once you have drawn up a diagram of your network, it is time to determine your integration strategy. There are several tasks that need to be completed before your system will be fully functional, all of which will be detailed in your implementation plan. Prior to that step, you must outline which tasks need to be completed and in what order. If your organization is like most, you have someone who is responsible for every aspect of the network service or function that the infrastructure is dependent upon, including DNS, WINS, DHCP, routing, power, HVAC, procurement, and so on. During this stage, it is a good idea to get these people together for an integration strategy meeting.

The goals of the meeting should be simple—to determine the tasks that must take place before the cluster server system can be put into production and to decide who is responsible for each task. Remember, there are many people involved in any project. You may not often see the person in charge of the heating and cooling of your LAN room, but that does not mean that his or her work is expendable. You must consider every aspect of your system before planning its implementation. Some of the questions to ask include the following:

- What are the power requirements of the cluster system?
- Do I need any special power outlets for the UPS system?
- How will the additional servers affect the temperature of the LAN room?
- How will the system be protected from physical intrusion?
- How will the system be protected from Internet threats?
- Who will be responsible for the system maintenance?
- Who will be responsible for maintaining content?
- Is there enough space for the new servers?
- Is the equipment being purchased compatible with existing systems?
- How will the system be backed up?

Bringing together a group of people to work on a project will be easier than trying to do it alone. By ensuring that your system will integrate with existing services and systems, you lower the amount of time and expense required to complete the project. The result of the integration meeting should be a set of notes that can be used to construct your project implementation plan.

3.1.8 Create Implementation Plan

As important as any step within the process, the implementation plan, once complete, will serve as a guide for the engineer that will be implementing the system. The best way to formulate an implementation plan is to write down all of the tasks that need to be completed before the system can be put into production. Order does not matter at this point; just write down the tasks as you think of them. Checking your network diagram will help, for there are many steps that need to be taken that you may forget. Document all of the tasks necessary to get the system online, even those for which you are not responsible.

Once you have all of the tasks written down, begin ordering them based upon the order in which the tasks need to take place to complete your project. After you get your list of tasks in order, go down the list and assign each task to a particular person. This provides an "owner" for each task, someone who is completely responsible for completing that action.

For those who have done project management, this method will be easily accomplished, but for those who are new to it, project planning takes some practice. There are many applications on the market that will assist you in the development of your project plan, including Microsoft Project. For those who are more advanced, Microsoft Excel can be used to plot out your course. Whichever application you use, just make sure your plan is comprehensive, covering every task that needs to be accomplished. Also be sure to review it several times for completeness.

After completing the task list and the ownership of each task, assign a start date to the first task and then assign duration to each task. This will be the time it takes to complete each task.

Note

Task duration has always been a common problem with project planning. If you assign the actual duration that it takes to complete to each task and then place the tasks in chronological order beginning with the start date you will end up with an unrealistic project completion date. Put it this way. If the first task is "purchase hardware," the actual time it takes to order the hardware may be only an hour or so, but the hardware does not actually arrive for two weeks. The next task is "install hardware." Obviously, you cannot install the hardware before it arrives, so the duration of the task has to be relative to the time it takes for the previous task to complete. Make sure you factor this into your project plan so there is plenty of time for each task to complete.

3.1.9 Create Contingency Plan

In addition to your implementation plan, consider creating a contingency plan. Building a cluster is a complex, time-consuming process and is not always free from complication. If your cluster implementation is the first set of hardware/software in your network, then a contingency plan may not be required, but if you are attempting to integrate your cluster system with an existing network, a contingency plan is a must.

The contingency plan is similar to the implementation plan, but rather than building a plan to install a system, it is constructed to give engineers a "way out." Contingency planning allows you to plan the reverse of the implementation so that you can roll back the changes that you have made in the case of a failure that prevents users from accessing the network. This can be advantageous when you are operating in an environment with minimal tolerance for downtime.

Although contingency planning sounds simple, it isn't. You can't just reverse the process that implemented your system (although that may work in some cases). To create a contingency plan, you must review the impact of each change you will be making as detailed in your implementation plan. Some changes can be easily reversed, but some changes are irreversible. Your best bet in building a contingency plan is to assume you have completed the installation of the cluster and it fails to function properly. What steps do you need to take to restore network services to the clients? You may find that you have not changed anything that affects the clients, but in the event you have, those changes need to be reversed as part of your contingency plan.

3.2 Hardware Requirements

Before launching out into the deep water of clustering, it is important to have a firm foundation of knowledge related to the hardware requirements of Microsoft clustering and network load-balancing products. In this section we will look at the specific requirements of both the Microsoft Cluster Server (MSCS) and the Microsoft Network Load Balancing (NLB) service.

3.2.1 Servers

The Microsoft Hardware Compatibility List (HCL) is the most definitive resource for determining what hardware will work correctly on Windows 2000. Any grasp at compatibility must start there. The clustering software has hardware requirements that are separate from the HCL, but you must ensure that your operating system will function properly on your hardware before reviewing the hardware compatibility of the clustering services. The Microsoft HCL for Windows 2000 and other Microsoft products can be found at *www.microsoft.com/hcl*.

3.2.1.1 CPU

Although disappointing to some dedicated Alpha fans, Microsoft removed support for the Alpha processor from the final release of Windows 2000 products. Clustering support for the Alpha processor platform has been removed as well. If you plan to build a cluster using Microsoft products, you will need to use an Intel x86 platform to do so.

Note

The Intel x86 architecture is a general term that refers to a particular kind of processor construction. Using this term does not imply that you can use only Intel microprocessors in servers that are going to be clustered. The AMD (Advanced Micro Devices) processor and the Cyrix processor are both Intel x86-compatible chips and offer similar performance and operation.

3.2.1.2 Memory

There are no specific hardware requirements for the cluster related to memory. As a rule of thumb, make sure you have a sufficient amount of memory for each server in your cluster so that memory does not become your bottleneck. As a designer, you are the only one who can decide how much RAM you are going to be using, but there are relative guidelines for choosing how much memory your server will need. Use this formula. Start with 256MB RAM, and add 256MB for each application you plan to run on your cluster. Then add 128MB for every 100 users that will be accessing the server cluster simultaneously.

For instance, suppose you are building a two-node failover cluster. You want to house SQL Server and file sharing on your cluster. There will be 1,000 people in your organization and approximately 500 users that will have simultaneous access to the cluster server. In this situation, the formula would look like this:

256MB + 256MB (SQL) + 256MB (File Sharing) + 640MB (500 users) = 1,408MB

This formula applies to each server within the cluster, based upon a two-node distributed failover cluster. Each server in this situation will run a different application. The first will run SQL Server and the second will run file sharing. The RAM needed is based upon the assumption that when one machine fails, the other will have to adequately support both applications. This is the standard memory capacity that each server within the cluster should run to maintain the clients without a performance decrease. Keep in mind that this is a relative formula and will obviously need to be adjusted to suit the needs of the applications you may be running.

3.2.1.3 Paging

As discussed in Chapter 1, "Climbing the Mountain: 24/7 Data Access," paging is the process of writing temporary working data to a hard drive due to a limitation of physical memory. Paging allows computers to run applications and programs that are larger than the memory resident in the machine. Paging is often referred to as *swapping*.

Paging is a double-edged sword. It greatly improves the memory management for computers that have a limited amount of RAM, allowing them to run programs that would not otherwise run. But it is also a very processor-intensive, time-consuming task that can cause a machine to slow. Balancing the right amount of paging with the operating system, applications, and services you are running is essential to the performance of your cluster server.

It is not typically necessary for you to adjust the size of the paging file that Windows 2000 Server implements by default, for it is calculated based upon 1.5 times the amount of physical memory in the machine. There are times, however, when you will want to adjust the default page file settings. You can access the page file settings by right-clicking on the **My Computer** icon and selecting **Properties**. Then select the **Advanced** tab (see Figure 3-2) and click the **Performance Options** button.

There are several items you can modify to increase the performance of your server, and consequently increase the performance of your cluster. The following recommendations will assist you in determining the best configuration for your paging file:

- Do not place your paging file on the same physical drive as your operating system files (c:\winnt).

- Set the minimum size and maximum size of your paging file to be identical.

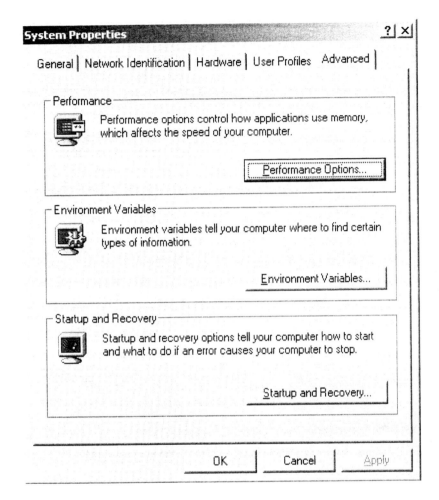

Figure 3-2
Accessing the paging file settings.

- If possible, make smaller paging files spread across multiple drives.
- Do not place paging files on fault-tolerance disk partitions (RAID 5).
- Place paging files on stripe sets (nonparity) when possible.

The object of the paging file placement is to allow the system to access the file without affecting the disk access time to other parts of the system. Obviously, placing the paging file on a disk drive separate from the system files will allow one disk to write to the paging file while the other is accessing system files, thus increasing the amount of data that can be written at one time.

Setting the paging file on a different partition of the same disk will not improve performance because the same disk still has to access the system files and the paging file simultaneously. Separate disks will improve performance, and separate disks on separate controllers will increase the performance even more. In Figure 3-3 you can see that a Windows 2000 Server with three separate physical hard drives has been configured with a paging file that is distributed across two separate disks. There is no paging file configured for the C: drive because it is the system partition. All three of the drives are Small Computer System Interface (SCSI) drives attached to the same controller. If you wanted to increase the performance of the paging file even more, you could add a second SCSI controller and place the last drive on the second controller, thus allowing the paging file (that is distributed across two disks) to be on separate disks and separate controllers.

When setting your paging file (see Figure 3-3), be sure to set the minimum and maximum paging file size to the same setting. Using different settings causes the paging file to expand the file as needed, which can bring unwanted processing during critical operations. A large difference between the minimum and maximum size can also contribute to disk fragmentation.

When using paging files on systems that utilize RAID (Redundant Array of Inexpensive Disks) controllers, it is important to note how performance can be affected. RAID is discussed later in this chapter in more detail, but in simple terms, RAID is the configuration of two or more drives to form one logical drive to the operating system. When a paging file is used on a nonparity stripe set (where data is written contiguously across three or more hard drives), performance can be increased. However, if that stripe set utilizes parity (which is present in RAID 5), you may experience a performance loss if your paging file is set on this volume due to the fact that the operating system must cache parity information related to every bit of data that it writes. To write parity information for every piece of data that is placed into the paging file can be time consuming for the processor and disk controller.

So, how do you know the correct size setting for your server(s)? Well, the truth is, it may take a bit of trial and error to find the right combination, but here is the process you should use to determine your paging level. Set the paging file to 1.5 times the size of the amount of memory you have in the machine and then review the Process(_Total)\Page File Bytes counter through Performance Monitor (see Figure 3-4). This will tell you the amount of the page file being used by your server. This is a byte count, so you may have to adjust the vertical scale to 1000 rather than 100. This activity indicates the amount of the paging file that is currently in use. Using the current physical memory, determine the percentage of the paging file being used. If it is more than 70%, increase the paging file size. Don't increase the size of the file too

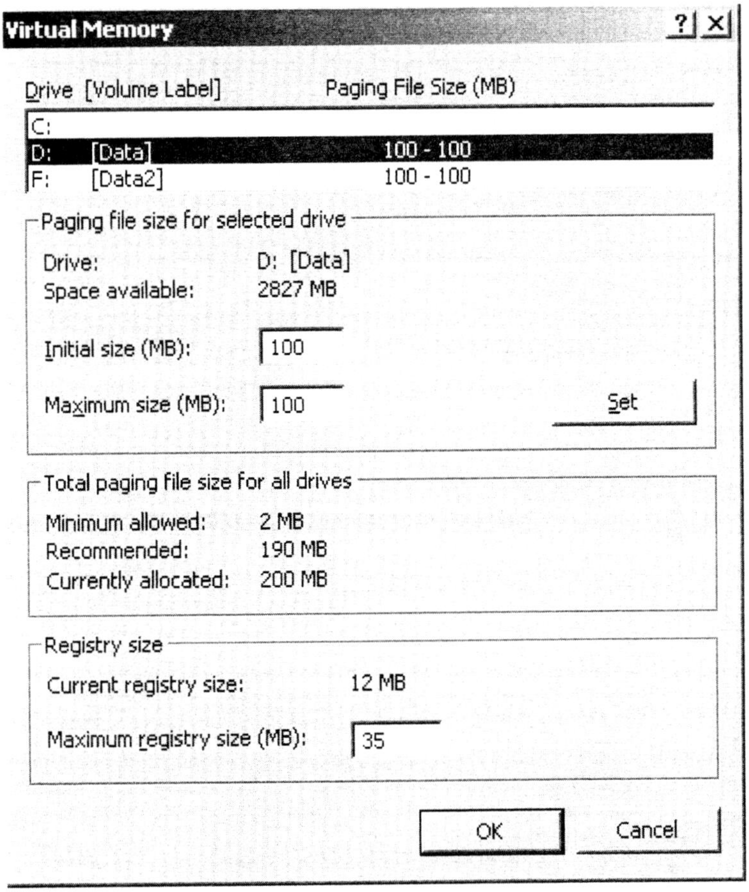

Figure 3-3
Setting the paging file properties.

much, because the paging file is actually a file, and uses valuable storage space. Change the file setting gradually until you have reached a balance that is optimal for your system. If you find that you have to increase the paging file far beyond the double amount of memory that is in the machine, consider adding more physical memory to the machine.

Also remember that adding physical memory to the machine does not change the paging file automatically, so be sure to adjust the paging file after adding physical memory to a server that is already running Windows 2000.

When adjusting your paging file settings on machines that are clustered, be sure to make similar changes to all machines. This will ensure that performance is consistent to all clients.

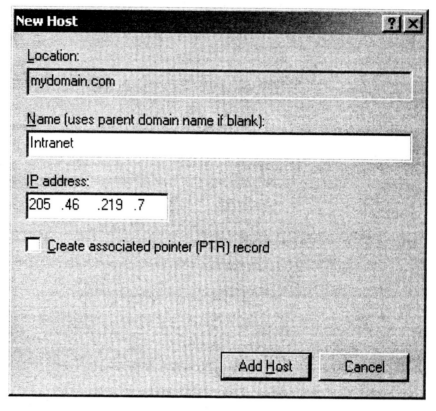

Figure 3-4
Using Performance Monitor to review paging.

3.2.2 Disks

Windows 2000 has robust support for multiple disk types, file systems, and architectures. Unfortunately, the clustering and load-balancing services are not as diverse; they require specific types of drives and file systems for correct operation. In addition, the placement of the operating system and application data in most single-server systems is trivial, but in clustering, you must place the operating system and the applications in the proper place or they will not function (or failover) properly.

In this section we will review the disk type requirements as well as the mandated file systems of MSCS. We will also discuss the placement of the operating system and types of storage devices that can be used for failover clustering.

3.2.2.1 Disk Types

Hard disk types can be categorized into three basic categories: IDE/ATA, SCSI, and fibre channel. As discussed in Chapter 1, the IDE/ATA standard is more common in desktop workstations and end-user computers due to their inexpensive price tag, even though they have a two-device limitation and limited fault tolerance options. SCSI is a more advanced architecture, allowing administrators to place up to seven devices on one controller (or channel). This increases the amount of storage possible and also boosts the fault tolerance options available. Fibre channel is a disk type that allows mass storage devices to transfer information, using 100 mbps fiber connectivity. Fibre channel drives are faster and more reliable than IDE/ATA or SCSI drives, but cost significantly more. Most SAN (storage area network) implementations employ fibre channel technology due to its fast transfer rate and flexible fiber connectivity.

The Microsoft NLB service is disk-independent and can be used with all three disk types. The MSCS, however; supports all three disk types for the system partition, but supports only SCSI and fibre channel connectivity for shared disk storage.

3.2.2.2 File Systems

A file system is the organizational structure that an operating system uses to keep track of files within a computer. One of the most popular file systems made common by *DOS* (disk operating system) is called *FAT* (file allocation table). This file system splits pieces of the hard disk into sectors; it writes data to the sectors and keeps track of the location within hidden files called "fat" files. Many enhancements and alternate file systems have been developed since the DOS days, including HPFS (OS/2), NTFS (Windows NT), and FAT32 (Windows 98). Detailing the intricacies of each of the file systems is beyond the scope of this section; however, it is important to note the performance benefits of using NTFS5, the Windows 2000 native file system, over other file systems.

- Fault tolerance using transaction logging and recovery
- Faster disk access times
- File and folder security
- Supports volumes of up to 2 terabytes in size
- Disk quotas
- Native encryption using EFS (Encryption File System)

In the days of FAT file systems, operating systems such as DOS and Windows 95 came bundled with disk maintenance tools. These tools were essential due to the way FAT stored data on the disk and a lack of fault tolerance within the design itself. Tools like checkdisk and defrag needed to be run routinely to keep the disk operating at an efficient level. NTFS is a more advanced file system design, which incorporates transaction logging and recovery into file system management. This allows fragmented files and missed transactions due to system failure to be handled correctly with a minimal amount of mess left on the disk. While it is optimistic to say that you will never need to run disk maintenance tools on an NTFS volume, the necessity of the tools has been greatly reduced, and disks formatted using NTFS can run more efficiently for longer periods of time than the same disks formatted using legacy file systems such as FAT.

NTFS requires less disk maintenance, and it operates more efficiently, requiring far less disk reads to find a file within the file system. This makes disk access faster for server applications.

NTFS also allows a greater amount of flexibility when securing folders and files. Within a single server or a network domain, administrators often choose to set permissions on a folder within a file structure to limit access. Unfortunately, on old files systems, you could set the permissions only on directories, which did not give much control to the administrator when trying to secure certain files. NTFS supports access control lists and permissions set at the directory level and the file level. This allows a more granular control over the files and folders within a file share or volume.

Building a SAN or cluster server that will be used to store large amounts of data requires large volume support. Older file systems had limitations that forced administrators to create many small volumes for file storage rather than a few large volumes. NTFS allows administrators to create disk volumes of up to 2 terabytes in size, shattering all of the previous limits. When disk space management is key to your enterprise, NTFS offers the ability to set quotas on disk volumes, limiting the amount of space any one user can consume.

In addition to the preceding advantages, the Windows 2000 NTFS file system also incorporates native file encryption called EFS, which uses symmetric key encryption in conjunction with public key technology to protect user files from unauthorized access. File encryption ensures that the file can be opened only by its owner. If the file were to be stolen opened without the private key assigned to the owner, the unauthorized user would see only unintelligible characters. This can be of great benefit to computers shared by multiple users or portable computers.

For clustering and load balancing, NTFS offers a variety of benefits that can increase the performance of the cluster system. Network load-balanced clusters do not require NTFS volumes to function, but you can lower your cost of ownership, broaden your administrative control, and heighten the performance of the system by using it. The MSCS does not require that the operating system partition on each node be formatted NTFS (although it is recommended), but it does require NTFS formatting on all shared disk storage between nodes.

Note

Windows 2000 supports a new type of disk model called dynamic disk configuration. The configuration of dynamic disks is different than the basic disk configuration, which was the standard until Windows NT 4.0. Dynamic disks do not have primary or extended partitions, but only "volumes." These volumes can be organized to build performance and fault tolerance into a disk set. For instance, using the dynamic disks, a server running three or more disks can create a spanned volume or RAID 5 volume that will allow data to be written across the disks simultaneously. This configuration gives an alternative to hardware-based RAID and can increase performance. The use of dynamic disks can increase the performance and fault tolerance of the operating system partitions on load-balanced clusters and failover clusters, but is not supported by failover clusters for shared disk storage.

3.2.2.3 OS Placement

As you plan to build your server cluster, it is a good idea to consider your data placement. In a load-balanced server cluster, most configurations will contain two sets of data: the operating system files and the data files. The machines that you add to a load-balanced cluster should be high-performance machines, and the configuration you use for your data storage can do a lot to help or hinder performance.

It is recommended that you have at least two separate disks within any machine that will participate in a load-balanced cluster. There are many different ways to configure your disks, but all of them seek to obtain the same goal: fast data access. Use the following rules to get the most out of your load-balanced cluster's disk configuration:

- Place the operating system and data files on separate disks.
- Use RAID 0 (stripe set without parity) to increase performance.
- Use RAID 5 (stripe set with parity) to increase fault tolerance.

Placing the operating system and data files on separate disks increases performance by allowing two disks to work simultaneously to access and display data. If you have two disks in the machine, use one disk as your operating system disk and use the other disk as your data storage. If you have three disks, consider using a SCSI RAID array controller to create a RAID 0 or RAID 5 array. A RAID 0 array is often called a stripe set without parity. This configuration writes data across the disks without maintaining parity information. This yields high speeds, but lacks any fault tolerance. If one disk in the array were to malfunction, the whole array (along with the data) would be erased. This may work well for you if you have a server farm where every machine runs the same data and it is easy for you to build new machines and add them to your farm, but if you require a more fault-tolerant system, you should use a RAID 5 array (which is discussed later in this chapter).

It is possible to use Windows 2000's dynamic disk configuration to create a software-based RAID 5 array, but software RAID never performs as well as hardware RAID and is more prone to failure. What is possible is not always the best solution. If the budget allows, stick with hardware-based RAID.

When building a Microsoft failover cluster, the rules are the same. The difference with the failover cluster is the external disk array. The shared disk storage will maintain all of the application data. For operating system placement, you only need to worry about what drives are in use on the local machine. Again, RAID 5 is the best fault-tolerant solution for the operating system, but if you are constrained by budget, software RAID or a mirrored drive will work in a similar way. Keep in mind that you are building the failover server cluster for fault tolerance, and neglecting to make your operating system fault-tolerant decreases the reliability of your system.

3.2.2.4 Cluster Storage

When planning your cluster storage placement, it is important to note the amount of space your applications require as well as the partitioning requirements of the cluster server. Because the load-balanced cluster server system does not use shared disk storage, this section applies only to failover clustering.

The most important requirement for the shared disk storage is application residence. The applications running on your cluster should each have its own physical disk. This allows each application to be owned by a particular server and failover-independent of the other applications running on the cluster. You will also need a physical disk for the quorum (cluster transaction logs) resource, which will be discussed in more detail later. For instance, consider a failover cluster that will run SQL Server and Internet Information Server (IIS.) Based upon that requirement, the MSCS software must see three separate drives on the external storage array. One will be used for the SQL Server files, the second will be used for the IIS files, and the third will be used as a quorum resource.

Note

Each application used in the cluster requires a separate physical disk. This may cause some confusion when configuring RAID 5 arrays. Because the RAID 5 array appears as one drive to the operating system, you must partition your RAID array, using the RAID BIOS configuration, to resemble three separate drives. To do this, configure three separate containers for your RAID configuration. This will appear to the operating system as three separate drives and allow each application to be owned and failover-independent of the other applications.

3.2.3 Storage Array Connections

As you plan to build your shared disk failover cluster, one of the most important decisions you will make is the type of connection you wish to have between your server(s) and your shared disk storage container. The two types of connections in use today are SCSI and fibre channel. Both of these technologies offer a robust, efficient connection to your shared storage, but their differences and limitations are important to note.

3.2.3.1 SCSI

SCSI is an industry standard interface for connecting peripheral computer devices such as CD-ROM drives, backup drives, and hard disks. SCSI has become popular due to high transfer rates and the ability to link up to eight devices on the same controller. As SCSI advanced, manufacturers began to distribute multichannel SCSI cards, allowing users to connect up to 16 devices to a single card. The flexibility of SCSI, in addition to the number of devices that can be connected to a single SCSI card, has made SCSI a solid choice for external disk arrays.

Before we discuss the specific requirements of a SCSI external disk array, let's look at SCSI technology in general so that you will have a solid foundation when constructing SCSI disk arrays for a server cluster.

Although often referred to as a controller, a SCSI interface card is not really a controller, but a system bus that interfaces with the system board via a host adapter. As stated before, a SCSI bus can host up to eight devices. Each device is configured with an ID, numbered 0 through 7. When a SCSI bus loads its BIOS (a small software component resident on the SCSI card), it scans the bus to determine what devices are present. As you boot a system that has a SCSI interface, you will see it detect devices and confirm their ID placement on the bus.

SCSI devices are typically "daisy-chained," meaning they all connect to the SCSI bus using the same cable. Some devices are external and some devices are internal, but the SCSI architecture stays the same. Although you can put up to eight devices on a SCSI bus, the SCSI card itself is considered one device and must use one of the IDs. The factory default for this setting is typically 7, although it can be changed to any ID you choose.

Because the SCSI bus operates on a chain, you must terminate the end of the chain properly for SCSI to function correctly. There are many ways to terminate a SCSI bus. For external devices, there is usually a small terminator device that is used on the last device in a chain. On internal devices, many drives offer internal termination or a built-in termination that is resident on the drive. As a rule, just remember that SCSI connections must always be terminated. A SCSI bus will typically alert you at boot up if it is not terminated properly.

When you build your cluster server system, always keep these rules in mind:

- SCSI devices on the same bus cannot share the same ID.
- SCSI chains must be terminated properly for them to function correctly.
- SCSI cards (or RAID cards) used for failover clustering should be identical.

A typical external SCSI drive array will come with two external SCSI connections. These cards are not SCSI cards, but are actually interfaces to the backplane of the device you are using to store your drives. Logically, you must connect the SCSI card in one server to the first drive array interface and the SCSI card in the second server to the second drive array interface. This placed both cards, and all drives in the array on the same SCSI bus. If you remember our first rule, SCSI devices on the same bus cannot share the same ID. Because both SCSI cards you buy will have the same factory default setting, one of them must be changed. You can use whichever ID you want, but it is recommended that you change one of the SCSI cards to ID number 6 rather than 7. This frees up ID 0 through 5 for remaining drives in your cluster array. If you plan to use more than six drives, you will need to make sure that your SCSI card is a dual channel card, or else you will run out of available IDs.

The second rule is met in this scenario because you are using one SCSI card at the beginning of the chain and you are using the second SCSI card at the end of the chain to act as a terminator for the bus. No further termination should be necessary.

The third rule is not so much a rule as a strongly encouraged guideline. It is possible to configure and run your external storage array using two different SCSI cards, but it is not recommended for a couple of reasons. The first reason is compatibility. You want to make sure the devices on your SCSI bus are compatible. Choosing the same card for both ends will help to ensure compatibility. The second—and probably the most important—reason is the transfer of the array configuration. If you choose to use a SCSI RAID array controller, which you most likely will if you are building a system with fault tolerance in mind, then you will need to be able to transfer the configuration you create on one machine to the other machine. RAID controllers store configuration information typically in two places: on the card itself, in nonvolatile memory, and on the disk array. When you are building your cluster it is important, before you even load your operating system, that both array controllers have the same configuration.

The process of transferring the configuration is simple and will be discussed in more detail in later chapters, but must be noted here for planning purposes. Before the cluster software is installed, you should never run both servers at the same time. This will cause disk corruption on the disk array. To configure your array, you will need to boot one server and enter the RAID array configuration. Configure the array and save the configuration. Then you will shut down the server. The second server will boot and then retrieve a copy of the saved configuration from the disk array and will save it to the card. This will ensure that both cards have the same configuration. This process works well if both array controllers are identical and read and write the configuration information in the same way, but two different controllers may not be able to read and write the configuration in the same way. This would hinder you from correctly configuring the RAID array.

3.2.3.2 Fibre channel

More common than SCSI for shared disk storage, fibre channel is becoming the industry standard for building large SAN implementations. Fibre channel is a serial data transfer architecture that employs both networking technologies and channel attachment technologies. Fibre channel is a flexible way to connect all devices and offers speeds over 1 GBPS. Fibre channel supports several standard protocols, including SCSI, High-Performance Parallel Interface (HIPPI), and IP.

Fibre channel uses single-mode or multimode fiber cable to connect devices such as servers, workstations, and shared disk arrays. Devices are connected point-to-point or through the use of a fibre channel hub or switch. The scalability of a fibre channel network is almost limitless.

The most common type of fibre channel connectivity is called *arbitrated loop* (FC-AL), which supports up to 127 addresses per loop, with one address being reserved for switch attachment. Fibre channel hubs can be cascaded to a fibre channel switch to integrate millions of devices into the same fiber fabric, but the realistic limit for each loop should be 6 to 12 devices. Multiple hubs can be linked using a fibre channel switch.

Fibre channel is expandable through the use of fiber-SCSI bridges—devices that allow fibre channel switches and hubs to connect to legacy systems based upon SCSI technology.

So, why isn't every network running fibre channel to the desktop? Mostly cost. It is much more expensive to implement a fibre channel cluster than a SCSI cluster. Many manufacturers have ceased production of SCSI-based clustering solutions, so fibre channel pricing should become more reasonable in the near future.

Fibre channel is fully supported (and recommended) for use on both the Microsoft NLB service and the MSCS.

3.2.4 RAID

RAID is a storage subsystem technology that allows several hard drives to be clustered together into an array that virtually provides one large drive to the operating system. RAID used to be an expensive endeavor, but has recently become a very inexpensive means of fault tolerance and performance, and can be implemented on SCSI and fibre channel platforms.

3.2.4.1 RAID History

RAID was developed at the University of California, Berkeley, in 1987. Scientists were hoping to improve the reliability and performance of storage subsystems by clustering small, inexpensive disk drives into an array that the operating system would recognize as a single drive. This technology worked well, but had a major flaw. They found that although the use of the array improved system performance, there was a higher chance of failure within the system, since a failure in any drive within the array causes the entire array to fail. To rectify this flaw, the scientists recommended six levels of RAID to provide a balance between system performance and data reliability.

3.2.4.2 RAID Versions

There are six RAID versions, labeled RAID 0 through RAID 5. Each RAID version maximizes certain areas of concern while minimizing another. All of them are valuable, but not all of them are suitable for every need. RAID 0, 1, and 5 are the only versions in common use today.

3.2.4.2.1 RAID 0

RAID 0 is often referred to as *striping*. When using RAID 0, a storage subsystem will write data across multiple drives simultaneously and consecutively. In a typical disk subsystem, an application will write to a single hard disk until it is full, and then write to a second hard disk. Using RAID 0, the operating system sees only one drive and writes "stripes" of data across the drives as needed (see Figure 3-5).

RAID 0 maximizes performance by utilizing several different drives simultaneously to read and write data to disk. The downside to RAID 0 is a lack of fault tolerance. Because the drives are all within the same array, the failure of one drive will cause the loss of all data on the stripe set volume.

3.2.4.2.2 RAID 1

RAID 1, often referred to as mirroring, is the storage of data redundantly across multiple drives. Mirroring ensures that if a disk fails, a second disk will have a complete copy of the data. Multiple disks can be configured to mirror another set of multiple disks, assuming the disks are similar in size. If they are different in size, the set will mirror the data equal to the smallest disk set within the group.

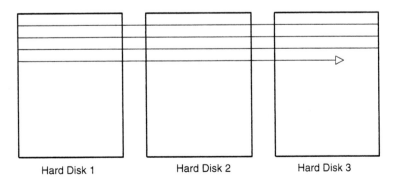

Hard Disk 1   Hard Disk 2   Hard Disk 3

Figure 3-5
RAID 0 striping.

73

A typical mirroring configuration would be two identical drives mirrored for the operating system files.

RAID 1 actually improves read performance on the disks because there are multiple locations for the data to reside. The disadvantage to RAID 1 is that you lose half of your disk space to the fault tolerance of the system. For instance, if you have two 18 GB drives on your RAID array controller and you choose to use RAID 1 to mirror the two drives together, you would have only 18 GB of actual space.

3.2.4.2.3 RAID 2

The RAID 2 model is not commonly used within commercial applications, but is mentioned here for reference. RAID 2 uses an ECC (error-correcting code) algorithm to determine checksum values for each data block on a hard disk. The verification data is then written to the end of each block. As data is read from the disk, the actual data is verified against the checksum values to determine data integrity. If the integrity of the data is compromised (incongruent with checksum values) then the data is discarded from that block and rebuilt using the data found within the checksum. Again, this is not a widely used RAID version.

3.2.4.2.4 RAID 3

RAID 3 is much like RAID 0, for it writes data across multiple disks simultaneously to improve disk performance. RAID 3, however, reserves one disk in the set to use for parity information. This information can be used to rebuild a lost drive in the event of a failure. The problem with RAID 3 is a disk-write bottleneck that takes place on the parity drive. Using RAID 3, system resources are occupied too frequently as the disk writes parity information to that one disk. RAID 3 is not in common use, being replaced by RAID 4 and RAID 5.

3.2.4.2.5 RAID 4

RAID 4 is an improvement upon RAID 3, but was designed more for "read-only" environments than for large contiguous file writes. Using deeper stripes for the stripe set, the disks achieve better read performance. RAID 4, like its RAID 3 cousin, still uses one disk as a parity disk, contributing to the bottleneck during writes to the disk(s). Like RAID 2 and RAID 3, RAID 4 is seldom used within commercial applications today.

3.2.4.2.6 RAID 5

Probably the most common and widely used RAID technology today, RAID 5 has become a standard in the server market and is slowly becoming more common on high-end workstations. RAID 5 builds on the concepts developed in

RAID 3 and RAID 4—the use of parity information to recover lost data. However, RAID 5 writes parity information within a stripe across all of the disks within the array rather than on a single disk. This improves read and write performance over the previous RAID versions and alleviates the bottleneck found within single-disk parity RAID.

RAID 5 holds many advantages over RAID 0 and RAID 1 technologies by providing fault tolerance without sacrificing disk space and without significant performance decreases. RAID 5 uses the space equivalent of one disk within the array to store parity information, thus decreasing the available space within an array only by the size of one disk. For instance, if you have four 18GB drives within a RAID 5 array, you will have 54GB of disk space available, while only 18GB of space will be used for disk parity information.

Some of the first implementations of RAID 5 were implemented on closed-disk systems—meaning you had to dismantle the system to replace defunct drives. Advances in the "hot pluggable" backplane market have allowed server manufacturers to offer hot swappable drive arrays. These arrays give administrators access to the hard drives without dismantling the machine. Even more helpful, the hot swappable drive array allows you to remove one drive from an array without disrupting the operation of the system!

To give an example of how RAID 5 can provide fault tolerance for production servers, let's consider a typical scenario. John is a systems administrator for a company that just purchased four servers, all equipped with RAID 5 hot swappable drive arrays. A few months after building the four servers with Windows 2000 and various applications, John comes into work to find a red light on one of the drives in server A, indicating that the drive has failed. The server is still running and responding to client requests, but the drive in the server has gone bad and needs to be replaced. John goes to a storage room where all of the information systems equipment is stored and grabs a drive identical to the one that is in server A. John pulls the bad drive out, puts the new drive in the drive array, and watches as the green light comes on and the array begins to restore the data to the drive. John did not have to restore data from a backup tape and he did not have to perform any type of maintenance. During the entire rebuild process, the server continued to function and respond to client requests.

If you are a system administrator and you have yet to work with RAID 5, consider purchasing a RAID 5 controller within each server you buy going forward. Although sometimes they are a bit costly, they are worth their weight in gold if you are using the server to maintain mission-critical information. Think about the process John would have had to go through to repair the server if he was not using RAID 5. He first would have noticed that the server was down and not responding to clients. After investigation, he would have deduced that one drive in the server was bad. He would have replaced the bad drive, reloaded the operating system, reloaded all of the applications, and restored all the data from a backup tape (assuming he had a current backup tape). Altogether, the server would have been down for approximately four to five hours, which could have been avoided by the use of a RAID 5 array controller card.

3.2.4.3 When to Use RAID

The next concerns are, When do I use RAID, and How does it fit into my clustering plan? To answer these questions, you have to determine which data needs to be fault-tolerant, and which data needs to be high-performance. Think about the following scenario.

Jennifer works for a popular national retail chain. Her company has decided to take all of their products online. Jennifer has been tasked with the design and deployment of the e-commerce system that will be used to host the Web site and product database. She has been given only two guidelines: Make the system as fast as possible with the ability to respond to several thousand requests per minute, and make the system as fault-tolerant as possible. Downtime is not an option. She decides to build the system using two technologies: the Microsoft NLB service and the MSCS. She designs a system that consists of eight load-balanced Web servers and a two-node cluster for the database.

As she begins to develop a required specification for the purchasing department, she considers the use of RAID and asks herself the following questions:

- Should I use RAID?
- Which servers should use RAID?
- Which type of RAID should I run on each server?
- How many drives will I need for each server?

She considers the eight Web servers and decides to order each equipped with three 9GB hard drives and a RAID array controller. She plans to use RAID 0 on each server. She then orders three 9GB drives for the two servers that will participate in the two-node cluster, along with two RAID array controllers for each server. One RAID array controller in each server will be used to configure a RAID 5 array for each machine's operating system. The other controller will be used for a shared external storage array.

Why did Jennifer decide to use RAID 0 on the Web servers and RAID 5 on the cluster servers? She decided that RAID 0 would give her the fastest disk access time for the front-end Web servers. Because each server within the load-balanced cluster will run the same content, fault tolerance for that volume is not necessary. If one server were to fail, she could easily build another server and add it to the cluster without taking the cluster offline. She chose RAID 5 for the failover cluster because it would allow the maximum amount of fault tolerance possible for those machines. And since they are running a mission-critical database, it made sense to make the data storage and the operating system storage fault-tolerant.

So, to answer the original question, you should use RAID on every server that is a part of your cluster. You should use RAID 0 (disk striping) or RAID 1 (mirroring) when you need fast disk access, and you should use RAID 5 (disk striping with parity) for every data store that needs to be fault-tolerant.

Note

There are many software programs, including Windows 2000, which will allow you to configure software-based RAID arrays. This is one way to achieve RAID performance or fault tolerance without the need for expensive hardware, but there are a couple of things you should keep in mind prior to using software based RAID. First, shared data storage for use in Windows 2000 failover clustering does not support software-based RAID. Second, most hardware-based RAID solutions come equipped with on-board RAM that allows the card to cache disk reads and writes, improving the speed of the system, but software-based RAID uses the operating system's resources for caching and can decrease the performance of a system significantly.

3.2.5 Network Interfaces

As with any application deployment, it is important to plan your network strategy during the design phase of your project. Many organizations may require a certain topology or protocol based upon what they are already using in each location. Other companies are more diverse. The network interface you use for your cluster server solution is very important, for it will dictate the speed at which your system will be able to communicate with other servers on the network, as well as its integration flexibility. When you consider this decision, keep in mind the following guidelines:

- Different topologies (e.g., fiber vs. CAT 5) can be significantly different in cost.
- Whatever you choose, you may have to integrate the technology into an existing network infrastructure.

- Your solution should scale to meet future bandwidth needs.
- Your solution must be conducive to your environment.
- Your network interface must be supported by Windows 2000 and the clustering software you choose to use.

There are two interfaces that you will have to provision when building a cluster server. If you choose to build a network load balancing cluster, you will most likely want to select two interfaces for each server: one that is used for cluster communication and one that is used for client connectivity. Network load balancing requires that regardless of how many network interfaces you use in each server, they all must be connected to the same network segment.

In a failover cluster, the interfaces are a bit more complex. The interfaces in a failover cluster can be used for public traffic or private traffic and can be in the same network segment or a separate network segment. You can use a single network card in each failover cluster node for both cluster communication and client communication, but this would not be efficient. Most implementations use a network connection for connectivity to the clients and a direct crossover cable connection between each server for the node-to-node cluster communication (see Figure 3-6). This is often referred to as a *heartbeat* connection because the cluster nodes communicate with each other using heartbeat type messages. Virtually, this is the same as having two separate network segments, but because your private network contains only two nodes, it

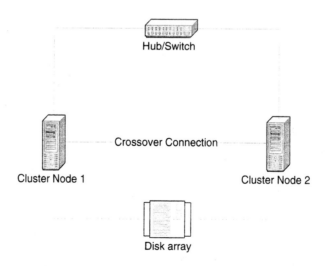

Figure 3-6
Typical failover cluster network interface configuration.

makes sense to connect them directly to one another. If you are constructing a cluster server with more than two nodes, then you will need to use separate network hubs or switches to ensure you have a private network and a public network for each connection.

In a Microsoft-based load-balanced or failover cluster, your choice of networking options is almost as wide as the Windows 2000 HCL. Let's discuss four of the most popular network protocols and how they fit into the implementation of a Microsoft cluster server.

3.2.5.1 Ethernet

Ethernet was one of the first network protocols to be developed and has the largest install base. It is based upon the CSMA/CD (Carrier Sense Multiple Access/Collision Detection) access method. This governs how network devices communicate on the network segment when they have information to send. If they "talk" at the same time that another device is talking, it creates a collision, and both cards timeout for a random period of time and then attempts to retransmit the data.

Ethernet can be used in both network load-balanced clusters and failover clusters. At speeds of 10 mbps to 100 mbps, Ethernet is the most common choice for cluster server implementations. Most cluster server implementations will be done in an effort to provide a service to a dispersed group of people, either on the Internet or across a WAN. When application data must travel across slow WAN links at speeds of 1.544 mbps or less, 100 mbps is typically more than adequate bandwidth for the system's local communication.

Note

Although Ethernet is supported on the MSCS, you must use a card with a PCI bus. EISA and ISA are not supported.

In some situations, you may wish to boost the connection speed between your clients and your cluster, or possibly the connection between the cluster nodes themselves. In this case, a higher bandwidth technology may be a better choice.

3.2.5.2 Gigabit Ethernet

A recent enhancement to the common Ethernet technology is the advent of Gigabit Ethernet. Gigabit Ethernet is similar in its operation to Fast Ethernet (100 mbps), but achieves speeds close to 1000 mbps. The first Gigabit

Ethernet technology utilized fiber connections between devices to achieve those high speeds, but recent enhancements have modified the technology to run across standard copper CAT 5 cables.

Like most new technologies, Gigabit Ethernet was very expensive when it hit the market, but became more affordable as people began to migrate their systems to the technology. Although we are probably not ready for Gigabit Ethernet to the desktop, the technology is very affordable for backbone server connections and building-to-building interfaces.

The advantage to using Gigabit Ethernet for your cluster server solution is the affordability, the speed, and the integration with existing systems. Most Gigabit equipment comes equipped with a 100-mbps uplink to Fast Ethernet hubs and switches for fast and painless integration with existing Ethernet networks. This can make implementing Gigabit Ethernet into your environment simple and cost effective. The only downside would be that all Gigabit controllers are not supported under Windows 2000, so make sure you check the HCL before investing in Gigabit hardware.

3.2.5.3 FDDI

FDDI (Fiber Distributed Data Interface) is a standard set of ANSI protocols used for sending digital signals over fiber optic cable. FDDI works in the same way that Token Ring does, but adds an additional ring to the topology, creating a more fault-tolerant ring. FDDI is used for backbone connections and high-speed communication between devices. FDDI runs at 100 mbps, which is not very impressive to most, but the power in FDDI is the fault-tolerant token-passing topology and the redundant rings.

FDDI is not in large use today due to the advent of technologies such as Fast Ethernet and Gigabit Ethernet, but does still hold a portion of market share. FDDI is supported on both the network load-balanced clustering and the failover clustering technologies, but there are some issues you should be aware of before implementing your cluster with FDDI.

The first and most obvious concern is the lack of support for the FDDI architecture. Although FDDI has market share, it is waning. Building a cluster server solution on an architecture that may be obsolete in the near future is not in the long-term interest of your company. Second, many FDDI controllers attempt to override virtual Media Access Control (MAC) addressing and will not work properly with the NLB service. You should check with the hardware manufacturer and the Microsoft HCL before attempting to implement your solution using FDDI.

3.2.5.4 Token Ring

Since its first introduction into the networking world by IBM, Token Ring has been the cornerstone of most mainframe environments, and despite its higher cost, has even held a good portion of market share in the client/server environment. Token Ring networks are fast, efficient, fault-tolerant, and easily integrated into source-routed mainframe environments.

With the addition of a fast Token Ring specification, Token Ring has made a good effort towards competition with its low-cost Ethernet cousin. Unfortunately, support for Token Ring has started to wane in the past few years, with several vendors dropping products designed for that market. The MSCS suite of services is not an exception. As disappointing as it is to all of the energetic Token Ring fans, neither the Microsoft NLB service nor the MSCS supports Token Ring networking environments.

3.2.6 Network Equipment

As important as the choice of networking interfaces is the choice of networking equipment. If you stay within the environments we just discussed (Ethernet, Gigabit Ethernet, FDDI), you will be safe, but there are a few things you should be concerned about before you rush out and buy equipment.

Cluster software is unique because it interoperates with network services to simulate server names and addresses on the network. Although you may think that networks deliver data to machines on a local network based upon an IP address, most network equipment uses *MAC* addresses and *ARP* (Address Resolution Protocol) to deliver content. Every machine on a network has a unique address that is burned into its network card. This network address is often referred to as the physical address of the card. This MAC address is the address that is broadcast on a local subnet to allow other machines on the segment to deliver messages.

If you have 10 machines on a network (all running TCP/IP) and a machine wants to send information to another machine, it determines, based upon the destination IP address, whether the machine is on the local subnet. If it is not, it forwards the request to the gateway address. If the address is on the local subnet, the machine will broadcast the request on the local segment to see which machines responds to the request. This broadcast is known as an ARP request. In lay terms, the machine is shouting, "I have a message for IP address 192.168.4.56. Can someone please tell me who that is?" The machine that has that address will respond, "I have that address. Please forward the request to me. I am at MAC address 00-50-04-94-75-23." The requesting machine will then forward the request to the destination machine by broadcasting the request to all the machines in the network. The machine that the packet is destined for will retrieve the packet and the other machines will ignore it.

To make things a little simpler, operating systems and routers use what is known as an ARP table to keep track of MAC address-to-IP address resolutions. If you are using a Windows NT or Windows 2000 machine, you can view your ARP table by typing *ARP –a* at a command prompt (see Figure 3-7). Whenever your machine connects to another machine on a local subnet, an ARP entry is made for that machine, listing the machine's MAC address and IP address. This allows your machine to make further requests to the destination machine without the need for a broadcast ARP request.

You may wonder what difference it makes to have an ARP table if the machine is going to send the packet to the machine as a broadcast request anyway. Well, that is a good question. In the traditional communication we discussed earlier, a machine would have to make two broadcasts requests on the network to get the packet from machine A to machine B. The first request would be to determine the destination machine's MAC address and the second would be to send the actual request. The first obvious use of the ARP table is that it eliminates the need for the first broadcast. Because the machine already knows the MAC address of the destination machine, it can skip that

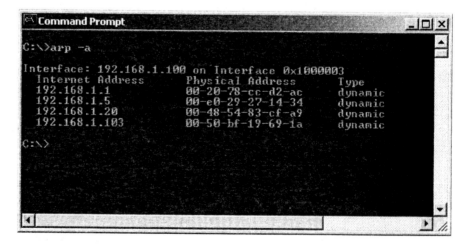

Figure 3-7
Viewing the ARP table.

step and send the packet directly. The second use of the ARP table comes into play when you begin implementing second-layer and third-layer switching and routing.

Let's take a look at how typical hubs and switches work on a network and how their features (or lack of features) might complicate or enhance your cluster implementation. The equipment you choose to use will mostly likely be based upon the network protocol you decide to run (Ethernet, FDDI, etc.). Regardless of the choice you make, the decision to use hubs, switches, or routers in conjunction with your cluster will raise some issues you need to be aware of.

3.2.6.1 Hubs

A hub is a networking device used to connect multiple machines to a central point. A typical hub is not intelligent; it passes all network requests to all ports, regardless of source or destination. If you were to place all 10 of the machines we discussed earlier on a hub, all traffic produced by those 10 machines would be broadcast to all other machines on the network. You can easily see how network traffic could become a problem very quickly—maybe not with 10 machines, but what if we added 10 more? And then 10 more?

As far as your cluster design is concerned, hubs do not add any complication to the configuration, but do require that you keep in mind a node limitation. Exceeding that limitation will cause application response to slow due to network traffic. Because hubs rebroadcast all request to all ports, you do not need to worry whether your virtual servers or network names will be available.

Hubs are good for connecting small workgroups together to share information or files and can be great for small cluster solutions, but they lose their value once the number of machines on the network hub grows beyond a small group.

3.2.6.2 Layer 2 Switching

In response to the limitation of network hubs, network equipment providers engineered a new type of hub that actually filters and forwards packets within a single LAN segment based upon MAC address. Layer 2 switches accomplish this in the same way machines retain an ARP table. However, instead of retaining the machine's MAC address and IP address, a layer 2 switch is concerned only with the MAC address and which port on the switch provides connectivity to that machine.

In our 10-node network, a machine that needs to contact another machine would send out the request in the same way, but because it is attached to a second-layer switch, the switch does not broadcast the address to the other machines on the network, but forwards the packets directly to the destination machine. Thus the switch actually will "switch" between each port, routing the traffic directly to the machine that should receive the request. If a layer 2 switch does not have a particular MAC address in its ARP table, it will broadcast the address to the other machines on the network until it learns the location of the requested MAC address. This behavior is great for networking because it allows large networks to be built without having to route traffic between several small network segments.

Unfortunately, switching does cause problems for some cluster servers. Failover clusters are not typically affected by second-layer switching, for they retain the actual MAC address of the network card in use. Even though the IP address or network name may be virtual, the MAC address is real and associated with the network card in use for client requests. When a failure occurs, the application resources, along with the IP address resource, are transferred to another server in the cluster. When this happens, the new server performs a gratuitous ARP request, informing devices on the network that the MAC address for a specific IP address has changed. Many routers and network devices use this information to update their ARP table so that traffic can continue to flow to the clustered application.

Note

The only issue you may encounter with the use of failover clustering in a layer 2 switched environment is during failover. Even though the new server will broadcast a gratuitous ARP request when failover occurs, many routers and network devices are configured to deny the routing of ARP broadcasts by default. If you find that devices on one network segment have difficulty connecting to the new server after a failover, ensure that routers and switches in use have ARP forwarding enabled.

Network load-balanced cluster servers create virtual addresses for the clients to connect to, as well as virtual MAC addresses. This means that if you have five machines within a network load-balanced cluster, all five machines will announce that they have the same MAC address and IP address. Obviously, this is a problem for a layer 2 switch, which routes packets based upon MAC address. Some switches will attempt to assign the virtual MAC address to a particular port, causing requests for that MAC address to be forwarded to that one node, rather than being load-balanced across all nodes within the cluster.

To ensure that your NLB cluster operates correctly, you must choose one of the following configuration options:

- In Unicast mode, mask the source MAC address by editing the registry.
- In Unicast mode, use a hub for all cluster nodes, and then uplink the hub to a switch port.
- Use Multicast mode.

When configuring your network load-balanced cluster, you can use Unicast or Multicast mode. Unicast mode is the default mode and associates IP addresses to unicast MAC addresses. Unicast mode, by default, uses a "dummy" address for the source MAC address when sending packets through a switch. This prevents the switch from recording the virtual MAC address used for the cluster (because it is masked by a dummy address) and therefore will forward requests for that address to all ports on the switch.

Another way to use Unicast mode is to connect all cluster adapters within the network load-balanced cluster to a shared hub rather than to a switch, and then uplink the hub to a layer 2 switch. This will allow the switch to record the virtual MAC address as resident on a single port, ensuring proper operation. If you choose to use this route, you will have to disable the MaskSourceMAC value in the registry so that your hosts do not submit dummy MAC addresses to the switch. To do this, open the registry editor (regedt32.exe) and navigate to the following key:

`HKEY_LOCAL_MACHINE\SYSTEM\CurrentControlSet\Services\WLBS\Parameters`

Edit the MaskSourceMAC key to reflect 0 (disabled) rather than 1 (enabled). This will turn off the masking feature and allow the layer 2 switch to correctly identify the virtual MAC on the uplink port (see Figure 3-8).

As an alternative to using Unicast mode, Multicast mode uses a multicast MAC address (for the virtual address) and resolves it to the unicast IP address. Because the virtual IP address is associated with a multicast MAC address, the switch does not associate the MAC address with a single port, but broadcasts all requests to all ports. Although this may be the simplest method of rectifying issues with the layer 2 switches, it should be avoided. Multicast mode does not offer any performance benefit for the switch or the cluster servers, and the increased overhead caused by the use of a multicast address may burden your routers and switching equipment.

3.2.6.3 Layer 3 Switching

Layer 3 switching is similar to layer 2 switching, but packet delivery is routed to the appropriate port based upon IP address, not MAC address. If you remember, Windows 2000 NLB implements a MaskSourceMAC function to

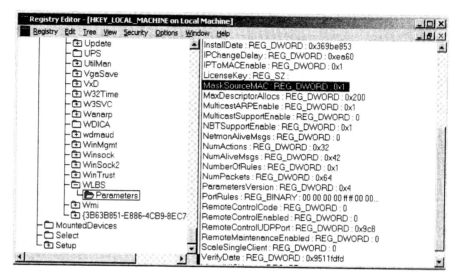

Figure 3-8
Editing the MaskSourceMAC registry entry.

fool the switch into believing it is using a unique MAC address for each card, when in reality all of the cards are using the same MAC address. Unfortunately, this type of feature is not available for the layer 3 switches. Neither the network load-balanced cluster nor the failover cluster will function correctly on layer 3 switches.

The workaround to this problem is simple. For your network load-balanced clusters and your failover clusters, plug your network connections into a hub and uplink that hub to a port on the layer 3 switch. This will allow the switch to route to the virtual IP address without conflict.

3.2.6.4 Routers

Using a router within your cluster environment is inevitable, assuming you want to connect your system to other network segments or the Internet. The configuration of your router does not rely heavily upon the configuration of your cluster, but it does have some scenarios that you should be aware of. However, before you assume that you are plagued by an undocumented problem caused by the interaction between the router and the cluster servers, ensure that you have the basics covered first.

Before troubleshooting your cluster server solution, put a simple workstation on the network segment you are using for the cluster and ensure you can ping the gateway address and addresses on other segments. Then locate a machine on an alternate segment and make sure you can ping the host on your local segment. If you have any problems pinging outside of the segment or pinging a host on the segment, then you have a routing issue you need to resolve before you begin to troubleshoot your cluster.

Regardless of which router you use, you will most likely be confronted with one of the following issues:

- Users on other segments cannot connect to a failover server after a failover.
- Users on other network segments cannot connect to network load-balanced servers.

If you have a failover server on one segment, computers on other segments may have trouble accessing your server after a failover. This is related to the ARP table entry that those machines have for the application owner. Remember, failover cluster servers retain the MAC address of the server offering the service. When an application fails, the IP address resource for that application fails over to another server in the cluster, but the IP address must bind to the new MAC address of the server that has gained ownership. To do this, Windows 2000 Servers will perform what is called a *gratuitous ARP broadcast*. This is a simple message to the other machines on the local segment informing them to update their ARP table. Machines local to the server will receive the request and update their ARP table, but machines on other subnets that may have connected to the server recently will have an incorrect MAC address in their ARP cache. Because most routers do not forward ARP broadcasts by default, the machines on other segments will have trouble connecting to the new server until they are forced to do a new ARP request. To solve this problem, simply enable the bridging of ARP broadcasts across your router's interfaces.

Note

Some network administrators disable ICMP (Internet Connection Message Protocol) on their internal and external networks as an additional security feature. Although the cluster can operate in this environment, it may cause problems with failover. When a failover cluster server loses connectivity with another server in the cluster, it will use ICMP to ping the other server. Once that fails, it will attempt to ping the gateway of the network that it is on. If that fails, it will failover to the other server and perform the process again. If ICMP is disabled on that segment, the ICMP ping to the gateway will fail in either case and could cause the application or service to failover indefinitely. To ensure it does not affect your cluster server, ensure that ICMP is enabled on the segment you use for your cluster server implementation.

As stated earlier, using network load balancing causes problems with layer 2 switches. To get around this issue, network load-balanced servers will mask their outgoing MAC address so that layer 2 switches will not attempt to record a virtual MAC address and therefore incorrectly load balance the traffic. Unfortunately, the use of source MAC masking eliminates the ability of the router to record an ARP entry for the load-balanced cluster. To correct this issue, you will need to add a static ARP entry to the router for the virtual IP address in use on the cluster. In most routers this is pretty straightforward, but you will need to check your router's user manual for the correct syntax.

3.3 Software Requirements

In addition to the various hardware requirements that have been cited, there are also some very specific software requirements that must be met in order for your cluster to operate properly. Let's take a look at the operating systems that are required to run Microsoft's clustering solutions and at the network services and applications that are critical dependencies of the clustering services.

3.3.1 Operating System

The most obvious software requirement is the operating system. Because the Microsoft suite of clustering software is available only in the Microsoft Advanced Server and Microsoft Datacenter Server operating systems, these products are obviously the most critical dependencies.

3.3.2 Cluster Software

Although there are several clustering products available, this book focuses on the Microsoft suite of clustering products, specifically, the MSCS and the Microsoft NLB service. As stated earlier, both of these products are included in the Windows 2000 Advanced Server and Windows 2000 Datacenter Server operating systems. The MSCS can be installed through the Add/Remove Programs applet located in the Control Panel (but don't install it yet!)

The Microsoft NLB service is installed by default in both the Windows 2000 Advanced Server and Windows 2000 Datacenter Server operating systems. To configure the NLB service, you must enable it through the Network

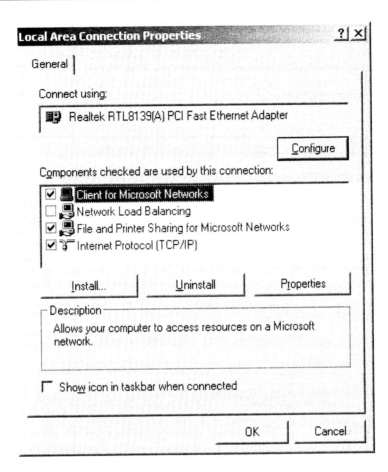

Figure 3-9
Enabling Network Load Balancing on a network adapter.

applet located in the Control Panel. You will notice that each interface on a Windows 2000 Advanced Server or Windows 2000 Datacenter Server will have a component called Network Load Balancing (see Figure 3-9). This is where you will enable and configure the NLB service.

3.3.3 Clustered Applications

Applications can typically be load-balanced without specific requirements. Because the NLB service operates at the network driver level, applications operate independently and do not exchange data. Although there are exceptions to every rule, generally, if your application can run on one server independently, it will most likely run just fine in a load-balanced cluster.

There are many applications that you may wish to cluster, due to their dynamic nature. Not all applications, however, can be used with the clustering service. The following is a list of Microsoft applications that can be clustered using the MSCS:

- Microsoft Exchange Server (5.5 and 2000)
- Microsoft SQL Server (6.5, 7.0, and 2000)
- Microsoft Internet Information Server (5.0)
- Microsoft BizTalk Server 2000
- Microsoft SharePoint Portal Server

There are many other applications that can be run on a cluster, but these are the Microsoft products you will typically be working with the most. There is also a variety of service that you can install on your cluster (which is discussed in the next section.)

To operate on a cluster, an application has to be cluster aware—meaning it has to communicate with the cluster API and be willing to transfer ownership of an application to the surviving node in the event of a failure. Just because an application will install on a cluster server does not mean that it will function correctly during failover. Be sure to check with your software manufacturer before you install software on a cluster.

3.3.4 Clustered Services

Aside from the applications you can cluster, there are many services that you can cluster using the NLB and the clustering services. There are many network services that can provide more reliability on a cluster than on a typical server. The following services can be run on a network load-balanced cluster:

- DNS (Non-Active Directory Integrated)
- Internet Security and Acceleration Server
- File Shares
- Print Queues

- WWW (World Wide Web)
- FTP (File Transfer Protocol)
- SMTP Relay

The key to running service on a load-balanced cluster is content consistency. Make sure that your content is consistent on every node. If it is a Web site, all pages should be identical on every machine. If you are running DNS, ensure that the zone(s) on each server are identical. On an FTP server, you must keep the data and the security consistent.

As an alternative to load balancing, you can run some services on a failover cluster. This provides more reliability than performance, but may be ideal for your situation. The following services can be clustered:

- File Shares
- Print Queues
- DHCP
- Distributed Transaction Coordinator
- FTP (File Transfer Protocol)
- WWW (World Wide Web)

When deciding whether to run your application or service on a load-balanced cluster or a failover cluster, always ask yourself which is more important for your needs: performance or reliability. If performance is more important, then choose load balancing. If reliability is more important, place your application or service on a failover cluster.

3.3.5 Generic Applications and Services

In addition to the applications and services that may be cluster aware out of the box, MSCS offers the ability to define custom parameters for services and applications that do not have specific cluster installation instructions.

Through the Cluster Administrator Microsoft Management Console Snap-In, you can define custom parameters for the generic service or generic application resource. Defining a resource this way allows you to cluster custom applications and services. The SDK (Software Development Kit) included with Visual Studio 6.0 and above includes the Cluster API so that programmers can write applications to be run on a cluster.

3.4 Placement Considerations

Before implementing your cluster, it is best to have a strong idea of where you want to place the system within your network and how that will affect other systems and services. Placement will be largely based upon the location of the clients. If your cluster serves an application to your internal organization, then you can place the cluster server on a segment within your network and it will have access to the network services it needs. If your clients are Internet users outside of your organization, then you will have a few more security issues to be concerned about.

3.4.1 Network Design

To decide where to place your cluster solution, determine which network services are dependencies and how clients will access the system. If your cluster system is dependent upon services such as WINS, DNS, or Active Directory, you will want those services in close proximity to your system. However, you don't want to compromise the security of your system by allowing Internet users to browse your network.

Let's consider a typical cluster system. AustrianAntiques.com is a company specializing in antique furnishings from Austria. It has a small company network based out of Salzburg, Austria, and wishes to move its e-commerce Web site from an outsourcing data center to an inhouse operation. AustrianAntiques.com currently run a Windows 2000 network internally, with approximately 23 workstations. Its Internet connectivity is currently a T-1, and its internal network is protected by a Cisco firewall.

Based upon its current hit count, the company estimates the need for four servers within the front-end cluster and a two-node failover cluster for the database. To protect the internal network, the network load-balancing cluster will be placed within a demilitarized zone—a secure zone between the Internet and the Internal network—and the failover cluster will be placed in the internal network for domain authentication. Placing the failover cluster internally will allow the cluster to participate within the network as a domain member and give the cluster WINS/DNS resolution as needed. The network load-balanced cluster will be placed within the demilitarized zone to prevent full access to the cluster (see Figure 3-10). The firewall will use filtering to ensure that only the necessary ports (i.e., 80, 443) can access the NLB cluster. It will also open a connection for the Web server (or servers) to access the database on the internal network.

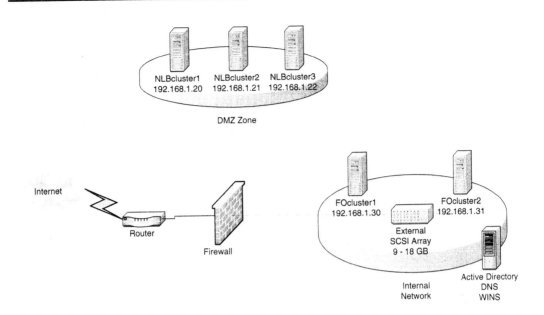

Figure 3-10
Example cluster placement.

This solution is secure and efficient, allowing fast access to network resources and secure access to the Web servers. Whenever possible, adhere to the following guidelines:

- Don't place servers directly on the Internet. Make sure there is always a firewall between your servers and the Internet.
- When you place servers on your internal network, make sure to allow access only to the servers from machines that you control.
- Don't place Active Directory domain controllers in a demilitarized zone (DMZ).

3.4.2 Scalability

Scalability is a design goal for clustering. Fortunately, Microsoft built the NLB service to be scalable to meet any need. Although there is a 32-node limit on network load-balanced clusters, the use of Round Robin DNS can provide a limitless amount of scalability.

Round Robin DNS is a setting that exists within DNS that allows more than one IP address to be resolved to the same name. For instance, you may choose to run two virtual private network (VPN) servers within your network. Megaserver1 and Megaserver2 are located in different parts of the country, so clustering is not an option. To load balance between the two servers you can add two A host records for the servers in the same DNS zone, using the same name (e.g., *vpn.mydomain.com*), and the DNS server will automatically load balance requests for those servers.

There is a downside to using Round Robin DNS. The DNS server has no way of determining if a server is up or down and will still forward requests to

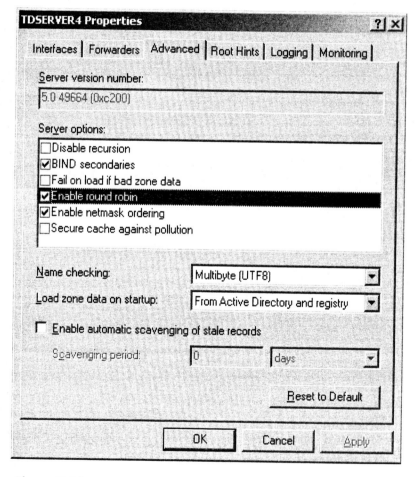

Figure 3-11
Enabling Round Robin DNS.

a server that may be down. This can be detrimental in a single server environment, but is tolerable in a cluster environment because the likelihood of all hosts within a cluster being inaccessible at the same time is unlikely.

To use Round Robin with clustering, you would set up two separate load-balanced clusters, then enter two (or more) records in DNS, both pointing to a virtual IP address of a cluster. This would load balance the traffic between two separate clusters.

To enable Round Robin DNS, simply open the DNS administrator (DNS-MGMT.MSC) and select the server you would like to edit. Right-click on the server and select **Properties**. Select the **Advanced** tab, and then select **Enable Round Robin** (see Figure 3-11). Click **OK**. Then add two records, with the same name, to the DNS zone (see Figure 3-12).

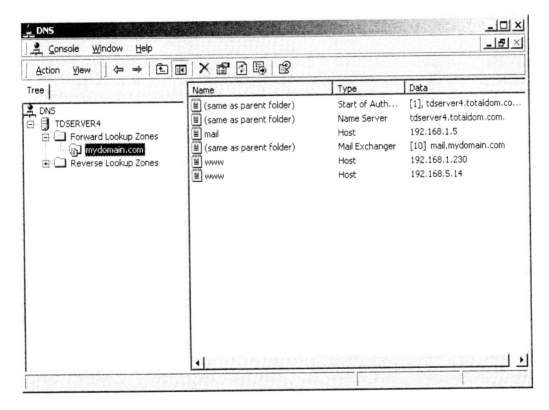

Figure 3-12
Add Round Robin records to DNS.

3.5 Network Services

The clusters that you decide to build will be dependent upon other services within your network. How you implement these services can severely affect the performance or effectiveness of your cluster solution.

3.5.1 DHCP

If you planned on using DHCP for any of the servers within your cluster, you will need to discard that idea, for DHCP cannot be used for nodes within a network load-balanced cluster or a failover cluster. Clients that connect to a cluster, however; can obtain addressing from DHCP.

3.5.2 DNS

The NLB service is the most independent service, for it really is not a service at all, but a single driver that interfaces at the network card level. There are no specific dependencies of the NLB service, but there are a few things you should keep in mind. If you are load balancing IIS servers, you will most likely want DNS entries for your Web site. If you have an internal application that you want to make available on the Internet, you will also want DNS entries.

Whether you are hosting a Web site on a load-balanced cluster or an Enterprise Resource Planning (ERP) application on a failover cluster, you need to ensure that your DNS server resolves the names correctly. Most networks today use what is called NAT (Network Address Translation). NAT allows the internal addresses of a network to be hidden from the outside by virtually assigning addresses to clients as they venture out onto the Internet to retrieve data. An internal network may have a 192.168.1.0/24 network address, while the external (public) network it is connected to is using 204.19.45.0/24. If your cluster is inside your network and has a network address of 192.168.1.25, you must have a translated address on the Internet for users to access, for the 192.168.1.25 address is a private address and is not routable on the Internet.

This puts a small wrench into the name resolution simplicity that once existed, for now the cluster server actually has two different addresses, depending upon where you are coming from. If you are inside the network, you must use the 192.168.1.25 address to access the server. If you are outside of the network, you must use the 204.19.45.32 address. To solve this dilemma, most network designers will place a DNS server inside the network for internal network name resolution and place a DNS server outside of the network to be used as the primary name server for the domain name in use. Internet users will query the external DNS server and receive the 204.19.45.32 address, while internal users will query the internal DNS server and receive the 192.168.1.25 address.

Note

When deploying a failover cluster, be sure that all nodes within the failover cluster have the same primary name server and/or primary WINS server entries in their network Control Panel properties. If these entries are different, the cluster nodes may not be able to communicate with each other or access the domain controller for authentication.

When entering host records into DNS, be sure you use the virtual IP address that the cluster shares, and not the actual IP address of the servers within the cluster.

3.5.3 WINS

Although WINS was the de facto standard for name resolution under Windows NT 4.0 and earlier, Windows 2000 can run just fine without it. However, legacy clients such as DOS, Windows 95, and Windows NT 4.0 don't have that luxury and are still dependent upon WINS.

When you create clustered application resources, a network name is created for each application. This name is registered in WINS and DNS so that clients can access the cluster resources by name. If WINS servers are not available, then legacy clients will not be able to access the clustered applications. As a simple rule of thumb, if you have clients other than Windows 2000 that need to access the applications running on your cluster, then you will need to run WINS on your network.

As far as placement, make sure to place a WINS server on the local segment with the cluster server. Although this is not a requirement, it may help to speed up name resolution functions on the cluster, thus raising the performance of the cluster.

3.5.4 Domain Authentication

As far as domain authentication goes, you can use a workgroup or domain configuration for servers within a load-balanced server cluster. Although it is possible to run servers in a workgroup and servers in a domain in the same cluster, it is not recommended. This may cause problems with applications you choose to run on your cluster, especially if those applications or services rely upon authentication. Plus, the design goal of a load-balanced cluster should be consistency across all machines. This ensures that all users experience the same result from the same action.

When you plan your failover cluster, you must pay closer attention, for the failover cluster has very specific needs and is not nearly as independent as the load-balancing service. Failover clustering requires domain membership. Nodes within a cluster can be either domain controllers or domain members, but must be a part of a domain. Because of the overhead caused by Active Directory and domain authentication services, it is recommended that you do not run your cluster servers as domain controllers.

Although optional on a network load-balanced cluster, domain authentication is critical to the operation of a failover cluster, so if you choose not to make your cluster servers domain controllers (which is the best way to go), make sure there is a domain controller on the local segment where the cluster is being run. The domain controller can be either an NT 4.0 domain controller or a Windows 2000 Active Directory controller, for both are supported environments for clustering.

Many organizations attempt to put their cluster server in a DMZ for security reasons, but you will quickly find that this is difficult to accomplish. If you must run your cluster server in a DMZ, make it a part of a new domain that is not connected (trusted). This will allow authentication to take place on that segment, but any security breaches will not compromise your internal network. The moment a cluster server cannot authenticate, the service will shut down, so the reliability of the domain controller used is as important as the reliability of the cluster.

3.6 Design Samples

It is always helpful to get a few examples of a system before you build it. This section presents descriptions and diagrams of a variety of systems that are in common use. This will help you to put together all of the pieces of a cluster and allow you to use these examples in the design of your own cluster.

Keep in mind that these are merely examples, not blueprints for each type of clustered system. Feel free to change the configuration to fit your environment. Just be sure to follow the guidelines set forth earlier in this chapter with regard to security and vital dependencies.

3.6.1 Single-Tiered System

A single-tiered cluster is simply a cluster that does not operate in conjunction with another cluster system. A single Web site on a network load-balanced server cluster would be considered a single-tiered system. If you added some dynamic content, a local database, and some COM+ components, it would still be a single-tiered system because all operations are running on the same cluster.

A single database running on a failover cluster would also be considered a single-tiered system, even though it is dependent upon authentication and name resolution. As long as the system does not span more than one cluster, it is considered a single-tiered system (see Figure 3-13).

3.6.2 Two-Tiered System

A two-tiered system is an application or service that has been broken into two distinctively different operating environments. Most e-commerce implementations fall into this category because they are running the Web site on one system (the first tier) and the database on a second system (the second tier). Many people refer to these two systems as a *front end* and a *back end* because clients do not access both systems. Clients access only the front-end server hosting the Web pages, and the Web servers access the database on the back end to retrieve data (see Figure 3-14).

Two-tiered systems are helpful because they allow more flexibility in placement issues and increased performance across the system as a whole. Because the database does not reside on the Web servers, they can concentrate on

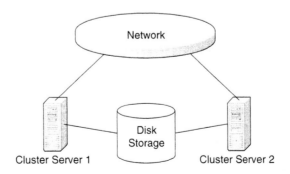

Figure 3-13
Single-tiered failover cluster.

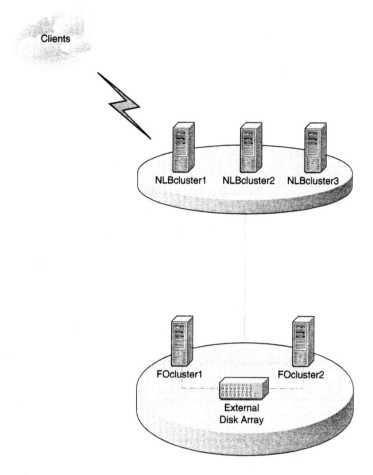

Figure 3-14
Two-tier cluster environment.

responding to user requests and accessing data from the database. Because the database does not respond to user requests, it can respond to the Web server requests in a more timely manner.

Two-tier systems have become the norm for most implementations, although you could choose to adjust the model to fit your needs. If you have a small group of clients accessing the system, it may be beneficial to run the system on a single node (single tier). If you have high amounts of traffic, it may be wise to split up the processing even more.

3.6.3 Three-Tiered System

A three-tiered system goes beyond the two-tiered system by adding another processing layer. This layer is typically a set of programming code that performs logical operations, or a set of COM+ objects that perform processing that is essential to the system (see Figure 3-15).

Most common today is the use of a COM+ cluster, which is a service available through Microsoft's Application Center 2000, a cluster management software package. This layer can be written to do anything, but typically is used to offset the processing of the system by allowing a third set of cluster servers to process all of the business logic for a particular operation.

Through the use of the COM+ cluster, the Web servers no longer need to be burdened with the overhead of processing COM objects and methods. This is an attractive platform for custom software development and high-end e-commerce portals, for it offloads the processing into three separate entities: one to respond to user requests, one to process business logic, and one to serve

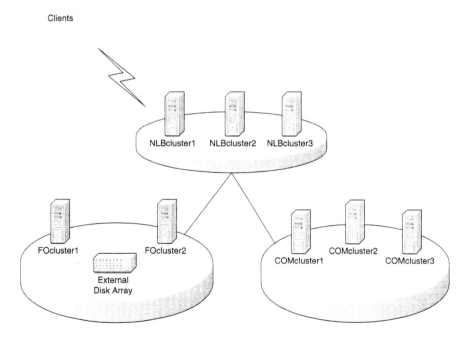

Figure 3-15
Three-tiered cluster system.

up data from a datastore. This type of clustering model has not been popular due to the high costs, but is becoming more and more common as COM+ development becomes more prevalent.

3.6.4 Round Robin System

The Round Robin system can be used with any system that includes a network load-balanced cluster. The object of the Round Robin system is the ability to provide a high level of fault tolerance along with unlimited scalability.

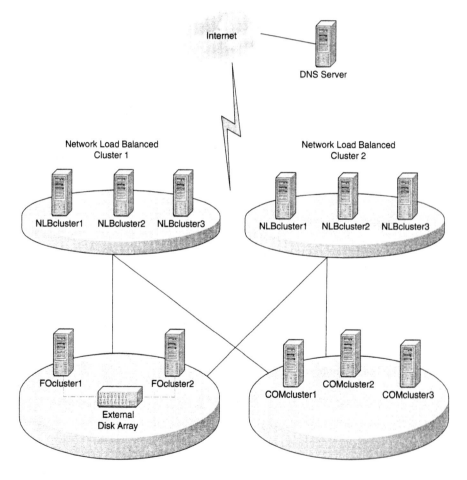

Figure 3-16
Round Robin system in a three-tiered environment.

As stated earlier, a Round Robin system is a system that utilizes Round Robin DNS to forward the same requests to two separate network load-balanced server clusters. By modifying the DNS records and enabling Round Robin on the DNS server, clients can access one name (myapp.mydomain.com) and be forwarded to the same application hosted on one of two separate load-balanced clusters.

Round Robin allows you to implement load-balanced clusters that exceed the standard 32-node limit and can be used with any of the three-tiered technologies mentioned previously. To allow the Round Robin model to reach its fullest potential and serve the greatest benefit, be sure to implement your network load-balanced clusters on separate network segments (see Figure 3-16). This will minimize the traffic on each network segment.

3.7 Summary

Designing a Windows 2000 clustering or a network load-balanced system is a complex process, but well rewarding. If you have taken the time to read through this chapter, analyze your requirements, plan your installation, and verify your configuration, then you are halfway to implementing a cluster. Most of the headaches that come from cluster installation and configuration are caused by a lack of planning.

Although most designers install a piece of software, configure it, test it, and work with it to learn its features, clustering is a different type of software and cannot be implemented that way. To do so would lead the designer down a path of total confusion. If you have not read this chapter thoroughly, you will not be able to implement your cluster successfully.

If you have planned your cluster carefully and obtained all the necessary equipment, then you are ready to implement your server cluster.

Chapter 4

BUILDING A FAILOVER CLUSTER

As the saying goes, knowing *how* to do something is one thing, but actually doing it is quite another. If you worked through Chapter 3, "Clustering Design Issues," then chances are you have a good idea about what your cluster will look like when it is complete, but you may be a little fuzzy on how to actually put it all together. Through this chapter you will learn how to construct a failover cluster server system from the ground up. This will allow you the hands on experience you need to comprehend the more advanced issues taught later in this book. It is recommended that you use this chapter as a guide while you physically build your failover cluster. Again, reading is one thing, but doing is another. You are much more likely to remember how to build a cluster if you actually apply the skill you are learning.

If you are like most, you probably don't have $50,000 lying around to invest in two servers, an external RAID array, and the other equipment you will need to build the failover cluster. If that is the case, then you will need to acquire the necessary equipment to build a "poor man's" cluster. This is not recommended for production equipment due to a lack of fault tolerance, but can be used as a learning tool to allow you to learn the art of clustering before actually buying production quality hardware.

To build the test cluster, you can use any two workstations. Most people in the IT business have a few machines lying around their garage or basement that will suffice. Just make sure they are x86-based and includes PCI slots. The machines should also have the required specifications necessary to run Windows 2000 Advanced Server.

Note

Although the specific requirements for Windows 2000 Advanced Server are high, Microsoft assumes you are actually using the machine in a production environment. Windows 2000 Advanced Server can be successfully installed on Pentium-class machines as slow as 75 megahertz. Your test server may run slowly, but it is only for testing.

For the external storage array, purchase two PCI-based SCSI cards, three 2 GB+ SCSI hard drives, and an internal SCSI cable that has at least five connectors and is long enough to plug into both machines simultaneously. You can plug the SCSI cable into the card in the first machine and run it out an open slot in the back to connect it to the three drives. Then plug the end of the cable into the SCSI card in the other machine. Yes, you can purchase an external cable instead and mount all three drives in a casing of some sort, but that includes unneeded additional cost. Keep in mind that you will also need to power the drives, so make sure you run a separate power supply so that the drives can have power regardless of which machine is running.

Regardless of whether you decide to build your own cluster or use higher end equipment, this chapter will walk you through the installation and configuration of your failover cluster and provide you with the information you need to manage a cluster and its resources.

4.1 Resource Configuration

Before building your cluster, you must plan your resources. If you worked through Chapter 3, you will already have some of the components necessary to compile your resource configuration. A network diagram, IP addressing allocation, and DNS entries are only a few of the items that must be completed before you can begin your cluster construction.

4.1.1 Network Drawings

In Chapter 3 you completed a network drawing relative to your cluster solution. Take the same drawing and delete any items that are not related to the failover cluster so that you can have a clear picture of the items you need to construct. Make sure that every server has an IP address listed. This will help you to construct your IP address table in the next section.

Also ensure that you have the necessary cables and networking equipment for all of the connections your network diagram represents. If your cluster implementation requires changes to a router or switch, be sure to have the login and password handy, or contact the engineer responsible for those changes.

4.1.2 TCP/IP Addressing

Using a spreadsheet or word processing program, make a list of IP addresses you will need to use for your cluster solution. You will need the following addresses:

- One IP address for every server used within your cluster.
- One IP address for every other server (DNS, WINS, domain controller) on the local network.
- One IP address for the virtual server provided by the cluster.
- One IP address for each application you choose to run on your cluster.

You do not have to assign addresses in order; you just need to make sure they are all on the same subnet, with the exception of the private node-to-node connection, which must be on a separate subnet. If you choose to run two network cards in each machine for node-to-node cluster communication (which is recommended), then you will also need to choose IP addresses for the private network. The addresses you choose for your private network are important, for they must be on a separate subnet, and must not conflict with any existing addresses in your network.

Note

If there are only two nodes in your cluster, you can use a crossover cable for communication between the nodes. A hub or switch would work as well, but there is no reason to waste money on additional network devices if the crossover cable will work just as well. You will not need a network (NetBIOS) name for these interfaces, for NetBIOS will be disabled on both interfaces.

You will also need a network name for each of the servers and applications in your cluster, for the cluster server actually assigns a network (NetBIOS) name to each application that it supports. Once your addressing table is complete (see Table 4-1), you are ready to assign DNS entries to the necessary addresses.

Table 4-1   TCP/IP Addressing

Node/Device	IP Address	NetBIOS Name
Domain Controller	192.168.1.20	DCserver
DNS Server	192.168.1.21	DNSserver1
Node 1	192.168.1.50	Cluster1
Node 2	192.168.1.51	Cluster2
Virtual Cluster	192.168.1.52	MyCluster
SQL Server Application	192.168.1.53	SQLcluster
IIS Application	192.168.1.54	IIScluster
Exchange Application	192.168.1.55	ExchCluster
Node 1 (Private)	10.1.1.1	
Node 2 (Private)	10.1.1.2	

4.1.3 DNS Entries

If you have done any work with Internet services such as Newsgroups, Simple Mail Transfer Protocol (SMTP), or WWW, then you are familiar with DNS. DNS maps names to IP addresses for Internet hosts. The top-level domains such as .com, .net, and .org are controlled and managed by a company called Network Solutions *(www.networksolutions.com)*. Network Solutions allows you to register second-level domains such as "mydomain" or "xyzcompany" so that you can have a presence on the Internet (e.g., mydomain.com). When you register your name with Network Solutions, you must tell them which DNS server hosts your domain name. This should be a DNS server located on your network (preferably outside of the firewall). Some ISPs (Internet service providers) will host the DNS for you and force you to make formal requests for changes.

Once your name is registered, you can add (or ask an ISP to add) records to your DNS zone. This could include "www" records or "mail" records. If you are building a cluster that needs to be accessed from the Internet, you should enter a specific record particularly for that application or service. For instance, say you want to run an intranet application on your cluster; you may create a record for "intranet" so that users on the Internet could access your clustered application using the name "intranet.mydomain.com."

If your application is internal to your organization and not accessible via the Internet, you can still create a DNS entry for the application. Most likely, you will be using an Internal DNS server rather than an Internet DNS server, but the process is the same.

To create your DNS zone, go to your DNS server and open the DNS administrator *(c:\winnt\system32\DNSmgmt.msc)*. If your DNS server is not listed, click on **Action** from the menu and select **Connect to computer.** Select **This computer** and press **OK.** Right-click on your DNS server and select **New Zone...** (see Figure 4-1).

The New Zone wizard will start. Click **Next** and the wizard will ask you what type of zone you would like to create (see Figure 4-2). If you are configuring an internal DNS server so that users on your network can access your clustered application, then choose **Active Directory-integrated.** If you are creating a zone for an Internet-based DNS server, select **Standard primary.**

Click **Next** and the wizard will ask you if you want a forward lookup zone or a reverse lookup zone. Select **Forward lookup zone** and press **Next.** Type in the name of the domain you would like to create. In our example, we used *mydomain.com.* When asked if you want to create a new zone file or copy a file from somewhere else, select **Create a new zone file with this name** and select **Next.** The wizard confirms that the zone is about to be created and asks you to select the **Finish** button (see Figure 4-3).

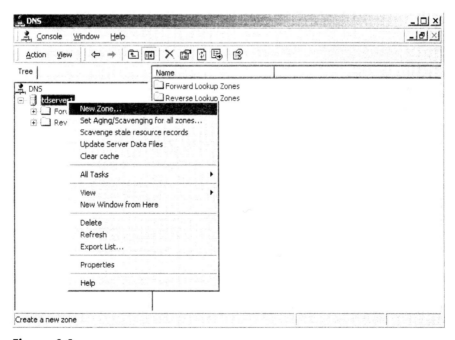

Figure 4-1
Creating a DNS zone.

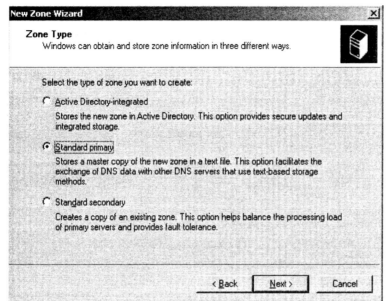

Figure 4-2
Select the zone type.

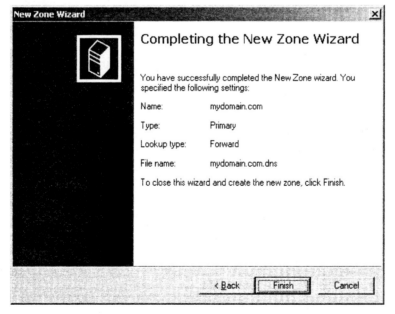

Figure 4-3
Finishing the New Zone
wizard.

Once the wizard creates the zone, select the *Forward Lookup Zones* folder to view the new zone. This process has created a zone on the DNS server to enable it to respond to requests for zone records. For this to be of any value, you must register your domain name with Network Solutions and make this server the authoritative DNS server for that domain. This way, requests for the domain will be forwarded to this server, which will respond appropriately.

Note

After creating your forward lookup zone, you should create a reverse lookup zone. The reverse lookup zone allows IP addresses to be resolved to names. The process of creating a reverse lookup zone is the same as for a forward lookup zone, except for the name. The reverse lookup zone will be named based upon the IP address of the domain hosts. For instance, in our DNS namespace, Intranet.mydomain.com resolves to 205.46.219.7. The reverse lookup zone for that domain would be 219.46.205.in-addr.arpa.

Once you have the zone created, right-click on the domain name and select **New Host**. The new host dialogue will ask you for the host name and IP address of the host you would like added to the domain. Type in the host name (without the domain name), and type in the IP address of the application you wish to register (see Figure 4-4). This will allow hosts to access your cluster

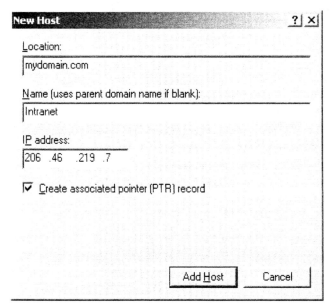

Figure 4-4
Add a host record.

server by name rather than by IP address. Repeat this process for all applications you choose to host on your cluster.

It may be a good idea to add a host entry for the cluster address itself as well. This will allow administrators to connect to the cluster server (or servers) by name rather than by IP address. This is optional however.

Note

The IP address you assign to the DNS record will be the IP address of the cluster application, not an individual cluster server. Also, if you are creating an Internet DNS zone, you will need to make sure you have some sort of network address translation (NAT) in place to translate the Internet-accessible IP address to the private IP address in use on your network (assuming you are using private addressing). This will typically be a firewall configuration change.

4.1.4 Domain Accounts

To ensure your cluster can operate in the domain, you will need to create a user account. This account should be a domain account within the same domain as the cluster server. The account does not need to have any particular privileges when created, for the cluster service installation will assign the appropriate permissions.

To add a new user to your Windows 2000-based domain, open **Active Directory Users and Computers (dsa.msc)** on the domain controller and select the container you would like to use to hold the user. Right-click on that container and select **New User**. In the New User dialogue, type in the name of the user account you would like to use for the cluster service. Then, under logon name, type the same name (see Figure 4-5).

Once complete, select **Next** and type in the user password you would like to use for the account. This password should be difficult to guess and include a combination of letters and numbers. Although you are not granting this user account administrator privileges at this time, the cluster software installation routine will modify the account to allow administrative rights on the cluster server. Also be sure that you select **User cannot change password** and **Password never expires** from the list of options (see Figure 4-6), for if you have applied a group policy to the container that the user resides in that forces password changes, the cluster service will quit functioning once the password expires. Once complete, click **Next** and then click **Finish**.

After you have added the user to Active Directory, you should consider adding other users that may be needed for your application installation. For

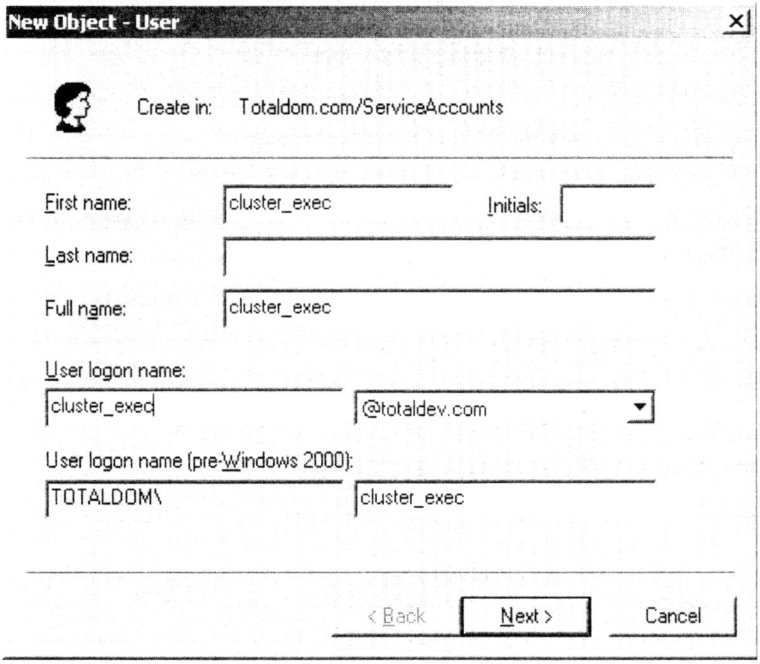

Figure 4-5
Adding the cluster user account.

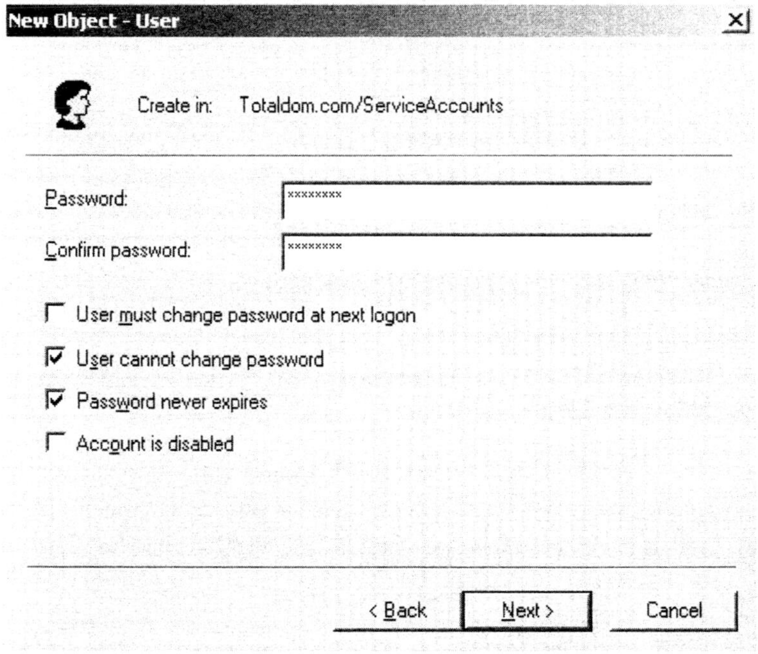

Figure 4-6
Assigning password options to the cluster user account.

instance, Microsoft SQL Server and Microsoft Exchange Server require a service account. Creating the accounts at this point will save you some time later. Make sure to add both of these accounts to the domain administrators group so they have the valid access they need.

When you create user accounts, try to follow a naming convention that will allow administrators to spot service accounts easily, such as *serviceaccount_EXEC* or *svc_serviceaccount*. This will prevent people from deleting your service accounts unnecessarily.

Also remember that the cluster service account must validate to a domain controller upon startup, so make sure your domain controller is present on the same segment as the cluster server and that it has ample fault tolerance.

4.2 Hardware Configuration

Constructing a cluster server system starts long before the software is installed. All machines in the cluster must be properly configured so that they operate correctly and, most importantly, share data consistently. Apart from the actual hardware requirements of the cluster server service, there are several items that need to be configured before the operating system can be installed on both nodes.

<u>Warning</u>

Under no circumstance should you ever have two servers powered up and connected to an external disk array prior to installing cluster software on the first node. Even though the disk is called a "shared" disk, the disk model being used is called a "share-nothing" model. If both servers are powered on at the same time and the cluster software is not installed, the servers will attempt to access the shared disk simultaneously, causing the disk to be corrupt.

4.2.1 Gathering Resources

Before you get started, make sure you have everything you need. If you are building a two-node cluster, you obviously need two servers equipped with two network cards, a local drive controller, and a secondary controller for the shared disk array, which will be either a SCSI controller or a fibre channel host bus adapter. If you are using fibre channel, make sure you have the necessary cables, fibre channel switches, hubs, and host bus adapters for each device.

You may also consider using a fibre channel bridge to bridge from fibre channel to a SCSI interface. Bridges are helpful when you wish to back up your cluster solutions.

If you are using a SCSI external array, make sure it is equipped with two interfaces—one for each node within the cluster—and that you have configured it for the manufacturer's recommended cluster-aware operation.

4.2.2 BIOS Configuration

Each machine you use in a cluster should have an identical BIOS configuration. Enter the BIOS configuration on node 1 and set to the factory default BIOS configuration. Most system boards allow a "reset to factory defaults." Once your BIOS is reset, disable any hardware you know that you will not need. COM ports, USB interfaces, and unneeded IDE interfaces should be disabled. This saves vital resources that your system may need for the shared disk array. Plus, if the operating system does not see it, it won't load drivers for it and will save on system memory. If you had previously added a system or boot password, make sure you remove it so that the cluster server can reboot itself unhindered in the event of a power failure.

Once you have completed your modifications to that server, complete the same process on the second node. This will ensure that both nodes are configured identically.

4.2.3 SCSI/Fibre Configuration

If you are using a SCSI external drive array, make sure that the controllers you are using in each machine are identical. Prior to inserting them into the machines, be sure to change one of the controllers' ID to 6 rather than 7. The default ID for most SCSI controllers is 7, and both of the controllers are going to be on the same bus, so you need to change one of the IDs to prevent conflicts. If you are not using an external drive array that assigns IDs to the drives automatically, make sure you assign manual IDs to the drives so that they are different than the controller IDs. This will ensure that all devices operate on the bus correctly.

If you are using fibre channel to connect to your external drive array, then you must connect your fibre channel host bus adapters to the fibre channel switch/hub, but configuration will not be necessary. Fibre channel uses a 3-byte address scheme for devices and communicates to other nodes automatically. Again, make sure you do not power on both nodes while they are connected to the external drive array or you will risk corrupting your disks.

4.2.4 RAID Configuration

If you are using RAID within your external drive array, you will need to know how to configure your RAID array prior to loading your operating system. Power on your external drive array and node 1 of your cluster. Upon boot up, you should see the option to configure the RAID array controller or fibre channel host bus adapter. This is typically a Ctrl key combination such as Ctrl + A or Ctrl + S.

Because all RAID software is different, it is difficult to give precise direction at this point, but use these guidelines to configure your RAID array.

- Verify that all drives are present within the cabinet through the configuration.
- Initialize all drives to ensure proper functionality.
- Create a RAID container for the quorum resource.
- Create a RAID container for each application you wish to host on your cluster server.
- Wait until the containers are created and scrubbed before continuing.

Once you have completed the configuration, shut down node 1 and power on node 2. Once again, enter the RAID array configuration for your system. Configuring node 2 is different than configuring node 1 because the RAID configuration is already present on the disks and must be copied to the new controller. Find an option that allows you to copy the configuration or restore the configuration from the drive array. Once this option is run, save the configuration and restart node 2. Enter the RAID configuration once again to verify that the configuration is present.

If you have completed this step correctly, you should have two RAID array controllers that are configured identically. Now power down node 2 so that you can load the operating system on node 1.

4.3 Operating System Install

If you have completed the hardware configuration, then you are ready to install your operating system on both nodes. Remember, the Microsoft Clustering Service (MSCS) is only available through the Windows 2000

Advanced Server and Windows 2000 Datacenter Server versions of the operating system, so be sure you have the appropriate version and the necessary license for each node within your cluster.

4.3.1 Smart Start Programs

Many servers come with a program that will help you to install the operating system. Vendors like Dell and Compaq have tried to streamline the process of installing an operating system on their hardware by creating "jump start" or "smart start" CD-ROMs that perform various tasks on the hardware prior to installation of the operating system. Often, these CD-ROMs modify the installation of the operating system with updated drivers and configuration information for the particular machine it is being installed on.

In most cases, it is better to use these programs than to attempt a direct install of the operating system. A direct install may neglect needed files or utilities intended by the manufacturer. If you do use a smart start program to prepare your system for installation, make sure that it supports the installation of Windows 2000 Advanced Server or Windows 2000 Datacenter Server. Also be sure to perform the same operation on all nodes within your cluster.

4.3.2 Loading the Operating System

If you used a smart start CD-ROM to load the operating system, then you're most likely loading the operating system already. If you are not using a smart start CD-ROM or your CD-ROM does not initiate the operating system install, place the Windows 2000 Advanced Server or Windows 2000 Datacenter Server disk in the CD-ROM drive and power on the first node within the cluster.

Installing the operating system is no different than usual, but pay careful attention to the following items:

- Do not install the MSCS with the operating system.
- Assign your designated IP addresses to the network cards during the installation, but don't set a gateway address for the adapter used for private cluster communication.
- Make sure your public network connection has the correct primary DNS entry so that the server will register its name with a DNS server.
- Name your server based upon the name you chose in the previous section.
- Do not join the server to a domain during the installation.

117

Once the operating system is installed, shut the machine down and repeat the process on node 2. Make sure that the steps you take to install the operating system are identical. The only difference should be the name of the server and the addresses you assign. Once complete, power down the second server.

4.4 Network Configuration

Configuring the network properties for the cluster server is important because the cluster server relies upon the connectivity provided, along with the name resolution services, to communicate with other nodes on the network. In many cases, a lack of connectivity can trigger a failover. To reduce timeouts, you must ensure that your network properties are correct.

Shut down the external disk array and disconnect it completely from both machines. Then boot both servers and perform the following network configurations on each machine.

4.4.1 Configuring the Private Network

The private network is the communication between all cluster nodes. The cluster nodes use IP to communicate with each other. The status of the cluster and the status of each node is derived through a heartbeat message that is sent at regular intervals.

When you install the cluster software, you will be given the option to configure each network interface for private cluster communication, public client communication, or a combination of both. The idea is to allow the cluster nodes to communicate with each other on any medium, but to allow clients to contact the application on the cluster through only one medium. Because the private network adapter is only physically connected to the other cluster node (if you are using a crossover cable between nodes), it cannot respond to client requests. Therefore it will be used for private node-to-node communication only. The public network connection, however, can communicate with both the cluster nodes and the clients; therefore it will be used for both private and public communication.

This builds extra redundancy into the system, for even though a private network card may fail, the failure would not affect the service to clients, so you do not want it to trigger a failover. To prevent the failover, the cluster nodes will begin communicating with each other through the public interface.

To configure your private interface, power on node 1 (only) and login as administrator. Right-click on the **My Network Places** icon and select **Properties**. This should show you two interfaces, **Local Area Connection** and **Local Area Connection 2**. Right-click the icon that represents the adapter that is connected directly to the second node, and click **Properties**. It may take some detective work to determine which adapter is connected to what, but you can figure it out by right-clicking on the icon and selecting **Status** as you connect and disconnect the cables.

Once you have entered the **Local Area Connection Properties,** click the **Configure** button to configure your network card. Click the **Advanced** tab (see Figure 4-7) and select **Media Type,** or **Speed** from the list. On the right hand side, pull down the menu and select **100BaseTX** (or the fastest speed

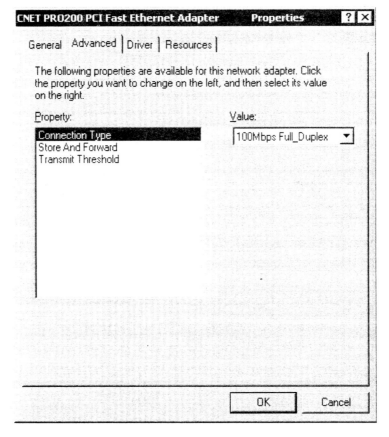

Figure 4-7
Configuring the private network adapter.

available, based upon what hardware you are using) then click **OK**. This will prevent the adapter from dropping unnecessary packets, for some adapters drop packets while negotiating speed.

It is recommended that you use the same network adapter in all cluster nodes, but if you must use separate adapters, make sure they are configured identically with regard to duplex mode, media type, speed, and flow control.

Select the **Internet Protocol (TCP/IP)** component and click the **Properties** button. Select the **Use the following IP address** option and enter an IP address for your private cluster adapter. This will be the address you chose in the TCP/IP addressing section of this chapter. You will also need to enter a subnet mask, but do not enter a default gateway address for this adapter (see Figure 4-8). The only traffic that will flow through this adapter is traffic destined for the other cluster server and therefore does not need a gateway address or a DNS address.

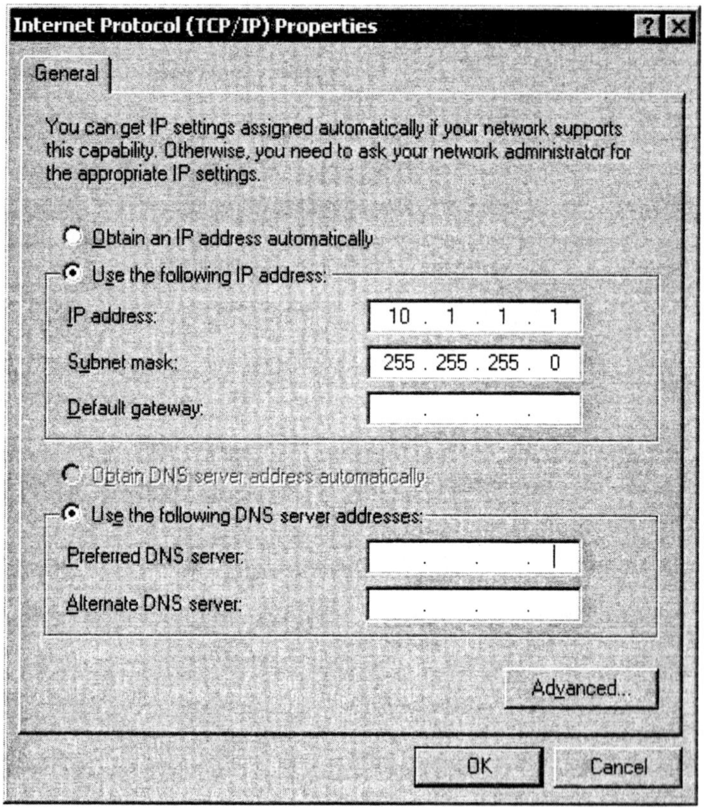

Figure 4-8
TCP/IP addressing.

Select the **Advanced** button and click the **WINS** tab. On this sheet, select the **Disable NetBIOS over TCP/IP** option and click **OK** (see Figure 4-9). You will get an error stating that you did not assign a WINS address to this adapter, but it is safe to ignore. The cluster nodes communicate via TCP/IP only, and are not dependent upon NetBIOS. If you don't disable the NetBIOS, it may slow down the boot time of your server and interfere with the node-to-node communication.

In the network Properties window, clear the check marks to disable the **Client for Microsoft Networks** and the **File and Print Sharing for Microsoft Networks** on this interface. Once you have completed that step, rename the connection so that it is called *Private Cluster* or *Heartbeat Connection*. This will make it easier to work with in the future and prevent confusion. To rename a connection, right-click on the connection and select **Rename** from the menu. The name of the connection is only a label and will not change the functionality of the interface.

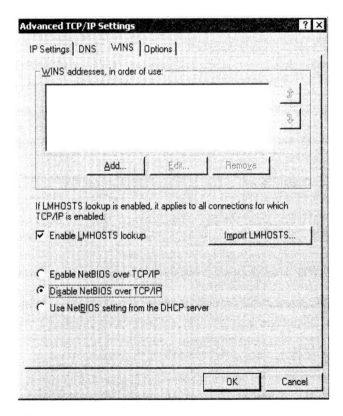

Figure 4-9
Disabling NetBIOS.

4.4.2 Configuring the Public Network

To configure the public network connection, right-click on the network connection and select **Properties.** Select the **Internet Protocol (TCP/IP)** component and click **Properties.** Select **Use the following IP address** (if you did not already assign one during setup) and put in the public network adapter address you chose in the TCP/IP addressing section (see Figure 4-10). For this adapter, you will need to put in a valid subnet mask address as well as a default gateway address. Then select **Use the following DNS servers** and type in the address of your primary DNS server. This should be a Dynamic DNS server (Windows 2000-based) so that the server can correctly register its name and IP address information. It's a good idea to have a secondary server listed as well so that in the event the first server is not available, the server can still register and receive responses to name resolution queries.

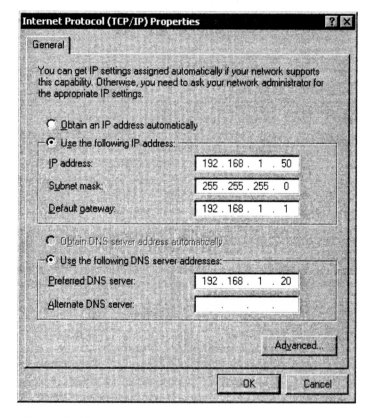

Figure 4-10
Configuring the public network adapter.

Note

It is important to note that even though this adapter is referred to as the "public" network adapter, it does by no means imply that it must have a "public accessible" or "Internet" address. The adapter is termed a public adapter because it is accessible to clients, not just cluster nodes. The clients that access the cluster can be internal (LAN) clients or external (Internet) clients. If you are making your cluster accessible to Internet clients, it is strongly recommended that you use private addressing and perform some sort of translation on a router or firewall for incoming client requests. This adds an extra measure of needed security.

4.4.3 Verify Connectivity

Once you have configured the private and public interfaces for all nodes within your cluster, you need to test each interface's connectivity to other hosts on the network. First, verify that you have the appropriate IP addresses assigned by opening a command prompt and typing *IPCONFIG /ALL* on each node within the cluster. This will show you the IP address that is bound to all of the cards in the system. Review the addresses and verify that both interfaces are correct (see Figure 4-11) for each machine.

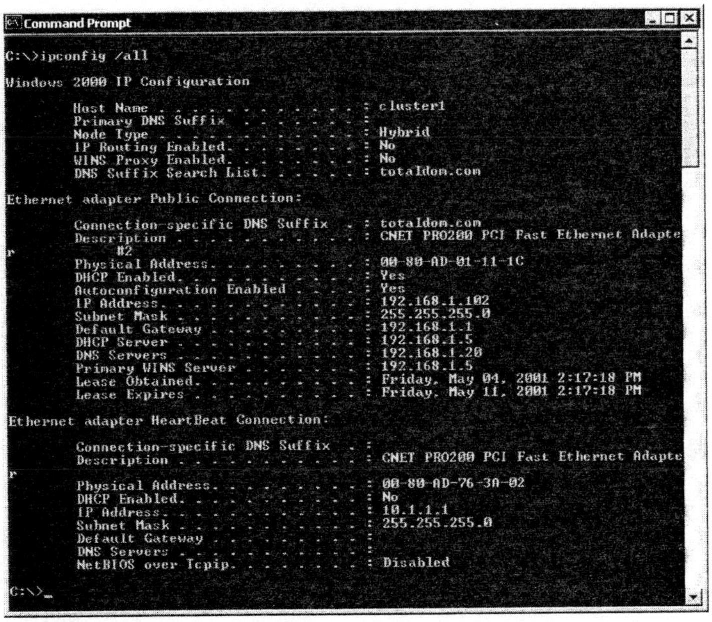

Figure 4-11
Reviewing IP addresses.

   If the IP addressing information is incorrect, repeat the steps in sections 4.4.1, "Configuring the Private Network," and 4.4.2, "Configuring the Public Network," correcting any mistakes that were made. If the information is correct, use the PING command to verify connectivity between the private network adapters. From a command prompt, type *PING X*, where *X* is the IP address of the other cluster node. In this example, the 192.168.1.0/24 network is used for the public network connection and the 10.1.1.0/24 network is used for the private network connection. Because the IP address 10.1.1.1 is assigned to cluster node 1, a PING command is used to send a packet to the other node (see Figure 4-12). If the other server responds, then connectivity between the two machines has been verified. If it does not respond, verify that you have the correct IP address assigned to both cards, and that you are using the necessary cabling to connect the machines. If you have multiple machines in your cluster, be sure you can ping each node in your cluster.

   Once you have verified connectivity on the private network adapter, use the same process to verify connectivity on the public network adapter. Be sure to ping the address you actually assigned to the adapter, not the cluster address. Also, ping the domain controller on your network and the gateway address you assigned to the card to verify that the public network adapter has connectivity to all machines on the network.

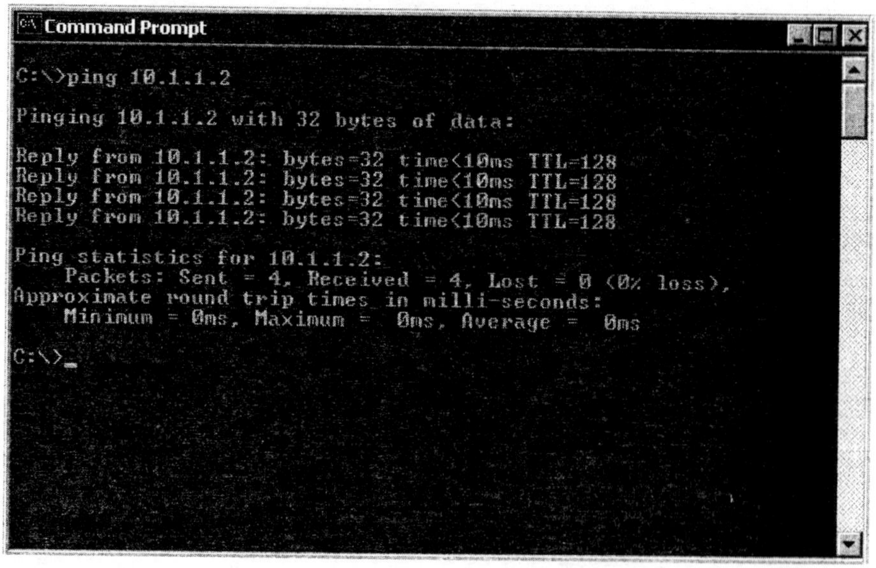

Figure 4-12
Pinging the private network hosts.

4.4.4 Joining a Domain

Once you have verified that all nodes within the (soon to be) cluster can ping other hosts on the network as well as each other, it is time to join the computers to a domain. Remember, cluster nodes can be domain members or domain controllers, but must be a part of a domain. Make sure that your external drive array is still powered off for this section.

To join the Active Directory or Windows NT 4.0 domain, right-click **My Computer** on cluster node 1 and select **Properties**. Select the **Network Identification** tab and then click the **Properties** button. This will bring up the **Identification Changes** window and allow you to add your computer to the domain. In the **Member of** section, select **Domain:** and type in the name of the domain you wish to join (see Figure 4-13). Once you click **OK**, it will

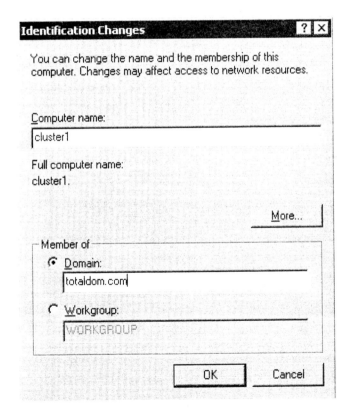

Figure 4-13
Joining a cluster node to the domain.

ask you for a username and password. This will be the user who has rights to add workstation accounts to the domain or directory. Type in the administrator account name and password for your domain and select **OK.**

You should receive a message that says, "Welcome to the *domainname* Domain." If you receive an error stating that the domain is not available, make sure that you have spelled the domain name correctly and that the domain controller is online. If you still cannot connect, try to verify the connectivity with the PING command once again.

If you successfully added your server to the domain, select **OK** when it asks you to reboot the server, and then repeat the process on all nodes within the cluster. Now power down both servers and continue the configuration process.

4.5 Configuring the Shared Disk Array

Power on the external drive array and then start cluster node 1. In this section you will configure each machine to correctly view the drives available on the disk array. This step is important, for if your operating system does not view the drives correctly, the cluster installation will not succeed.

4.5.1 Partitions

If you have a RAID disk array, you have already configured the containers necessary to house your data, but you must still create partitions and format those partitions for the operating system and the cluster software installation to be successful.

Login to cluster node 1 as the domain administrator. Access the disk administrator program by right-clicking on the **My Computer** icon and selecting **Manage** from the drop-down list. Once the computer management program has loaded, double-click on the **Disk Management** icon in the left pane to connect to the logical disk management service. This will show you the physical disks in your machine, along with any logical drives or storage volumes you have created (see Figure 4-14).

Under the Volume heading in the right pane, verify that you have a system drive and one drive for each container you created within your RAID configuration. The disk management program will not see your external array as

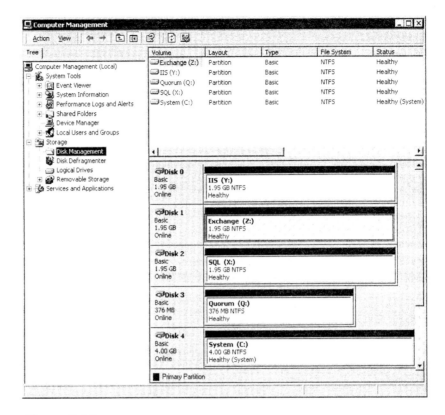

Figure 4-14
Viewing the cluster disks.

many separate drives configured as containers, but will see one physical drive
for each container you have created in your RAID configuration.

If the drives are not present, verify that your external disk array is attached
securely to the cluster node and that you have configured the RAID array correctly. In the bottom portion of the Computer Management screen, it shows a
more graphical view of your disks. If you look at the label to the left of each
drive, it will tell you whether your disk(s) are configured as dynamic disks or
basic disks. If your disks are configured as dynamic, you must change them to
basic. To do this, right-click on the label and select **Revert to basic disk**. This
will convert the disk to basic and prepare the disk for partitioning.

If you see the drives you were expecting, right-click on each drive and select
Create Partition to start the Create Partition wizard. Click **Next** at the wizard
startup screen and select **Primary Partition** for the partition you wish to create
(see Figure 4-15). Type in the maximum size partition it will allow and select

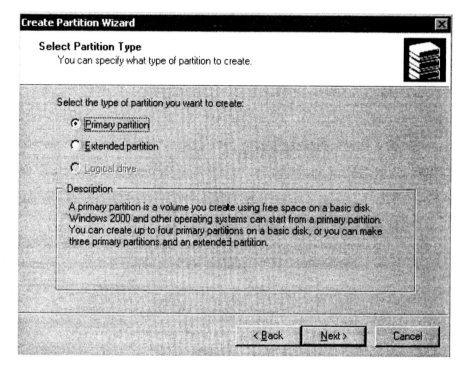

Figure 4-15
Selecting a partition type.

Next. When asked to assign a drive letter, accept the default. You will change the drive letter later. Click **Next** to reveal the **Format Partition** dialogue.

Make sure that **Format this partition using the following settings:** is selected. Also make sure that **File System to Use:** is set to NTFS. Click the **Perform a Quick Format** option and type in a volume label for this disk. Try to make the volume label consistent with the disk usage (Quorum, SQL, etc.). Select **OK** and then **Finish** to begin the format operation (see Figure 4-16). Repeat this process for all disks within the external storage array.

4.5.2 Assigning Drive Letters

Once you have formatted all disks within your storage array, you must assign drive letters to the drives. Even though the operating system will assign drive letters automatically, you will most likely want to change them. Because all nodes within the cluster will need to access the disks, they must all know the

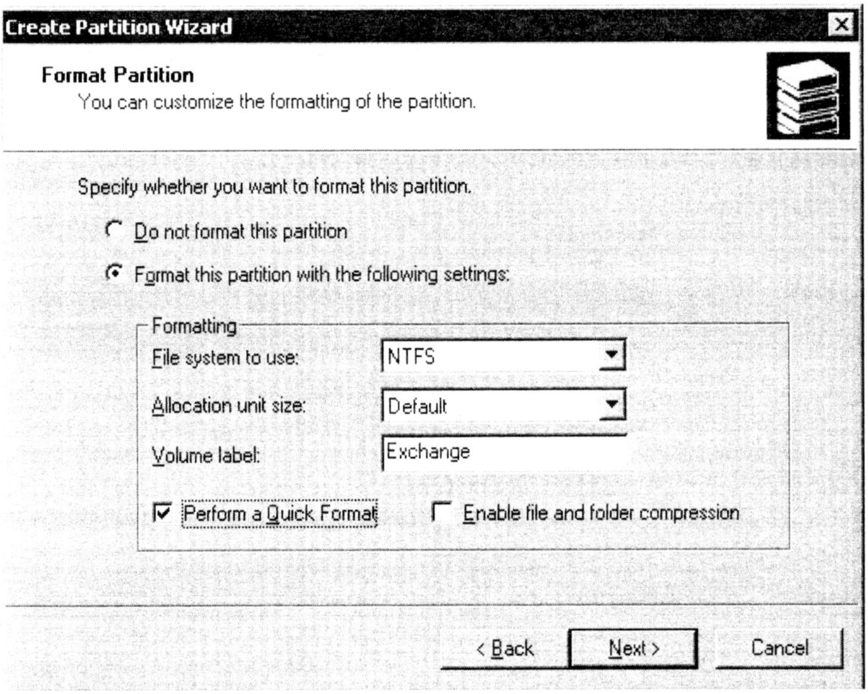

Figure 4-16
Formatting the cluster disks.

disks as the same letter. For example, if you have formatted three drives within your external drive array, and the operating system assigned E:, F:, and G: as the corresponding drive letters, then every node within the cluster must see all three disks as E:, F:, and G:. The operating system assigns drive letters in ascending order from D: to Z:. If you were to add an addition local drive to one of the servers, it would cause the operating system to adjust the drive assignments—causing your cluster to malfunction.

For consistency, and to prevent the shifting of drive letters, you should assign letters to your external disks that you know will not change. Use a descending order instead of an ascending order so that all of your external disks will be at the end of the alphabet and the local disks will be at the beginning of the alphabet. If you have three disks within your disk array, name them X:, Y:, and Z:.

To change the drive letter, open Disk Administrator through the Computer Management application and right-click on the drive you wish to change. Select **Change Drive Letter and Path.** A dialogue showing the current

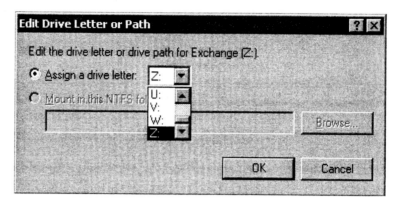

Figure 4-17
Assigning drive letters.

drive letter is revealed. Click the **Edit** button and select the letter you wish to assign to the drive (see Figure 4-17). When you click **OK**, you will be given an error message stating that some programs on the volume may no longer function. It is safe to ignore this message for now. Click **Yes** to apply the change.

You need to repeat this process for each drive in your external array. Once you have completed the drive letter assignment, shut down node 1, make sure the drive array is powered on and connected to both nodes, and start up node 2. Open Disk Administrator through the Computer Management program and view the drives on your external storage array. You will notice that all drives are already formatted (because you did that through the first node), but that they do not have the drive assignments you gave them. That is because drive assignments are native to the operating system, not to the drive itself.

You need to change the drive letters on node 2 to match the drive letters you assigned to the disks through node 1. It is imperative that these drive letter assignments match, so make sure you know which disk should be assigned which letter. If you need to power up machine number 1 to view them again, you can do so, but make sure you power down node 2 before you do so.

If you have other nodes in the cluster, repeat the process for those nodes as well so that all nodes have the correct drive letter assignments.

4.5.3 Verify Read/Write Ability

After configuring the external drives for each node, bring each node up, one at a time, and complete the following process to verify access to the drives.

1. Open **Windows Explorer.**
2. Click on the first drive in the external storage array.
3. On the right side, right-click and select **New**, then **Text File** from the menu.
4. Name the text file and hit **Enter**.
5. Double-click the text file to open it, and type a few words.
6. Click **File** and **Save** from the menu.
7. Click **File** and then **Close** from the menu.
8. Select the file and hit the **Delete** key to delete the file.
9. Click **Yes** to send it to the Recycle Bin.
10. Repeat the process for each of the external drives.

This process verifies that the operating system can read from the drive and write to the drive. It is possible for the drive to be visible, but not accessible. This step prevents your cluster installation from failing due to a failure within the disk access.

4.6 Clustering Software Install

If you have completed the preceding steps, then you are ready to install the cluster software. Shut down all of the equipment. Power on the external storage array and start up the first node within the cluster.

4.6.1 Preparation

Before you begin the software installation, there is one action that you must complete that will make the installation easier. When installing the software, it will review your disks and your network connectivity. If you have used a crossover cable between node 1 and node 2 (assuming you are only running two nodes within your cluster), you will need to ensure that there is power to both machines, without actually booting the operating system on both machines.

That sounds a bit tricky, but here is how you do it. Boot node 1 to the Windows 2000 logon screen. Then boot node 2, but prior to the Windows 2000 startup screen, hit **F8**. This will give you a boot menu. If you leave the machine in this state, it has power to the network card but is not running the operating system. At this point you can login to node 1 and begin the cluster software install. Make sure that node 2 does not boot during this process or you will corrupt your drives.

If you happen to make the mistake of running both operating systems at the same time prior to cluster software installation, power up your external disk array and one node and delete all partitions on the external disks. After recreating all the partitions, format them and assign drive letters. Then shut down the first node, boot the second node, and assign drive letters to the disks. Once complete, verify connectivity and you will be ready to install the software once again.

4.6.2 Node 1 Install

To install the MSCS, click **Start**, then **Settings**, and then **Control Panel**. In the Control Panel, select the **Add/Remove Programs** option. This will allow you to view the installed components. Select **Add/Remove Windows Components** to open the Windows Components dialogue box. Select **Cluster Service** (see Figure 4-18) and hit **OK**.

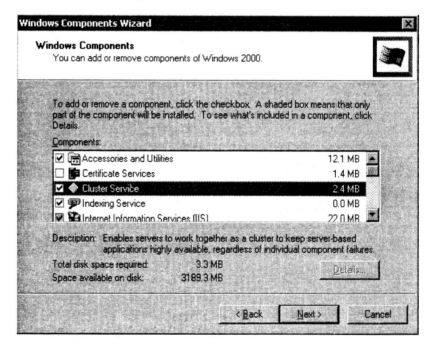

Figure 4-18
Installing the Microsoft Cluster Service.

The installation will ask you for the Windows 2000 Advanced Server CD-ROM. Insert the CD-ROM into the drive and select **OK**. The install will then copy several files from the CD-ROM and start the Cluster Service Configuration wizard (see Figure 4-19).

Select **Next** to continue the installation. The wizard will then show you the hardware configuration screen (see Figure 4-20). This screen does not verify your hardware, but alerts you to check the clustering section of the hardware compatibility list (HCL) to ensure your hardware is supported. You should have completed this step in an earlier chapter, but if you did not, the wizard presents a link to the Microsoft HCL Web site so you can do so at this time. If you know your hardware is compatible, select the **I Understand** button, and then select **Next**.

The next screen asks if you are creating a new cluster or joining an existing cluster. Since this is the first node in your cluster, select **The first node in the cluster** and click **Next** (see Figure 4-21).

Figure 4-19
Cluster Service Configuration Wizard.

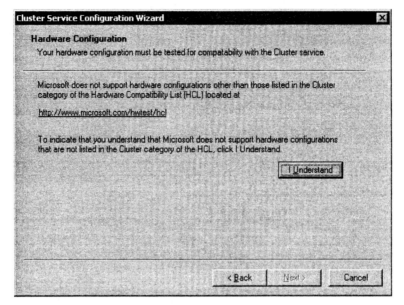

Figure 4-20
Hardware Configuration screen.

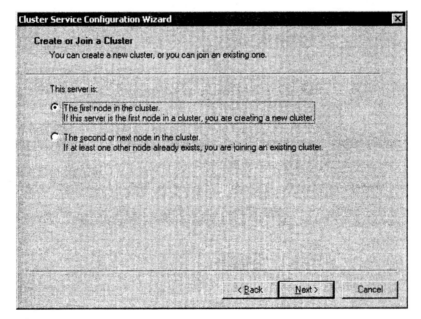

Figure 4-21
Creating or joining a cluster.

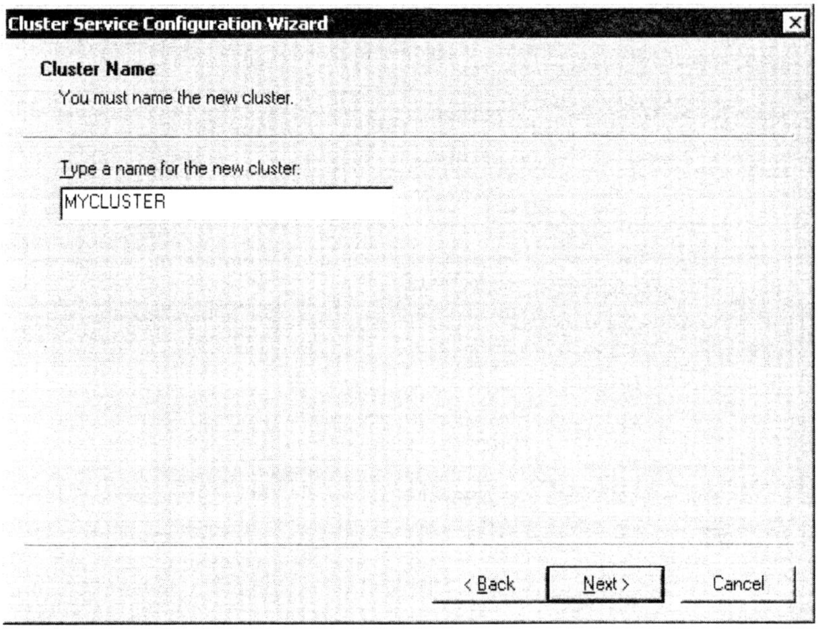

Cluster Service Configuration Wizard

Cluster Name
You must name the new cluster.

Type a name for the new cluster:

MYCLUSTER

< Back   Next >   Cancel

Figure 4-22
Assigning a cluster name.

Next, select the name you would like assigned to your cluster (see Figure 4-22). This name will be the NetBIOS name of the cluster on the network. This will be the name you use to manage your cluster from remote workstations on the network. The name is not really that important, but should not be the same name as any other device on your network. Once you have entered the cluster name, click **Next** to continue the installation.

The next screen will ask for a domain account that will be assigned to the cluster services for all nodes within the cluster. You should have created this account earlier in this chapter. Type in the name, password, and domain of the service account you created (see Figure 4-23) and click **Next**. If the user you created is not a member of the local administrator group for that node, the configuration wizard will ask if you would like to add that member to the group. Select **Yes** to continue.

Note

Make sure you do not assign the "administrator" user as the service account for the cluster service. This creates more overhead than necessary when password changing policies are in effect and will require you to reconfigure your cluster every time you change the user account.

135

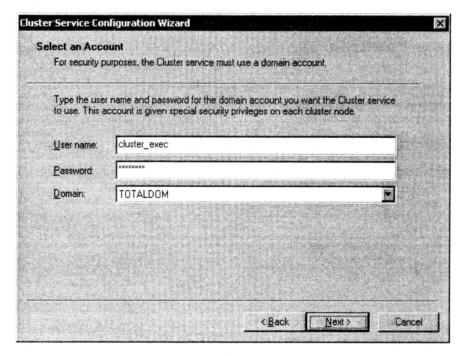

Figure 4-23
Assigning the cluster service account.

Next, you will see the Managed disks dialogue (see Figure 4-24). The cluster service needs to know which disks are part of the external storage array so that it will know which disks to manage. Verify that the disks that are part of the external storage array are listed under Managed disks. If there are any non-shared disks in the list, move them to the Unmanaged disks section so that the cluster service does not attempt to control them. Local disks that contain system files should not show up in the list, but if they do, make sure they are also moved to the Unmanaged disks section. Once you have verified that everything is correct, select **Next** to continue.

The next dialogue is the Cluster File Storage screen (see Figure 4-25). This screen allows you to specify which disk you would like to use for the quorum disk. The quorum disk holds transaction logs and cluster status information for the cluster. If you followed the instructions in the earlier section related to disk partitioning of the external disk array, you should have a disk of at least 100 MB that is assigned the letter Q. This will be your quorum disk. Select the letter Q from the drives listed, and click **Next**.

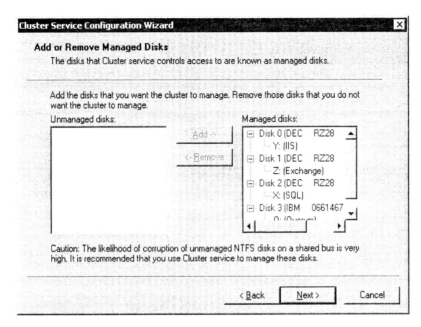

Figure 4-24
Assigning managed disks to the cluster.

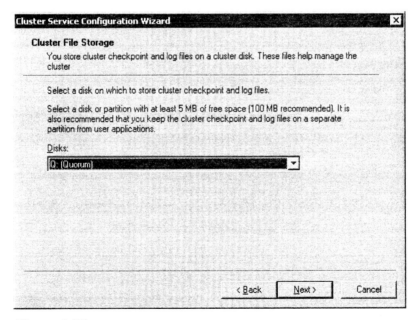

Figure 4-25
Assigning a disk for quorum storage.

The next screen is the Configure Cluster Networks screen. This screen does not require that you select any options, but discusses the use of public and private network adapters. It is recommended that you read this section carefully, and then select **Next**.

The wizard will then prompt you to configure each of your network cards for the cluster service. As stated before, an adapter can be a private adapter, which communicates only with other cluster nodes; a public adapter, which communicates only with clients on the network; or a combination of both, which communicates with both the cluster nodes and the clients. You may also choose to disable a network adapter for cluster use if you do not need to use it for your cluster service.

Previously, you configured two network cards: one for public communications and one for private (cluster only) communication. Through the next two (or more) screens, configure your private network connection for **Internal cluster communications only (private network)**, as shown in Figure 4-26. configure your public network connection for **All communications (mixed network)**, shown in Figure 4-27. Once you have completed the configuration of each device, select **Next**.

After configuring your network adapters for the cluster service, the Internal Cluster Communication dialogue (see Figure 4-28) asks which network

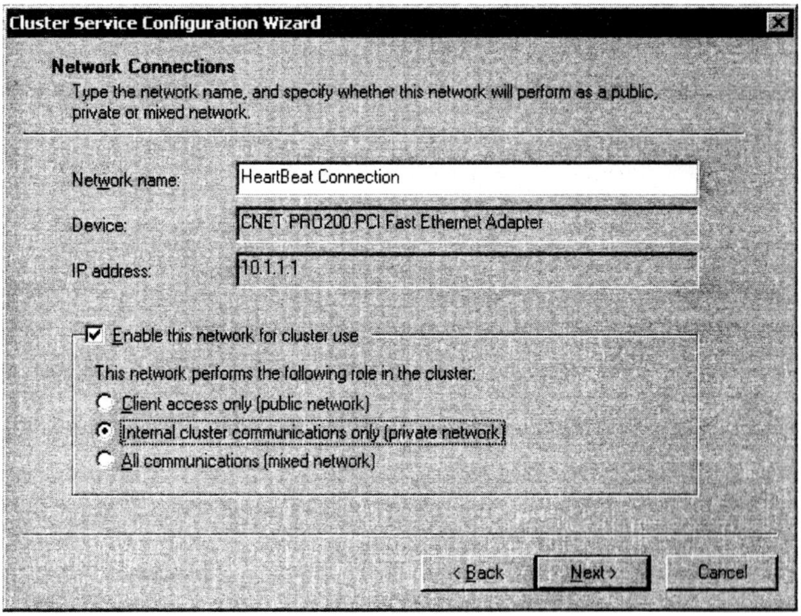

Figure 4-26
Configuring the private network connection.

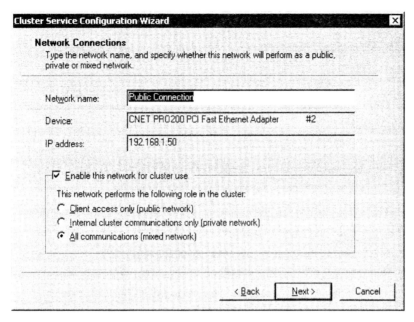

Figure 4-27
Configuring the public network connection.

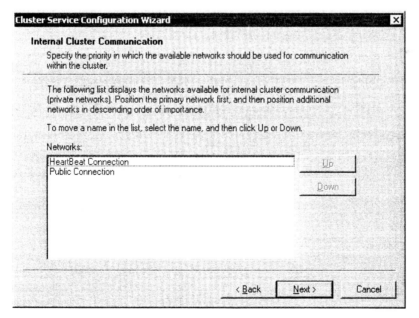

Figure 4-28
Configuring the internal cluster communication priority.

adapter should be the primary network adapter for node-to-node communications. Make sure the Private (HeartBeat) connection is the first in the list, and select **Next**.

The next screen asks for the cluster IP address (see Figure 4-29). This will be the IP address you wish to assign to the cluster. Remember, this IP is a virtual server and should not be the same as any other cluster node or device on your network. You will also need to type in a subnet mask. Make sure the subnet is consistent with the network segment you are on. Type in the IP address you wish to use for the cluster, along with a subnet, and select which network will host the virtual server. This should be the public network connection—the network connection through which the clients access the server.

Once you have assigned an IP address to the cluster, hit **Next**. The cluster wizard will then inform you that all of the configuration data has been complete (see Figure 4-30). Select **Finish** to have the wizard complete the installation of the cluster service on the first node. After making several configuration changes, the wizard will inform you that the setup is complete. Press **OK** to complete the cluster service installation.

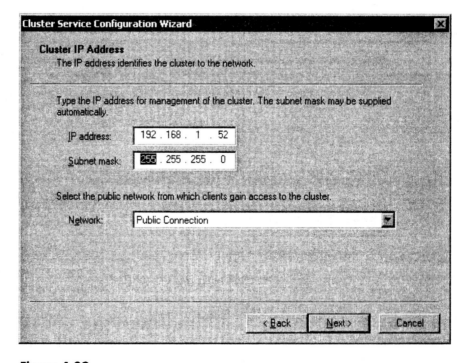

Figure 4-29
Assigning an IP address to the cluster.

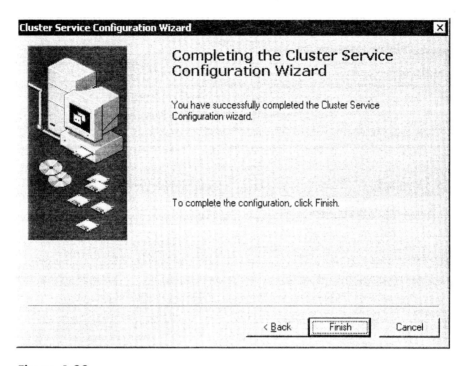

Figure 4-30
Finishing the Cluster Service Configuration wizard.

To confirm that you have installed the service correctly, open the Cluster Administrator program *(c:\winnt\cluster\cluadmin.exe)* and connect to the cluster using the name you created in the previous steps. Verify that each group under the Groups section is listed as online.

4.6.3 Node 2 Install

Once you have verified the installation of the cluster service on node 1, leave node 1 and the external array powered on and start node 2. Once you have started the second node, select **Start**, then **Settings**, and then **Control Panel**. In the Control Panel, select the **Add/Remove Programs** option. This will allow you to view the installed components. Select **Add/Remove Windows Components** to open the Windows Components dialogue box. Select the **Cluster Service** and hit **OK**.

The installation will ask you for the Windows 2000 Advanced Server CD-ROM. Insert the CD-ROM into the drive and select **OK**. The install will then copy several files from the CD-ROM and start the Cluster Service Configuration wizard.

Select **Next** to continue the installation. The wizard will then show you the Hardware Configuration screen (see Figure 4-20). This screen does not verify your hardware, but alerts you to check the clustering section of the HCL to ensure your hardware is supported. You should have completed this step in an earlier chapter, but if you did not, the wizard presents a link to the Microsoft HCL Web site, so you can do so at this time. If you know your hardware is compatible, select the **I Understand** button, and then select **Next**.

The next screen asks if you are creating a new cluster or joining an existing cluster. Since this is the second node in your cluster, select **The second or next node in the cluster,** and select next (see Figure 4-31).

The next dialogue asks for the name of the cluster you wish to join (see Figure 4-32). Type the name of the cluster you used in the installation of cluster node 1. Do not check the Connect to cluster as checkbox. The cluster installation will use the username you provided during the initial installation on cluster node 1. Click **Next** and enter the password for the service account used in the installation of cluster node 1 (see Figure 4-33).

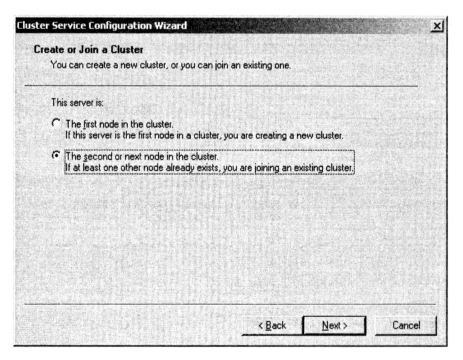

Figure 4-31
Adding the second node to the cluster.

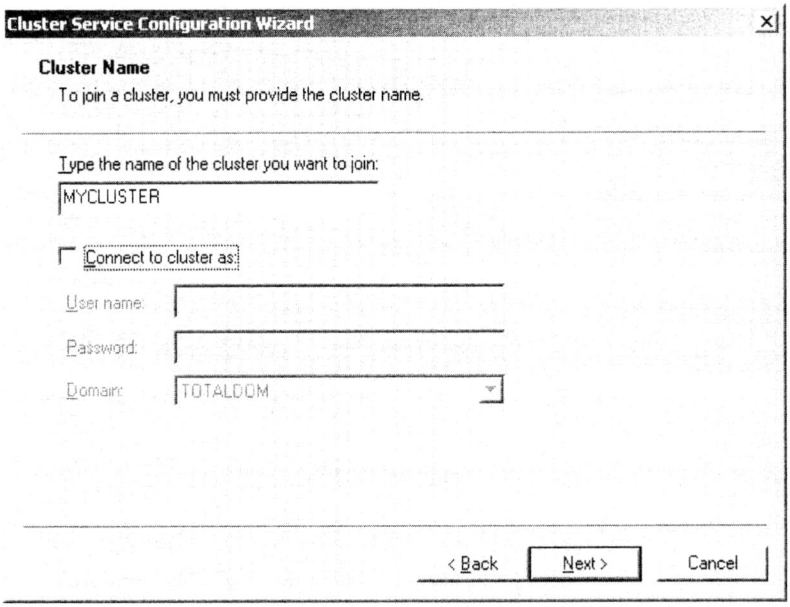

Figure 4-32
Joining the cluster.

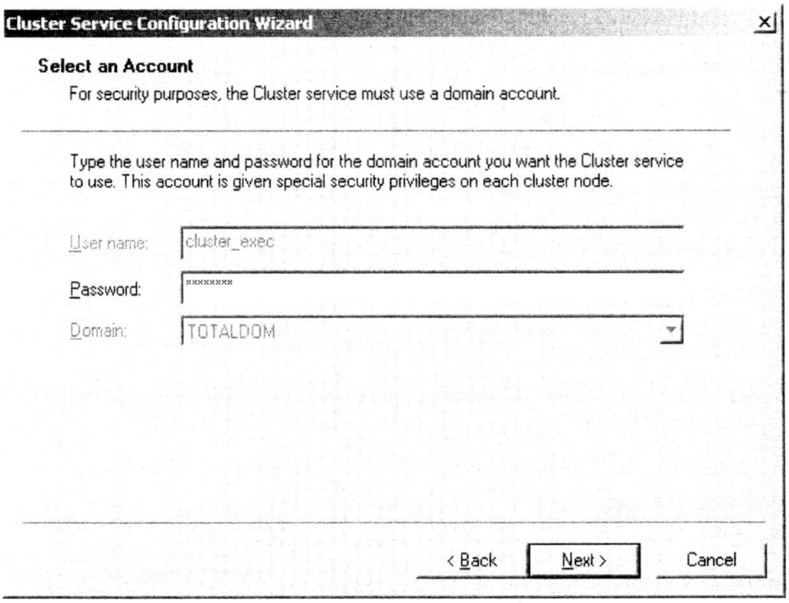

Figure 4-33
Entering the service account password.

Click **Next** and the wizard will inform you that the selected account is not a member of the local administrator's group for that machine. Select **Yes** to add this account to the administrator group. Then select **Finish** to complete the installation.

4.6.4 Remaining Node Installs

At this time you should repeat the process you completed on the second node to all remaining nodes within the cluster. This will join each node to the cluster and allow it to operate as a part of the group.

4.6.5 Cleaning Up

Once the installation is complete, there are a few items you should do to ensure your cluster server is up to date with the latest changes at Microsoft. The first step is to apply the latest service pack for the Windows 2000 Advanced Server operating system. This can be obtained from Microsoft by visiting *http://windowsupdate.microsoft.com*.

Once the service pack is complete, install any other patches or components that are suggested by Microsoft through the Windows update site. This will ensure that your server is secure and up to date.

4.7 Testing the Installation

After you have installed your cluster server software, it is important that you test your installation for proper operation. To test the installation, open the Cluster Administrator program on all nodes within your cluster.

On cluster node 1, select the Groups folder and select any group other than the cluster group. Right-click on the group and select **Move Group** (see Figure 4-34). You should see the owner of the disk within the group shift from cluster node 1 to cluster node 2. If have multiple nodes within your cluster, you will be able to choose which cluster node to move your group too. Pick any node and verify that the group moves to the other chosen node.

Another way to test your installation is to unplug one of the network cables attached to the public network segment. For instance, view the Cluster Group in the cluster administrator. Verify that the cluster group is owned by cluster node 1. Then unplug the public network cable from cluster node 1 to see if the

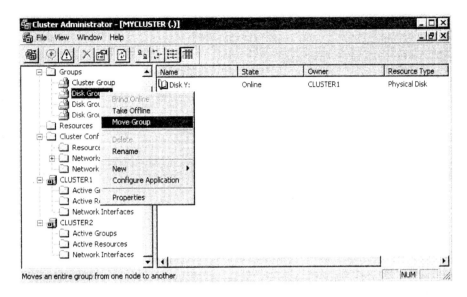

Figure 4-34
Moving a group.

cluster group will fail over to the other server. This should take approximately five seconds to fail over.

   If you see the owner of the resources located within the cluster group, change from cluster node 1 to cluster node 2. Congratulations—you have successfully installed the cluster server software.

4.8 Managing the Failover Cluster

Once your cluster server is online, it is important that you know how to manage the system. Although the Cluster Administrator program is where you perform most management, it is not the only tool available. This section will allow you to become familiar with many cluster management processes.

4.8.1 General Cluster Administration

Cluster administration is typically performed through the Cluster Administrator, a program installed with the Windows 2000 Advanced Server operating system. If you wish to manage the cluster from a Windows 2000

145

Professional workstation, you must install the *adminpak.msi* file, a Microsoft installation file located on any Windows 2000 Server in the *%systemroot%\sys-tem32* folder. If you run this file on a Windows 2000 Professional workstation or server, it will install the administrative tools necessary to manage the Active Directory, Network Services such as DNS, WINS, DHCP, and cluster server implementations.

Open the Cluster Administrator program on a workstation or server. If the program asks which server to connect to, type in the NetBIOS name of the cluster you wish to manage. Once connected, right-click on the cluster name and select **Properties** (see Figure 4-35).

The first tab on the Cluster Properties sheet is the General tab (see Figure 4-36) and shows the cluster name and the cluster description. You can change the NetBIOS name of the cluster from this screen if you wish to, but you must be sure to take the name resource for that group offline and then back online for the name to re-register with WINS and/or DNS. The description field is a text field for general information. Some large groups that manage multiple cluster servers may wish to use this field as an identifier of some sort. The field is optional, however.

The second tab is the Quorum tab (see Figure 4-37) and allows you to con-figure your quorum disk and its parameters. The quorum resource is the disk that hosts the quorum log file *(quolog.log)*, and the root path is the path to the file on that volume. It is possible to change the location of the quorum

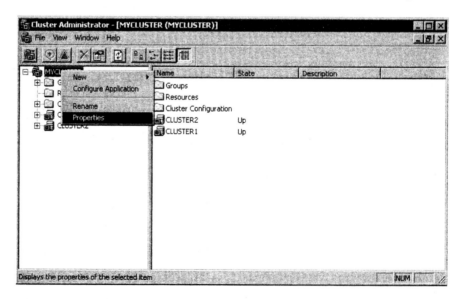

Figure 4-35
Viewing cluster properties.

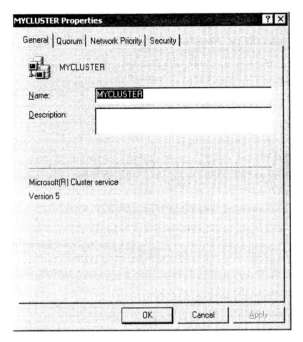

Figure 4-36
General properties of a cluster.

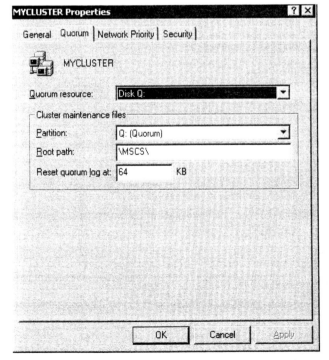

Figure 4-37
Configuring the quorum resource.

resource by simply changing the disk that the file resides upon. Once the change is made and the service on both nodes is restarted, the cluster service will create the necessary path and log files of the quorum. The quorum resource, at installation, is placed in the Cluster Group and is associated with the network name and IP address of the cluster. Although this is not necessary for proper operation, it is recommended that you retain this relationship. If you must move the quorum resource, be sure to move the IP address and network name of the cluster to the new group as well.

The next tab is the Network Priority tab (Figure 4-38). This is the configuration you completed during installation. It defines which network interface the cluster nodes should use to communicate with each other. If you set one interface to private communication only and one node to public communication only, the private interface will be the only adapter in the list. If you set one to private communication only and the other to communicate both private and public, both adapters will be listed. The adapter that communicates on the private network only should always be first in the list of networks used.

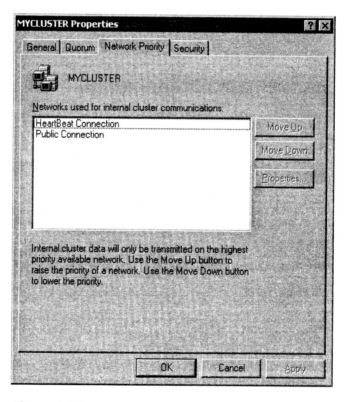

Figure 4-38
Network Priority settings.

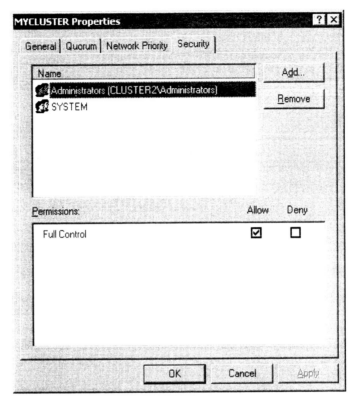

Figure 4-39
Cluster security.

The next tab is the Security tab (see Figure 4-39) and allows you to dictate which users should have administration rights over the cluster configuration. To add a user, just select **Add** and select the user from the domain or directory.

4.8.2 Groups and Resources

As you view your cluster configuration through the cluster administrator, you will notice that there is a Groups folder as well as a Resources folder. A group is a collection of resources that compose the necessary components to run an application. You will find that the number of groups you have is consistent with the number of shared disks that were available to the cluster installation. It is intended that you place one application on each disk. The groups allow you to pool other resources, such as IP addresses or network names, into a collection that defines components within an application.

As you begin to install applications, you will have to choose which disk the application will be hosted on. The installation of most programs will automatically create the resources necessary to run that application and place them in the same group as the disk you selected.

4.8.2.1 Creating New Groups

Although it is not common, it is possible to create new groups. Because the installation creates a disk group for each physical disk that is used on the shared disk array, you will only need to create a new group if you choose to add a new shared disk to the cluster. To create a new group, right-click on the **Groups** folder and select **New** and then **Group**. The New Group wizard starts to walk you through the creation of the group (see Figure 4-40). Name your group and select **Next** to continue. The **Preferred Owners** screen allows you to select which server should be the default host of the group. This does not exclude the other servers from being the host of the group in the event of a failure; it just dictates which machine the group should be running on when all hosts are operational. Select the preferred owner you would like and click **Add** to add it to the list (see Figure 4-41). Click **Finish** to complete the group creation.

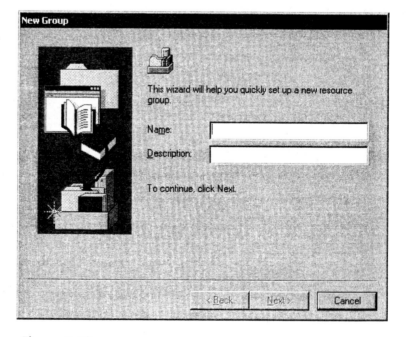

Figure 4-40
Adding a new disk group.

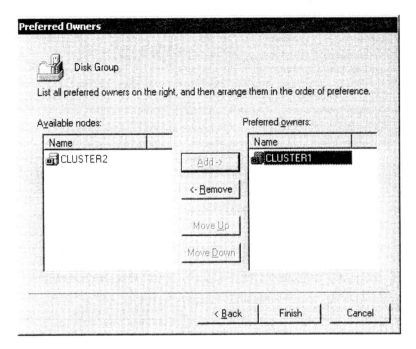

Figure 4-41
Selecting a Preferred Owner.

4.8.2.2 Renaming Groups

Once you have applications installed into the appropriate groups, you may want to change the name of the group to signify which application it hosts. To do so, double-click the **Groups** folder to view the configured groups, then right-click the disk group you want to rename and select **Rename**. Type in the new name and select **OK** to change the name.

The name of a disk group is strictly for organization and does not affect the configuration of the cluster.

4.8.2.3 Setting Group Properties

Within any group, there are properties that govern how the cluster server assigns ownership of the group. To access the properties of a particular group, right-click on the group and select **Properties** from the menu. Within the Group Properties there are three tabs. The first tab is the General tab (see Figure 4-42) and lists the name of the group and the preferred owner. As stat-

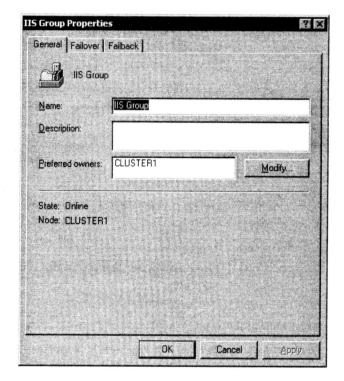

Figure 4-42
Viewing the general properties of a group.

ed before, the preferred owner is the server that should be the default host for the group under normal circumstances.

The second tab is the Failover tab and allows you to configure how the group fails over to another server (see Figure 4-43). The Threshold parameter is the number of times a group will fail over to another server within a specific period of time. The default setting is a threshold of 10 and a time period of 6 hours. This means that if a failure occurs and, during a period of six hours, the group fails back and forth between two servers (due to a problem with the application or service), it will not fail over on the eleventh time. This prevents the server from failing back and forth, consuming vital resources that may be needed for other applications running on the cluster. The default setting is typically sufficient, but if you have a troublesome application, you may want to lower the threshold.

The next tab is the Failback tab (see Figure 4-44) and allows you to configure how a server returns service to an original owner once the failure has been repaired. For example, if you have two servers within a failover cluster and one server is a high-performance server while the other server is an older machine

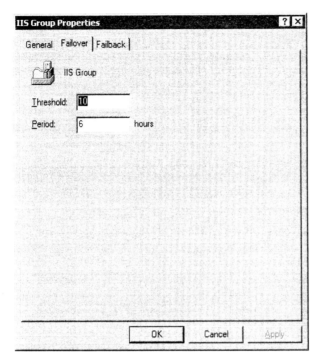

Figure 4-43
Configuring failover properties.

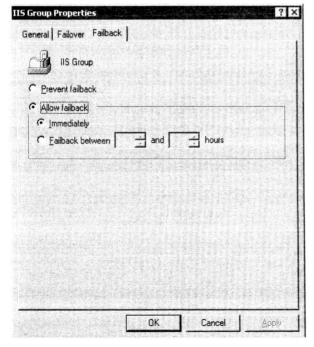

Figure 4-44
Configuring failback properties.

153

with fewer capabilities, you want to ensure that if the disk group fails to the low-performance server, it will return to the high-performance server once it is back online.

Failback can be configured to occur immediately, during specific time periods, or not at all. The default setting for all groups is Prevent failback. This is useful if you are running one application and both servers are equal in size and power. In this case you may want to manually move the group from server to server. If you choose to allow failback, then you can choose to allow an immediate failback or choose to allow failback only during a specific time of day. The Failback between __ and __ hours option allows you to define an hour in the day between midnight (0) and 11:00 p.m. (23) that failback is allowed to take place, using military time. You may want to use this setting if you have periods of inactivity or low activity that would be more conducive to a failback operation.

Note

For failback to take place, a server must be specified in the Preferred Owners section of the Group Properties. Be sure to restart the cluster service if you change a preferred owner setting.

4.8.2.4 Resource Objects

Within the Resources folder you will see a complete list of the resources that have been configured on your cluster server. Resources are objects that are managed by the cluster server or node. A resource object is implemented through native .dll (dynamic-link library) files. These files allow the cluster service to communicate with the resource monitor for a particular object.

An IP address, disk, and network name are all examples of objects that can be implemented on a cluster server. Each resource object is grouped with other objects to form the working pieces of an application. For instance, to implement a file share on your cluster, you need four objects: an IP address, a network name, a disk, and a path to share.

4.8.2.4.1 Resource Object Options

If you right-click on any resource within the Resources folder, you will see the following options related to that object:

- Bring Online
- Take Offline
- Initiate Failure

- Change Group
- Delete
- Rename
- Properties

It is helpful to understand the function of each option so that you will be able to manage your cluster effectively. If an option is grayed out or unavailable, it is typically because the operation would be redundant.

The Bring Online option is only available when a resource has been taken offline. When this option is selected, the cluster service first verifies that all resources that this object is dependent upon have been started. If the service finds that a dependent service is not online, it will attempt to start the dependent resource. Once the dependent service(s) are online, the service will start the requested resource.

The Take Offline option is the opposite of the Bring Online option. When you request a resource be taken offline, the cluster service checks the items that are dependent upon the resource you are taking offline and takes them offline first. Once those items are offline, the original request is processed and the resource is taken offline. Be careful with this option because the cluster service does not give you any warning that it is taking other resources offline; it does it without question.

The Initiate Failure option allows administrators to test the failure of a particular resource to see how a failure may affect the operation of a system. Keep in mind that this option does not cause a failover, but the system attempts to restart the resource on the local node before failing it to another cluster node. Since there isn't anything wrong with the local node, the resource, along with the resources that are dependent upon it, restart. The Initiate Failure option is good for testing buggy resources or dependencies.

The Change Group option allows an administrator to move a particular resource from one group to another. Be careful, though, for the cluster service will also move any resources that are dependent upon the resource you move to the new location. There are many situations when you may want to move a resource. If you were to add a new shared disk to the disk array, for example, and you want to move an existing file share along with its IP address and network name resource to the new group, you could move the IP address resource and it would move all three resources into the new group due to the dependencies.

The Delete option works in the same way. If you delete a resource that has other resources that depend upon it, they will also be deleted to maintain consistency in the cluster. This option does prompt you for confirmation, which allows you to view which items will be deleted as a result of the action.

The Rename option allows you to rename the object, but does not change the properties of the resource. It is suggested that you use names that are descriptive of the object to allow for easier administration. For example, an IP address resource for a virtual SQL Server may be called SQL_IP or SQL_IPaddress.

The Properties option allows you to configure the parameters of the resources and will be discussed in more detail.

4.8.2.4.2 IP Address Resource

For users to access an application or service, they must have an address. You cannot send mail to a relative without a street address, and you cannot access an application without an IP address. The IP address resource is the core of the virtual server, for it is the presence of the server on the network. When an IP address resource is added, the IP address that is configured is bound to the card of the server hosting the disk group. This allows users to access the service or application that is associated with that disk group.

When an IP address is assigned to a disk group (and ultimately to a cluster node), two things take place. The first is the binding, or initiation, of the IP stack on the local machine, and the second is the broadcasting of an ARP request on the local network, informing all machines to update their ARP table with a new IP address-to-MAC address mapping.

Creating an IP address resource is detailed in later chapters as a foundation for implementing other services, such as DHCP, file shares, and IIS on the cluster.

4.8.2.4.3 Network Name Resource

Most clients don't access servers on a network via an IP address, but use a more familiar method—name resolution. Name resolution allows computers to resolve names to IP addresses so that the requested server can be located. The table of names can be located in several different places. Typically, networks use a centrally located server to do name resolution. A WINS server or a DNS server would be sufficient to perform this task. You can also hard code network name mappings into a file called a *host* file on each machine. On Windows machines, the *hosts* and *lmhosts* files both perform this function and are located in the *%systemroot%/system32/drivers/etc* folder.

Creating a network name resource allows you to associate a network (NetBIOS) name with an IP address that is associated with a service or application hosted on your cluster. Face it—it is much easier to tell your clients to visit a Web site called *mysite.mycompany.com* than to tell them to visit 216.23.49.2.

Although not required, network name resources should be dependent upon an IP address resource, for the name has to associate with an address, and if the IP address fails, you do not want the cluster to attempt to bring the network name resource online. Network name resources are actually NetBIOS names that are registered with a central server such as a WINS or DNS server. If you are not running a WINS or DNS server on your network, then a network name resource is not really required.

4.8.2.4.4 File Share Resource

A file share resource is a shared network directory that is offered as a service by the cluster, allowing the file share and the files that are available to fail over to alternate nodes within the cluster. File shares correspond to a directory located on a shared disk array and are dependent upon a disk resource for proper operation. Because you cannot access a file share without an IP address, the IP address (and network name, if you choose) is also a dependency. Because the file share is created as a cluster resource, directory security and the number of users that can connect simultaneously to the share are both managed by the cluster through the configuration of the resource.

File shares are discussed in greater detail in Chapter 10, "Clustering File and Print Services."

4.8.2.4.5 Physical Disk Resource

A physical disk resource is a disk located on a shared disk array that is available to all nodes in the cluster. When the cluster service installs, it should place each disk within your external disk array into a disk group. If you add new disks to the disk array at a later date, you will need to create a physical disk resource before the disk can be used. If you place the new disk into an existing group, the disk will fail over with the resources located in the target group. Remember, groups fail over to other cluster nodes, but resources do not. The better solution is to create a new group and then create a disk resource within that new group for the new disk. This will allow you to manage the disk group (and application resources) independent of the other disks within the cluster.

A physical disk is the first resource to be started and therefore has no dependencies.

4.8.2.5 Resource Dependencies

The cluster service manages groups and resources based upon dependencies. There are many resources that are dependent upon other resources before they can operate correctly. For example, you cannot have a network name resource without an IP address to assign it to, and you cannot have a file share without a disk to assign it to. It is important to understand dependencies so that you can assign each object its dependencies correctly.

The best method of defining dependencies is to assign each item one dependency and daisy chain all necessary dependencies together (see Figure 4-45). Let's consider a file share on a cluster server. You have the following resources: disk, IP address, network name, and a file share. The disk is the first item to start and therefore is not dependent upon anyone, so disk is not assigned any dependencies. The IP address is the only resource that can operate without the others, so we will make it dependent upon the disk, for if the disk does not start, you know the file share will not be available and the IP address is meaningless. The network name has to be dependent upon the IP address, for it has to register a name-to-IP address mapping. The remaining file share resource can then be configured as a dependency of the network

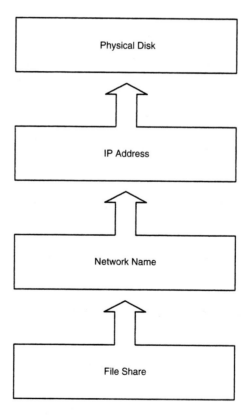

Figure 4-45
Daisy-chain dependencies.

name, for even though the file share is dependent upon all other resources for proper operation, you only need to assign a network name dependency due to the daisy chain of dependencies.

This type of dependency configuration allows for easier management and a clear understanding of how your resources are configured. Nevertheless, you should always keep your dependencies well documented so that you are aware of the configurations you have made.

4.8.3 Service Logging

The MSCS writes information about its operations in two different places; the Event Viewer and the Cluster Log.

4.8.3.1 Event Viewer

The event viewer is a Microsoft Windows 2000 application that has been standard in the operating system platform since the early days of Windows. The Event Viewer allows you to view error messages output from the system, the security manager, and various applications that run on your system. You can access the Event Viewer through the start menu by clicking **Start**, **Programs**, **Administrative Tools**, and then **Event Viewer**.

The Event Viewer in Windows 2000 is divided into three distinct logs (see Figure 4-46): the application log, the security log, and the system log. The application log records error messages and informational messages from applications running on the system. The security log records security events that are observed based upon auditing parameters set by the administrator. The system log records events that the operating system reports.

Because the MSCS is a service that functions as a part of the operating system, the events that it writes to the Event Viewer will be found in the system log. The events that it logs range from startup and shutdown notifications to severe disk corruption issues. The event log is a good place to begin troubleshooting any issues you may encounter with your cluster.

4.8.3.2.4 Cluster Log

The cluster log is a file that the cluster service writes to by default. Each cluster node within a cluster will write to a log file located in the *%systemroot%\cluster* directory. This file details the operation of the cluster node and provides extensive help in troubleshooting problems with a cluster server.

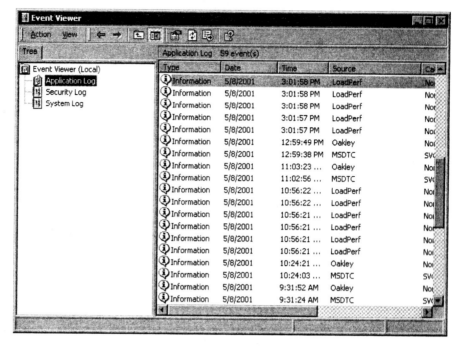

Figure 4-46
Event Viewer.

The location of the cluster log can be changed by modifying the environment variable called *clusterlog*. To view or modify the environment variable, right-click on **My Computer** and select **Properties**, then select the **Advanced** tab. Select the **Environment Variables** button to access the Environment Variables screen. Locate the clusterlog variable and change the value as you wish (see Figure 4-47).

By default, the cluster log will grow until it reaches 8 MB. Once that size is reached, it will begin to overwrite the file with new data. You can, however, modify the maximum size of the file by editing the registry. The following registry key holds that value:

```
HKEY_LOCAL_MACHINE\System\CurrentControlSet\ClusSvc\Parameters
```

The cluster log itself can be difficult to read, but does contain some valuable information. Look at Figure 4-48. You can see the date and time of each event, along with other useful information such as initialization, service domain account being used, name of the cluster being joined, and IP address

Figure 4-47
Modifying environment variables.

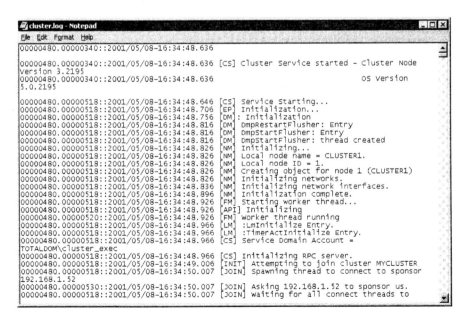

Figure 4-48
Examining the cluster log.

it is attempting to use for the virtual server. This is only a sample, but by reviewing the log file, you can trace every action of the cluster node from start-up to shutdown. This is helpful for troubleshooting failover problems.

4.8.4 Cluster.exe

The *cluster.exe* file is included within the *adminpak.msi* installation (the installation file used for loading administrator tools to Windows 2000 Professional workstations and servers). Cluster.exe is a command-line utility that allows you to perform cluster administration. Command-line utilities are helpful for creating batch files, managing applications through remote telnet sessions, and quickly obtaining information without the overhead of a GUI (graphic user interface).

The cluster command has various options and can be used to view configuration details, add groups and resources, or change existing settings. Although all of the commands are a child of the cluster command, the commands are broken into the following groups:

- Cluster
- Cluster Node
- Cluster Group
- Cluster Resource
- Cluster ResourceType
- Cluster Network

4.8.4.1 Cluster

The cluster command is used to view general information about the cluster. Using the cluster command, you can rename the cluster, query for the version of the cluster software, or view/change the quorum resource properties. The syntax for the command is as follows:

```
CLUSTER [Cluster Name] /option
```

The cluster name is optional if you are running the cluster.exe program on one of the cluster nodes, but is required if you are running the cluster.exe program from a remote workstation. Table 4-2 lists the available options.

Table 4-2   Cluster Command Options

Option	Description
/Rename: newclustername	Changes the network name assigned to the cluster
/Version	Displays the version number of the cluster software
/Quorum	Displays the current quorum configuration
/Quorum_resource: resourcename [/path: path] [/maxlogsize: size]	Changes the name, path, or maximum size of the log file for the quorum resource

4.8.4.2 Cluster Node

The cluster node command (see Table 4-3) is used to view or change information related to each individual cluster node. The node name is required for all options, with the exception of the /Status option. The syntax of the command is as follows:

```
CLUSTER [Cluster Name] NODE [Nodename] /option
```

Table 4-3   Cluster Node Command Options

Option	Description
/Status	Displays the status of all cluster nodes
/Pause	Pauses a single cluster node
/Resume	Resumes a node that has been paused
/Evict	Evicts a node from a cluster
/Properties	Views or changes the properties of a node

4.8.4.3 Cluster Group

The cluster group command is used to view or configure cluster groups. If your disk group contains spaces such as disk group 1, be sure to enclose the group name in quotes. The syntax of the command is as follows:

```
CLUSTER [Cluster Name] GROUP [Group Name] /option
```

Further Cluster Group command options can be viewed in Table 4-4.

Table 4-4   Cluster Group Command Options

Option	Description
/Status	Displays the status of a group
/Create	Creates a new group
/Delete	Deletes a group
/Moveto: *nodename*	Moves a group to another node
/Node: *nodename*	Displays all groups owned by a particular node
/Online: *nodename*	Brings a group online
/Offline: *nodename*	Takes a group offline
/Properties [propname = *newvalue*]	Views or changes the properties of a group
/Privproperties [propname = *newvalue*]	Views or changes the private properties of a group
/Listowners	Lists the preferred owners of a group
/Setowners : *node list*	Sets new preferred owner

4.8.4.4 Cluster Resource

The cluster resource command is used to view or change information related to individual cluster resources. The syntax of the command is as follows:

```
CLUSTER [Cluster Name] Resource [Resource Name] /option
```

Additional Cluster Resource command options can be viewed in Table 4-5.

4.8.4.5 Cluster ResourceType

The cluster resourcetype command is used to add or modify an existing cluster type. Don't confuse this command with the cluster resource command, which deals with specific created resources. The cluster resourcetype command is used to add new *types*, not new resources. For instance, if you have a

Table 4-5   Cluster Resource Command Options

Option	Description
/Status	Displays the status of the specified resource
/Create	Creates a new resource
/Group	Specifies which group should own the resource
/Type: *resource-type*	Specifies the type of resource to create (IP address, etc.)
[/Separate]	Specifies whether the resource should run in a separate resource monitor (optional)
/Delete	Deletes a specific resource
/Rename: *newresourcename*	Renames an existing resource
/Addowner: *node*	Adds a possible owner
/Removeowner: *node*	Removes a possible owner
/Listowners	Displays list of possible owners
/Moveto: *group*	Moves a resource to a different group
/Properties	Lists the properties of a resource
[Propname = *newvalue*]	Use propname = *newvalue* to change properties
/Privproperties	Lists the private properties of a resource
[Propname = *newvalue*]	Use propname = *newvalue* to change properties

generic application and you wish to add a new resource type so that the resource can be added to a group and configured, you would copy the .dll file to the appropriate location and then run the cluster resourcetype command to add the new resource. Once complete, you could run the cluster resource command to add the resource to the appropriate group.

You may also wish to alter the default settings for a particular resource type. Every resource that is created has default settings. Through the cluster resourcetype command, you can change the default values so that they will be assigned each time a resource is created.

The syntax for the command is as follows:

```
CLUSTER [Cluster Name] RESOURCETYPE [Resource Type Name] /option
```

Additional Cluster ResourceType command options can be viewed in Table 4-6.

Table 4-6   Cluster ResourceType Command Options

Option	Description
/List	Lists all resource types
/Create	Used to create a new resource type
/dllname: *filename*	Name of library
/Type: *typename*	Type of resource
/Isalive: *interval*	Default Isalive value
/Looksalive: *interval*	Default Looksalive value
/Delete	Deletes an existing resource type
/Properties [Propname = *newvalue*]	Views or changes properties for the resource type

4.8.4.6 Cluster Network

The cluster network command is used to view or modify the networks in use by the existing cluster nodes. As you may recall, the private and public adapters in each cluster node are connected to a network. Each of these networks has properties that can be viewed or modified through the cluster network command.

The syntax of the command is as follows:

```
CLUSTER [Cluster Name] NETWORK [Network Name] /option
```

Further Cluster Network command options can be viewed in Table 4-7.

Table 4-7   Cluster Network Command Options

Option	Description
/Status	Displays the status of the network(s)
/Rename: *newname*	Allows an administrator to change the name of a network
/Listinterfaces	Displays a list of cluster nodes for a given network and the status of each node
/Properties [Propname = *newvalue*]	Views or changes the properties of a network, such as address, addressmask, or description.

Chapter 5

BUILDING A LOAD-BALANCED CLUSTER

L oad balancing is the process of distributing multiple client requests across multiple nodes to minimize the possibility of overworking one particular machine. Within business environments, this has been called *server clustering, server farms,* or *Web farms.* Regardless of the name, the technology and the goal, are the same—to distribute the load of client requests across multiple nodes to prevent slow response times.

Windows 2000 Advanced Server and Windows 2000 Datacenter Server both include NLB. This service allows multiple machines to be configured as a cluster, or group of machines that respond to client requests as one virtual server. This prevents timeouts, increases the speed of the application, and adds a significant amount of fault tolerance to the application. Through this chapter you will learn the components that make load balancing work, the differences between a load-balanced cluster and a shared-disk cluster, as well as how to implement a load-balanced cluster within your own environment.

5.1 How Does It Work?

Enterprises worldwide have implemented load-balanced clusters to help serve customers and employees. Prior to recent efforts, load balancing was not available as a software component, but required expensive hardware to implement.

Although the hardware served its purpose, it lacked many features that integration with the operating system can provide. The Microsoft implementation of load balancing, NLB, offers the following benefits:

- Load balancing of client requests across multiple machines
- High availability and fault-tolerance
- Unlimited scalability
- Ability to perform maintenance without affecting service

The NLB service is really not a service at all, for it runs as a single driver called *wlbs.sys* that interfaces with the network driver. This driver (using a statistical mapping algorithm) allows the server to communicate with other hosts within the cluster, to determine cluster state/membership, and to select which packets to respond to and which packets to drop. The machine makes these decisions based upon rules that it has been given by an administrator.

Machines within an NLB cluster do not take direction from a single host, or "master" host, as do other software programs, but every machine within the cluster receives every request, and through the application of port rules, decides whether or not to respond. This is why (as you will see shortly) it is essential that all machines share the same rules.

Note

The term cluster *is used throughout this book loosely and can refer to a group of machines or a set of machines configured for a specific purpose. It is important that you do not confuse the use of the generic term* cluster *with the Microsoft Cluster Service, for it is much different than the Network Load Balancing service.*

Before we launch into a deployment of NLB, let's look at some of the components that make up the NLB operation and how they will affect your implementation. As you read, make note of how you wish to configure your own NLB cluster.

5.1.1 Cluster State

Much like the other clustering technologies available through Windows 2000 Advanced Server and Datacenter Server, the NLB hosts exchange messages, often called heartbeat messages, that determine cluster state. This allows each host to record which hosts are online and which hosts are offline. Once a node is determined to be offline, the cluster performs a process called *convergence*, where the server is removed from the cluster and the client load is distributed across the remaining machines. Once a server that is offline is brought back online, convergence takes place again, and the node is added to the cluster once again. The management of cluster state helps the cluster to determine which requests to respond to and which requests to ignore.

5.1.2 Port Rules

The TCP/IP specification dictates that applications that operate using the protocol must use a particular TCP port. A TCP port is a virtual "channel" within the protocol that allows for communication to take place separate from other operations within the protocol stack. Services like the World Wide Web and File Transfer Protocol operate on a particular port. When building an NLB cluster, you have the option to define port rules that will specify which network requests the servers respond to as a cluster. Remember, the cluster creates a "virtual" server that responds to client requests. You can allow the servers to respond to all client requests, regardless of port, or you can configure it to respond only to requests on a certain port. The choice is yours, for the software is very flexible. When making your choice, remember that the more ports that the cluster responds to means more overhead and wasted resources.

Using port rules, it is possible to configure a cluster server to respond to particular requests in three different ways. You can define a port or range of ports and specify that the particular node within the cluster

- load balance the requests among all nodes within the cluster,
- respond to all client requests unless a failure occurs,
- ignore all client requests on that port.

Within the first option, you can define what percentage of traffic you wish for each machine to handle. For instance, you may want to load balance a Web site across three different machines, but the first machine is much more powerful than the other two. In this situation, it would make sense to configure the first server to load balanced 60 percent of all traffic and configure the other two to each load balance 20 percent of all traffic. This allows the faster machine to handle more data, while the slower machines still help balance load for the application.

The second option allows you to configure a failover scenario. Similar to a failover cluster, a load-balanced cluster can be configured to fail over in the event of a failure. For example, if you have two servers that you wish to use for

171

an application, but the first server is a much more powerful server than the second, you can configure the first server to respond to all client requests and configure the second server to respond to client requests only if the first server is offline. This allows you to use older hardware within failover configurations, thus making a better use of your investment in hardware.

The third option allows you to configure the cluster to ignore traffic to a particular port or range of ports. This may be valuable if you receive undesirable traffic on a particular port and you do not want the traffic to use up vital resources. This configuration option will instruct the cluster to drop all packets destined for a particular port or range of ports.

5.1.3 Affinity

For each port rule setting that applies to multiple machines, you must define an affinity setting. The affinity setting defines the relationship between a client IP address and the cluster hosts. Affinity is used to manage state within a load-balanced cluster. Many applications manage session state as a client moves within the application. If you have used the Internet to navigate a dynamic Web site portal or to buy a book online, then you have experienced session state. Although you did not know it, the server was keeping track of your actions: the buttons you clicked and the information you entered. These bits of information are called session variables and are used in most Web sites today.

This presents a problem to the load-balanced cluster, for session variables are stored in server memory, a piece of storage that is not shared across several machines. Affinity is a way for the load-balanced cluster to deal with the session state issue. By understanding and correctly configuring affinity, you can correctly manage state across multiple machines. There are three possible affinity settings: none, single, and class C.

If your affinity setting is set to none, then all client requests will be distributed across the multiple nodes based upon your configuration settings with no regard to IP address. If you host an application or Web site on your load-balanced cluster that does not manage state, then this setting is the right choice for your environment. This setting allows the NLB cluster to operate more efficiently than any other setting, for it does not have to read host header information.

If your affinity setting is set to single, then all packets received by the cluster hosts will read the host header to determine the source IP address and maintain state for that client based upon further requests from that IP address. For example, if a client from 24.92.45.67 visits your Web site, which is utilizing affinity set to single, the server that first responds to the client will note the

IP address of the client and continue to respond to client requests for that session. Using this setting, the server maintains session state for the client associated with that IP address. This is typically the best setting for intranet applications, where the IP address of a client does not change dynamically. It is not necessarily well suited for Internet applications, for there are many network firewalls that change the client IP address during a session.

The class C affinity setting performs the same function as the single affinity setting, but does so for IP addresses within a class C subnet. Using the previous example, if a client connected to the cluster with IP address 24.92.45.67, and then connected again during the same session from IP address 24.92.45.4, both sessions would be handled by the same server and session state would be maintained. So, rather than the server responding to hosts with the identical IP address consistently, the server will respond to hosts that have an IP address anywhere within the same class C subnet.

Note

A class C subnet is defined as a segment of addresses that share a 24-bit network address. This allows for 254 different addresses to exist within a class C subnet. A network address of 24.92.45.54 is a part of the 24.92.45.0 network. Hosts within that network would include any host between 24.92.45.1 and 24.92.45.254.

5.2 Preplanning

Prior to setting up your load-balanced cluster, there are several planning tasks that you should complete. A good plan will ensure that your cluster is implemented with the minimal amount of difficulty.

5.2.1 Network Drawings

In Chapter 3, "Clustering Design Issues," you may have put together a network drawing that reflects the design of your network. If you completed this network design document, retrieve it and keep it handy, for you will need it in later steps. If you did not create your network design document, go ahead and document the number of servers you wish to cluster, the IP address of each node, as well as the cluster server IP address. If you are building your server in conjunction with a component load-balanced cluster or a failover cluster, be sure to document their placement, IP addressing, and other vital information.

5.2.2 TCP/IP Settings

Before you configure network load balancing, you should have your network adapters configured correctly. For optimal performance, you should have two network adapters present in each cluster server. These two adapters, operating on separate subnets, will allow the cluster nodes to communicate cluster state, port rules, and affinity settings to other nodes within the cluster without affecting the client-to-cluster traffic. The network load-balanced cluster can operate with single adapter systems, but it is not recommended due to the performance hit that the system will take.

To prepare for the network load-balance configuration, once you have installed the operating system, you will assign an IP address to the first network adapter on the first node. This adapter should be connected to the subnet that is Internet-enabled and has access to name services such as DNS and WINS. Then you will assign an address within the same subnet address to the first network adapter in each machine that will be a part of the cluster. In our example, we used 192.168.1.50 for the firstserver, 192.168.1.51 for the second server, and so on.

Once you have assigned IP addresses to each machine, you will assign addresses within a different subnet to the secondary adapter in each machine and connect all of those adapters to a hub or switch that is different from the other adapters. This should be a private network consisting of only the secondary cluster adapters. In our example, we used 10.1.1.1 for the first server, 10.1.1.2 for the secondserver, and so on.

Keep in mind the following network load-balancing limitations:

- NLB will not work in a Token-Ring network.
- TCP/IP should be the only protocol bound to the adapters utilized for the NLB service.
- NLB will not function properly on a layer 3 network switch. Use a shared hub or layer 2 switch instead.
- All network cards used must be PCI–based.

Once you have all of the adapters configured, you should open a command prompt and make sure that you can ping each machine on the network. This will confirm connectivity between the hosts and prevent problems that may arise during the configuration of the NLB service.

Note

The NLB service does not correctly operate with all network switches. Layer 3 switches will not work at all because of the way the NLB service assigns virtual IP addresses to cluster nodes. Layer 2 switches will work because by default the source MAC address is masked for load-balanced nodes in Unicast mode. However, layer 2 switches will cause a switch flood during every transmission because the switch cannot associate the virtual MAC address with any particular port. Due to these interoperability problems, it is a better idea to plug all public network adapters from the cluster nodes into a shared hub, and then uplink that hub to a layer 2 switch.

5.2.3 DNS Settings

If you plan to use DNS to direct your clients to the clustered server solution, then you will need to make sure you enter the appropriate DNS entry into the DNS server and assign it to the cluster IP address. If you are building multiple clusters to produce a round-robin cluster (as discussed in Chapter 3), you will need to make sure that round-robin DNS is enabled on the DNS server and that there are multiple entries for the same host in the DNS zone. Whatever hostname you use to direct clients to your cluster server, make sure you note it, for you will need it later in the configuration of your network load-balanced cluster.

5.2.4 Domain Authentication

The NLB service is a domain-independent service, meaning you do not need domain authentication to run the service. The servers that you use for network load-balancing hosts can be domain controllers, member servers, or workgroup servers. There is no part of the NLB service that requires domain authentication. However; if you have a Web site, FTP site, or VPN solution that you are trying to load balance, then you may need domain authentication. If you do need domain authentication and the servers you are using are a part of the domain, make sure that there is a domain controller available at all times on the same network segment as the load-balanced cluster. If there isn't one available, or it's on a different network segment, you may find that your services fail to start or function properly.

5.2.5 Planning for Heavy Loads

When you are building a network load-balanced cluster, it is typically because you want to provide fault tolerance or performance to an application or service. In some situations, you may find that clustering multiple machines together is not enough processing power to handle the load. Consider Microsoft's Web site or Symantec's Web site. Companies that have such large market share receive millions of hits per hour on their Web sites. To handle this type of load, you need to scale your cluster for increased performance and fault tolerance.

The NLB service supports a total of 32 nodes within the same cluster. This is typically sufficient for most implementations, but what if your load exceeds the 32 machine mark, or the local network traffic generated by the 10 nodes or 20 nodes is too great to achieve optimal performance? The answer employs the use of an older technology known as round-robin DNS. Round Robin DNS is an optional setting on a DNS server that allows a DNS server to direct clients to different IP addresses associated with the same DNS name entry. For instance, you may have two Web servers, and you would like the entry for *www.mydomain.com* forwarded to both servers equally to manually balance the load between the servers. To do this, a DNS administrator would enable round-robin DNS on that server and create two records for *www.mydomain.com,* one pointing to one server while one points to another.

Using round-robin within a clustered environment can be beneficial and extend the scalability and performance of an existing cluster solution. In this scenario, you would create two separate cluster servers in two separate locations. Each cluster would be assigned an IP address, which would then be added to the DNS server and assigned to two identical records. This allows the load to be balanced at the DNS server, for it directs clients to each cluster equally. Once the request reaches the cluster server solution, it will be load-balanced again across multiple servers.

Warning

Although round-robin DNS is a good way to extend the scalability and performance of a cluster, it does have a downside. The DNS server has no way of knowing which IP addresses are online and which IP addresses are not. Incoming client requests will be sent to "dead" IP addresses, so it is essential that if you use round-robin DNS, you ensure that the clusters will not go offline, or your clients will not reach the application.

5.3 Operating System Install

The NLB service is included with the Windows 2000 Advanced Server and Windows 2000 Datacenter Server operating systems. The system requirements are consistent with the Microsoft hardware compatibility list (HCL) located at *www.microsoft.com/hcl*. Keep in mind that even though you may be load balancing the same application across multiple machines, you will still need to purchase a license for Microsoft Advanced Server or Microsoft Datacenter Server for each node within your cluster. Also, if you plan to run third-party software on your cluster, be sure to check with third-party software vendors for their cluster licensing requirements; they're all a bit different.

There are not any special requirements for the operating system install, but if you choose to use any components that are not installed by default, you may want to make sure they are selected during the installation.

Note

It is possible to run Microsoft's NLB on Windows 2000 Server, but you will need to purchase Application Center 2000, a software tool developed by Microsoft for deploying and managing cluster nodes. Application Center 2000 is discussed in detail in Chapter 6, "Microsoft Application Center."

5.4 Configuring NLB

The first step to configuring NLB is to enable the driver. Right-click on **My Network Places** and click the **Properties** button. Right-click the network connection that represents your public network adapter, then click Properties. In the local area connection properties, you should see an option that says Network Load Balancing that is not checked (see Figure 5-1). If you do not see this option, then you are not running Windows 2000 Advanced Server or Datacenter Server.

Check the box next to the **Network Load Balancing** option, select it so that it is highlighted, and then click the **Properties** button.

The properties of the NLB configuration reveals three tabs: Cluster Parameters, Host Parameters, and Port Rules (see Figure 5-2). Make sure that the **Cluster Parameters** tab is selected.

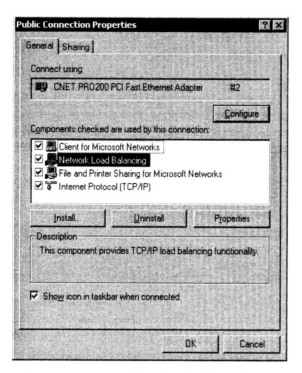

Figure 5-1
Enabling Network Load
Balancing.

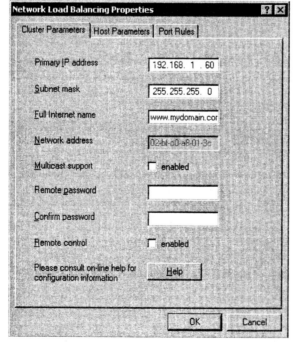

Figure 5-2
Configuring cluster parameters.

The first address is the Primary IP address, and this is where you configure the IP address that will be assigned to the cluster. The subnet should be consistent with the subnet of the adapter address. The Full Internet name option allows you to type in the fully qualified DNS host name for the cluster. If you are using your cluster to host a Web site or some other application, type the name you are using within DNS.

Selecting the Multicast support option specifies whether the server will use a multicast MAC address for the cluster. If this option is selected, the server will convert the existing MAC address into a multicast address. Keep in mind that some routers do not associate multicast MAC addresses to Unicast IP addresses correctly and will need a static ARP entry to enable connectivity. NLB does not support the use of cluster nodes in different modes. All nodes must be in either Unicast or multicast mode.

The Remote password and Confirm password options allow you to specify a required password for remote administration of the cluster configuration. If a password is entered, administrators using the WLBS.EXE utility remotely to manage the cluster server will be required to use the /PASSW option.

The Remote control option allows you to turn on the remote control features of the cluster. If this is enabled, users running Windows 2000 on remote machines can use the WLBS.EXE utility to view and modify configuration settings. This option is disabled by default. It is recommended that if you choose to enable the remote control option, you also assign a remote control password to limit access.

Note

If you wish to remotely manage the cluster servers using the WLBS.EXE utility through an Internet firewall, be sure you open the cluster control ports for UDP. The ports are 1717 and 2504. If you have an open connection to the cluster and wish to add additional security, make sure you filter those ports from outside access.

Next, click the **Host Parameters** tab. These settings are unique to the local machine and do not need to be replicated on other hosts (see Figure 5-3). The priority ID is a unique host ID that allows all machines within a cluster to differentiate themselves from each other. This ID setting must be different for each machine. Cluster nodes that start and that have conflicting host IDs will be prevented from joining the cluster until the error is resolved. This setting also dictates which host within the cluster handles the default network traffic for the cluster. Typically, port rules will determine which hosts respond to which requests, but there are times when the cluster receives traffic that is not

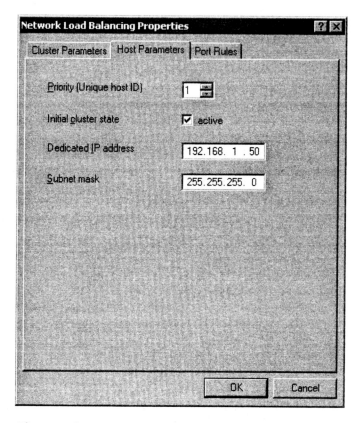

Figure 5-3
Configuring host parameters.

defined by a port rule. In this case, the cluster node that is online with the highest priority (lowest number) will respond to the traffic.

The initial cluster state is an option that allows you to configure NLB without actually enabling it. If you choose to configure the service, but you do not wish for it to participate in the cluster yet, clear the **Initial Cluster State** checkbox.

The dedicated IP address is the IP address of the cluster server itself; not the cluster IP address that all hosts will share, but the IP address of the actual node that is being configured. Type in the necessary information, including the IP address and the subnet, and then click the **Port Rules** tab.

The Port Rules tab allows you to configure how cluster traffic is processed (see Figure 5-4). The default setting allows all traffic on all ports to be equally balanced among all servers. This may fit your need, but it is recommended

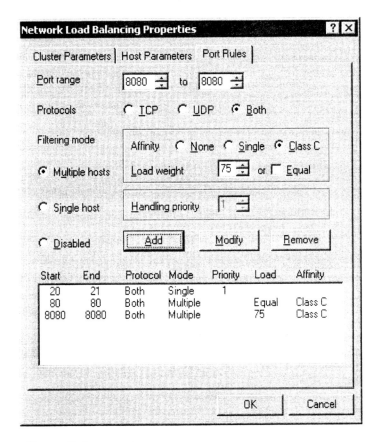

Figure 5-4
Configuring port rules.

that you change this setting so that the cluster server does not respond to all ports, creating unneeded network traffic. To remove the setting, select it and then click **Remove**.

Configure each port rule as you wish, and click **Add** to add each rule to the list. Port rules must be the same on all nodes. The port range specifies which ports that rule will apply to. To select a single port, make the first and second port addresses the same (i.e., 80-80). The protocols section allows you to determine which protocol you would like to load balance. The filtering mode can be Multiple, Single, or Disabled. Multiple is for port rules that load-balance traffic across multiple machines. The Single option is for failover scenarios where you wish one machine to respond to requests all of the time, passing ownership of the application to another host only due to a failure.

Once you have finished configuring all of the port rules, click **OK** to continue. Then select the **Internet Protocol (TCP/IP)** option and select **Properties**.

Within the TCP/IP settings dialogue, select the **Advanced** button. This reveals the **Advanced TCP/IP Settings** dialogue (see Figure 5-5). Click **Add** and type in the IP address of the cluster, then hit **OK**. This will bind the cluster IP address to the network adapter. Click **OK** twice to save the setting.

Once you have completed the configuration, repeat the process on all nodes within the cluster. Then return to node 1 and open a command prompt window. Using the cluster configuration utility, type the following command:

```
WLBS QUERY
```

This will display the cluster state. You should see the host IDs of all the cluster nodes you have created in the list of hosts that are part of the cluster (see Figure 5-6). If you do not see a particular host, open the event viewer on any node within the cluster and probe the Application log for details regarding the failure.

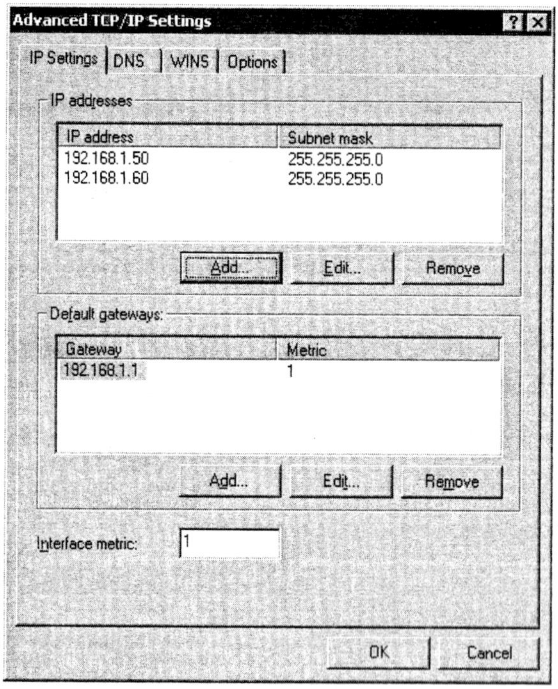

Figure 5-5
Adding the cluster IP address.

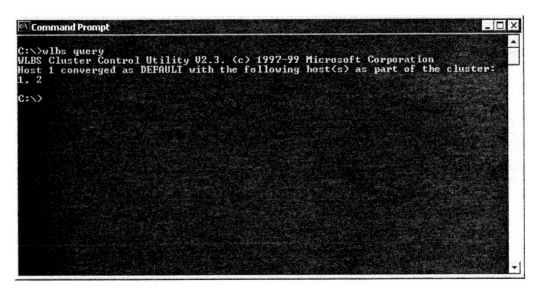

Figure 5-6
Verifying cluster memberships.

The most common problem is a port rule conflict. If you check the event viewer and find error messages related to inconsistent port rules (see Figure 5-7), then you have port rules within the different nodes that are not consistent. To troubleshoot the problem, disable the network load balancing on all machines within the cluster that are experiencing failures and attempt to correct the problem by configuring them one by one. As you bring one online, resolve the issues it may have to ensure it comes online, then work on the next one.

As for the NLB configuration, you are done! Traffic will be load-balanced based upon the rules you set up in the NLB configuration. There are, however, a few things that the cluster software does not do that you will have to tend to. The software does not automatically configure any applications you wish to load balance, so if you are running an application on all nodes, it is your responsibility to install and identically configure all nodes the same way. The software also will not synchronize data, so if you have changing data that you need to synchronize between hosts, that burden is on you.

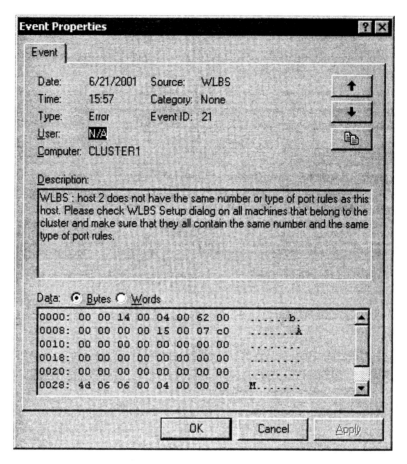

Figure 5-7
Cluster error.

5.5 Configuring Internet Information Server

You can run any application you choose to run on a network load-balanced cluster, mainly because the data is not shared and therefore does not require that you build your application to be cluster-aware. However, there are drawbacks to that. Because the data is not shared, you must ensure that the data between the different servers is consistent. Dynamic applications and applications that store data in a database are not ideal programs to run on a load-balanced cluster and would probably be a better fit for a failover cluster. More commonly, administrators will use the NLB service to cluster services such as FTP, WWW, and SMTP—services that have static content or configurations. Fortunately, these services are all found within Microsoft's Internet Information Server (ISS). Although you are not required to use IIS for these services, it is an ideal application for this environment. In this section we will discuss some issues that you may encounter clustering IIS and its services on a Network Load-balanced Server.

The first step is to ensure that IIS is installed. Click **Start**, **Settings**, **Control Panel**, and then **Add/Remove Programs**. Then click the

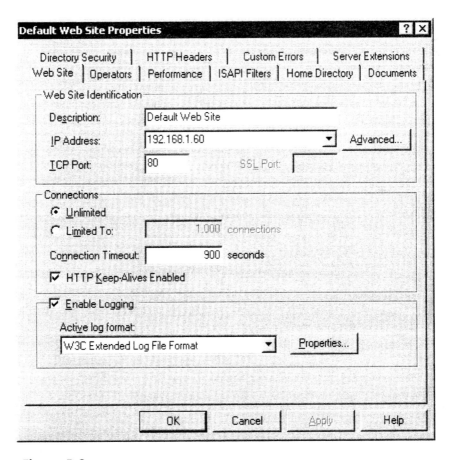

Figure 5-8
Configuring the WWW service.

Add/Remove Windows Components button. Make sure that the option that says **Internet Information Server** is selected. If it is, hit **Cancel** to exit the install. If it is not installed yet, continue with the installation.

Once the application is installed, click **Start**, **Programs**, **Administrative Tools**, and then **Internet Services Manager**. Right-click on the **Default Web Site** and click the **Properties** option from the menu (see Figure 5-8).

In the **IP address** field, pull down the list and select the IP address you are using for the cluster. This assigns the Web site to the cluster address so that users cannot access the Web site by typing the IP address or name of a single host within the cluster. Once you have completed this step, select **OK**. You will need to repeat this step for any FTP or SMTP services hosts on this server. Once you have completed the configuration, repeat the process on all other nodes within the cluster.

The hardware part of running a World Wide Web server on a load-balanced cluster is the synchronization of data. If your Web site is static and the pages never change, then you can copy the data to the root directory of the Web site and you are done with it. Unfortunately, most sites are not this simple. You may not have complex databases to load balance (because that should be on a failover cluster), but you may have programmers that need to update the Web site. In many organizations, the Web developers and systems administrators are in different departments, and teaching the Web developers to upload their data to several machines can be a management nightmare. So what is the solution? There are several available.

- Through the use of cluster tools such as Application Center 2000, you can distribute applications to each machine in packages and keep them synchronized.
- Through the use of batch scripts, you can have developers upload all data to one machine, and schedule a batch file to execute a file copy to all other machines.
- Configure all Web servers to use a shared directory on a backend server for the Web root.

Although all of these solutions will work, they have their pros and cons. The use of third-party tools such as Application Center 2000 can be expensive to implement. Batch files work well, but must be monitored to ensure proper synchronization, and batch files that execute too frequently can cause unneeded overhead for the cluster system. Locating the data files on a backup server works as well, but in many ways defeats the purpose of a load-balanced server, for it places all critical data on one machine.

5.6 Testing the Installation

To test your installation, there are several steps you can take. The first is a simple PING command. If you can ping the IP address of your cluster from a remote network, then you have successfully configured the load-balancing properties.

Another option is to place in the root of each Web server an HTML page that looks something like this:

```
<html>
<head>
<title>Test Page</title>
</head>
<body>
Cluster Server Node 1
</body>
</html>
```

Save the page into the Web root of each Web server as *default.htm,* and in each Web server, modify the page to reflect the number of host IDs for each server. From a client, open a Web browser and type the IP address of the cluster server, followed by the */default.htm* filename. Continually hit refresh to see which host responds. Most likely, the same server will continue to respond because the traffic is so low, but have someone pull out the network cable attached to each cluster node one at a time and you will see the page change from one node to another.

5.7 Managing a Network Load-Balanced Cluster

Unlike the other clustering services provided through the Windows 2000 Advanced Server and Datacenter Server operating systems, the NLB service does not include a GUI. The only means of managing the NLB cluster is through a command prompt utility called *WLBS.EXE.*

Note

It is called the WLBS *because Windows NT 4.0's implementation of load balancing was called Windows Load-Balancing Service.*

The syntax for WLBS.EXE is as follows:

```
WLBS command [Cluster:[host] [remote options]]
```

Table 5-1 lists the available commands that can be used with the WLBS program.

Table 5-1   WLBS Commands

Help	Displays the NLB online help for WLBS.
Suspend	This command ceases all functions within an NLB cluster and pauses operations until a resume command is issued.
Resume	This command enables a cluster server to receive commands after a suspend command has been issued. It does not start the cluster services.
Start	Starts the cluster server operations.
Stop	Stops the cluster server operations.
Drainstop	This command issues a stop command to the cluster server but will only execute after all client connections have completed.
Enable *port* [all]	This command enables the handling of all traffic for a specific port rule. If the All option is used, all port rules containing the specified port are enabled to receive traffic.
Disable *port* [all]	This command disables the handling of all traffic for a specific port rule. If the All option is used, all port rules containing the specified port are prevented from receiving traffic.
Drain *port* [all]	This command stops all new incoming connections for a specific port. If the All option is used, all port rules covered by the specified port stop new incoming connections.
Query	Displays the current cluster state along with node priorities and host IDs.
Reload	This command reloads the NLB service, using the existing configuration from the registry. This command cannot be executed remotely.
Display	This command displays extensive information about the cluster state and previous event logs, including binary data, along with node priorities and host IDs. This command cannot be executed remotely.
Ip2mac	Displays the current (cluster) MAC address. This command is helpful for configuring static ARP entries.

5.8 Summary

The Windows 2000 NLB service is a powerful, robust, flexible platform for deploying load-balanced applications. In the past, hardware load-balancing solutions were the only option for administrators who wanted to load balance applications and services, but with the advent of Windows 2000 and the NLB components, administrators can easily and inexpensively deploy load-balanced applications.

Chapter 6

MICROSOFT APPLICATION
CENTER 2000

T he development world has gone through many changes in the last few
   years. The legacy mainframe system has been replaced with the
client/server model, and the traditional client/server application development
is slowly being replaced with Web-based applications. Although limited in its
original implementation, Web-based applications have advanced to the point
where they are comparable to the client/server systems in use today. With the
advent of application platforms such as Macromedia Flash and assorted
streaming media solutions, Web application programming has become a standard within the industry that may shortly replace the client/server systems
widely in use.

In Chapter 5, "Building a Load-Balanced Cluster," you learned about the
Microsoft NLB service and how that service can be used to deploy a fault-
tolerant, load-balanced infrastructure for today's advanced applications. The
product itself is flexible, but the tasks that are necessary to deploy and manage
an application through the NLB service are tedious and lack the automation
necessary to handle a Web application implementation of any size. Microsoft
realized these issues early on and began developing a product that is now
called Application Center 2000 (AC 2000).

AC 2000 is a suite of tools designed to help you build, deploy, and manage
Web-based applications and services. Although one chapter is not sufficient to

cover the vast array of tools and solutions available through AC 2000, a cursory look at the application is necessary to appreciate the usability and functionality.

6.1 Product Overview

Microsoft's AC 2000 is a management tool, a product that allows cluster administrators to manage large cluster implementations from a central console. Through the use of AC 2000, cluster servers can be added to or removed from the cluster at will, the health of the cluster can be monitored, and the deployment of applications can be done easily. Although AC 2000 has many features, which will be discussed in a moment, its power is in

- The ability to easily deploy load-balanced servers within a cluster.
- The ability to monitor the health of a load-balanced cluster from a central console.
- The ability to load balance COM+ components for applications.
- The ability to synchronize content and publish applications across the load-balanced cluster.

AC 2000 works within Microsoft NLB as well as third-party load-balancing solutions to allow administrators to manage the cluster as a single entity. Synchronization becomes a much easier task because the configuration of the Web server and the data are synchronized between the cluster controller and all of the machines in the cluster. There is a downside to this, however, if you consider it a downside. AC 2000 makes the first machine in a cluster the *cluster controller*. This machine becomes the staging server for all changes within the cluster. If you make changes to other machines within the cluster, the changes will be overwritten by the next synchronization. So all changes must take place on the cluster controller.

AC 2000 also provides the ability to load balance COM+ components within their own cluster, taking application deployment to the third tier. COM+ components are typically used to apply business rules or logic to an application, processing information from a Web site and returning the result set to the application. By load balancing the COM+ components, processing of application rules is offloaded, providing faster response time on the front end of the application. Used in conjunction with a database back end, applications can be deployed in three tiers, with the front end serving the Web site, the middle component serving the COM+ processing, and the back end being used for data storage through *RDMS* (Relational Database Management Systems).

6.2 Product Features

AC 2000 provides many features that have not been available before. The following is not a comprehensive list, but a survey of the more popular features.

- Simplified cluster creation
- Data and configuration synchronization
- Local or Web-based administrative tools
- Centralized management of cluster nodes
- Request forwarding (affinity)
- Application deployment
- Performance/health monitoring and notification
- Microsoft FrontPage integration
- Component load balancing

AC 2000 simplifies cluster creation through the New Cluster wizard, an application within the administrative console that allows you to create clusters through a point-and-click interface. AC 2000 creates and maintains information related to the cluster and then designates a cluster controller—a server that will serve as the primary server within the cluster. This cluster controller acts as a central point of contact for all other nodes within the cluster. Once the cluster is in place, you can use AC 2000 to add members to the cluster through the Add Cluster Member wizard. Minimal configuration is necessary to bring multiple machines online.

AC 2000 makes use of a cluster controller to deploy application changes to all nodes within the cluster. The first node that is added to a cluster becomes the cluster controller by default, but this setting can be changed by promoting any node within the cluster to this position. The cluster controller is responsible for synchronizing all data and configuration information with other hosts within the cluster.

For your convenience, AC 2000 includes both a local administrative tool and a Web-based administrative tool. Using either tool, you can monitor all nodes within your cluster, view error logs, inspect performance issues, and reconfigure load-balancing percentages.

Prior to AC 2000, the only administrative console for managing a network load-balanced cluster was a command line through the WLBS.EXE program. AC 2000 greatly enhances the ability to manage and configure clusters through the AC 2000 administrative console, which is installed as a Microsoft

Management Console (MMC) snap-in. Now, through the AC 2000 console, you can view cluster status and events; monitor applications, server health, and synchronization; and perform functions such as adding members to a cluster, creating new clusters, and configuring COM+ application deployments.

Affinity is the ability to manage client state across multiple machines within a cluster. The NLB service deals with affinity by providing the service of client requests based upon IP address (i.e., a server that responds to a particular IP address will continue to respond to the same IP address for the duration of the session). AC 2000 expands this functionality through the addition of request forwarding. Request forwarding manages client state through the use of *cookies*. The initial server that responds to a client request is written to a small file on the client's machine, and for the duration of the session, the same server will continue to respond to requests.

Application deployment is a feature that allows a cluster controller to publish configuration and data to servers within the cluster. Unlike synchronization, which takes place automatically, application deployment allows administrators to deploy NT file system (NTFS) file and directory permissions, COM+ applications, and Internet Server Application Programming Interface (ISAPI) filters to Web sites within the cluster. Using the Application Deployment wizard, you can easily and reliably deploy applications to all nodes within a cluster. Because many services need to be restarted after configuration changes related to COM+ components and ISAPI filters, the Application Deployment wizard can be configured to perform rolling upgrades, where each machine is configured and restarted consecutively.

AC 2000, through the same administrative console, allows administrators to view real-time performance data as well as the applications deployed on all machines within the cluster. Through its integration with the performance monitor, you can view statistics on all nodes within the cluster, and set monitors to alert you to specific threshold violations. Through the alerting options, you can be notified of errors and anomalies through various channels. AC 2000 monitors not only server performance, but the actual services hosted on your cluster as well as the server event log for errors and warning messages.

In addition to the robust server support for COM+ applications and ISAPI filters, the server also includes tight integration with Microsoft FrontPage and Web DAV (distributed authoring and version) publishing. Publication of FrontPage data to a cluster controller will initiate synchronization between the cluster controller and all cluster nodes where FrontPage configuration data will be distributed.

Component load balancing was originally released within the beta version of Windows 2000 Server. Due to the response from beta testers who requested more features and greater control, Microsoft decided to release the final version within the AC 2000 product. Component load balancing is used for creating COM+ application clusters. These clusters host COM+ objects that are load balanced for maximum performance, reliability, and fault tolerance. Using this platform, systems administrators can deploy three-tiered applications that scale to meet demand and outperform previous infrastructures.

The feature set of AC 2000 is comprehensive and includes all the necessary tools for deploying, managing, and scaling Web-based enterprise applications. The next section presents the installation process for AC 2000. Although the vast array of features and administrative tools included with AC 2000 is far beyond the scope of this book, the next section will teach you the basic installation process and how servers are used within the cluster for synchronization, administration, and integration with the AC 2000 suite of tools.

6.3 Installing AC 2000

AC 2000 must be installed on any machine that will participate in an AC 2000 cluster. To install it, you must be running Windows 2000 Advanced Server or Windows 2000 Datacenter Server. You can run an AC 2000 cluster on Windows 2000 Server, even though the NLB components are not installed on the Windows 2000 Server, for AC 2000 will install them as needed during the setup process.

Each server that you install AC 2000 on has three installation options. You can install the server only, the client only, or the server and the client. The server component allows a server to be managed as a cluster node, while the client portion installs the AC 2000 MMC snap-in for the management of clusters throughout your organization.

Prior to installing AC 2000 on your servers, make sure that you are running the latest service pack. AC 2000 is not compatible with Windows 2000 running a service pack prior to Service Pack 2. The following list presents a guideline for your installation:

- Install necessary service packs on all machines that will be used as cluster nodes.
- Configure the network properties of the first node.
- Install AC 2000 (server and client) on the first node.
- Using the first node, create a new cluster and add the node to the cluster.
- Configure the network properties of the remaining nodes.

- Install AC 2000 on all remaining nodes (server and client).
- From the first node, add each server as a member of the cluster to complete the configuration.

The decision to install server and client on each node is yours. If you don't believe you will need to manage the cluster from each server, just install the server portion. If you install only the server portion on all the servers, be sure to install the client portion on a workstation or server outside the cluster in case the first node with the management snap-in becomes unavailable.

Installing the service pack on the servers is something you should already know how to do, so this will be assumed. Always remember, you can obtain service packs and other product updates from *http://windowsupdate.microsoft.com*.

After you have installed the necessary service packs on each machine, you will need to configure the network properties of your first server to prepare it for the AC 2000 installation. You should have two network adapters within each node you plan to use; AC 2000 will not install if two adapters are not present. The first adapter should be connected to the public network and will be used for client connectivity. The second adapter should be connected to a private network and will be used for cluster management traffic only.

Right-click on the **My Network Places** icon and select **Properties**. Right-click on the adapter that will be your public network adapter, and then select **Properties**. Select the **Internet Protocol (TCP/IP)** option and press the **Properties** button. This will reveal the TCP/IP properties for this network interface. Select the **Use the following IP address:** option and type in the IP address you wish to use (see Figure 6-1). This IP address should be unique to each machine (you will assign the cluster IP address in a moment). Also enter the subnet mask address and the gateway address for your network.

It is important that you use a dynamic DNS server for the DNS server listing. The cluster nodes rely upon name resolution to communicate with each other, so they all must have the same primary DNS address listing. Enter the address of your DNS server, and then click the **Advanced** button.

In the advanced section (see Figure 6-2), under IP addresses, select the add button and type in the IP address that you wish to use for the cluster. This will be the cluster virtual address that is shared by all other nodes in the cluster. Once you have typed an address and a mask, click **OK** to add it to the list. The address you use for the cluster must be within the same subnet as the interface address you assigned in the previous section. Click **OK** once you are finished. Click **OK** twice to return to the network places window.

Right-click on the interface you will be using for the private interface. Select the IP address and press the **Properties** button. In the **TCP/IP Properties** dialogue, make sure that both **Obtain an IP address automatically** and

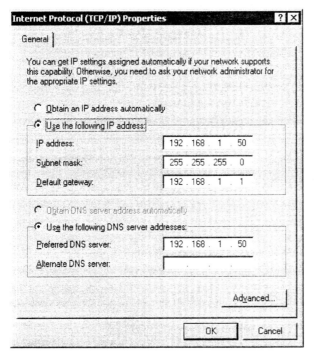

Figure 6-1
Configuring network adapters.

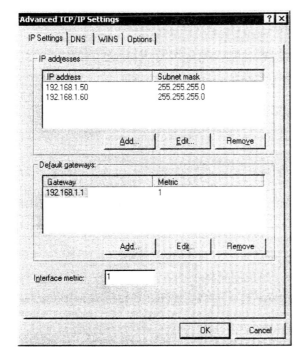

Figure 6-2
Advanced TCP/IP settings.

Obtain DNS Server address automatically are selected. This sets the interface to Dynamic Host Configuration Protocol (DHCP). Obviously, there will not be a DHCP server on the private network. This option allows the system itself to assign a private 169.254.x.x address to the interface. All nodes within the cluster will be configured in this way. Once you have verified the setting, click **OK** twice to exit **Network Properties,** and then close the **My Network Places** window.

Insert the AC 2000 CD-ROM into the drive. The autorun feature should show you the installation menu (see Figure 6-3), but if it does not, you can run the *autorun.hta* file from the CD-ROM to open the menu. This menu allows you to view the release notes and the help files. Select the **Install Microsoft Application Center 2000** option to begin the installation.

The next screen reminds you that Windows 2000 requires Service Pack 1 and additional fixes for proper operation (see Figure 6-4). All of the necessary fixes are included with Service Pack 2. If you have installed Service Pack 2 or higher prior to this point, select **Install Microsoft Application Center 2000** to continue. If you have not installed Service Pack 2 or greater by this point, exit setup and install it, then return to this point to install AC 2000.

The Application Center 2000 Setup wizard will start if you have properly installed all of the necessary service packs and hot fixes (see Figure 6-5). Click **Next** to continue.

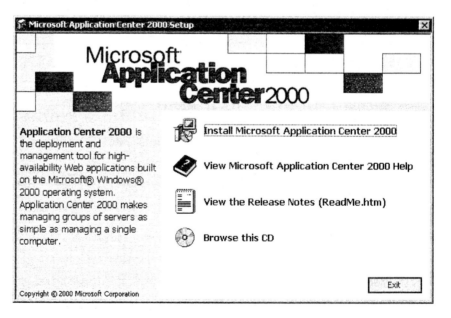

Figure 6-3
AC 2000 menu.

Figure 6-4
AC 2000 setup options.

Figure 6-5
AC 2000 installation wizard.

The next screen displays the license agreement (see Figure 6-6). Please read the license agreement completely, then click the **I accept the terms in the license agreement** option and select the **Next** button to continue. The AC 2000 licensing requires that you purchase a license for each processor that is used. This means that if you are running a network load-balanced cluster of three machines, and each machine has four processors, then you will need to purchase 12 licenses to comply with the licensing model.

The next screen requests user information (see Figure 6-7). Enter the username and organization name as you wish. These are for description and licensing information only and will not affect the configuration. Click **Next** to continue.

The next screen asks which type of installation you would like to perform (see Figure 6-8). If you select Typical, the wizard will install the server component, the client component, and the sample monitors. It is recommended that you always select the Custom option so that you can tailor the installation to your needs. Click the **Custom** option and select **Next** to continue.

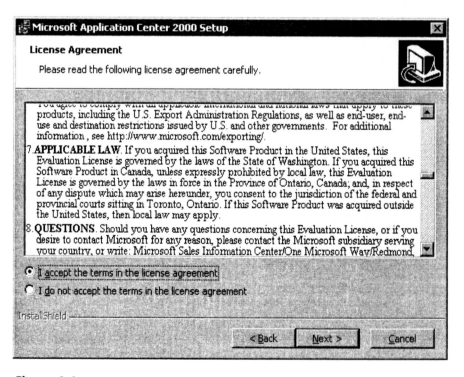

Figure 6-6
License agreement.

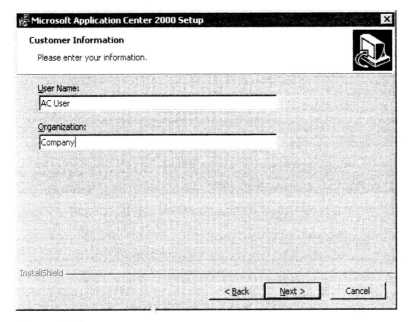

Figure 6-7
Entering user information.

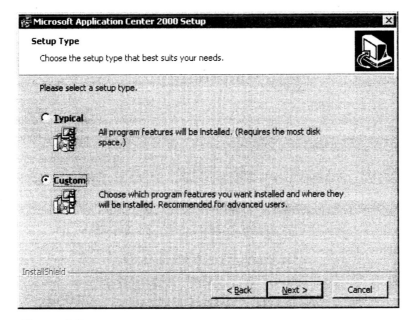

Figure 6-8
Selecting setup type.

201

If you selected the **Custom** setup option, then the next screen allows you to customize the features that will be installed (see Figure 6-9). If this is the first server within your cluster, you will need to select **Server** and **Client**. Under **Server**, you can select the monitor samples, if you wish. You can also select **Change** to alter the installation path of the application, but this is not recommended. If you do change the path, make sure to change the path of every installation across all nodes within the cluster.

The wizard will inform you that installation is about to begin (see Figure 6-10). Select the **Next** button to begin copying files.

Once the wizard has copied all of the necessary files, you will see the **Completing the Microsoft Application Center 2000 Setup wizard** screen (see Figure 6-11). Select **Finish** to complete the installation. Keep in mind that this installation only allows you to run the administrative console and to add this machine to a cluster (or create a new one); it has not configured this server for load balancing through this installation.

Once the software is installed, click **Start**, **Programs**, **Administrative Tools**, then **Application Center 2000** to open the administrative console. Right-click on **Application Center** and select **Connect**. The **Connect to**

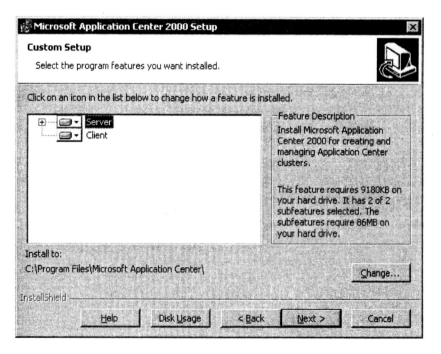

Figure 6-9
Selecting setup options.

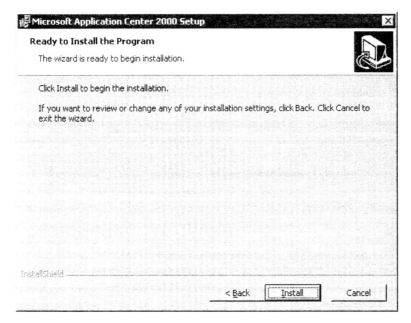

Figure 6-10
Beginning installation.

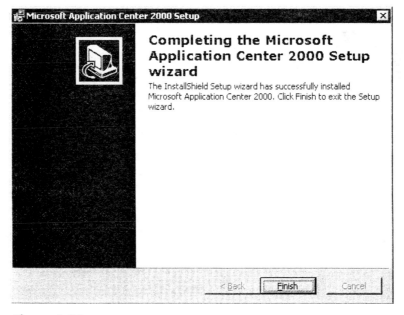

Figure 6-11
Completing the installation wizard.

Server dialogue is displayed (see Figure 6-12). The dialogue gives you the option of connecting to a specific server or a cluster of servers. There is no value in connecting to a specific server unless you are performing a quick operation or troubleshooting an error only on that machine. Click the **Manage cluster for the specified server** option to connect to a cluster. The wizard will connect to the specified server and see that there is no cluster configured, and will return an option to create a new cluster. The **Connect as** option is for managing a cluster from a machine that is not a node within the cluster. To connect to a cluster using a specific local account or domain account, click the **Connect as** check box and fill in the necessary credentials. This will not be necessary if you are building a cluster on the local machine. Click **OK** to continue.

Once the wizard sees that there is no cluster present on the server it is connecting to, it will give you the option of joining an existing cluster or creating a new cluster. Click the **Create a new cluster** option (see Figure 6-13), and then click **OK** to continue. This will create a new cluster and add the local machine as the first node within the cluster, thus making it the AC 2000 cluster controller.

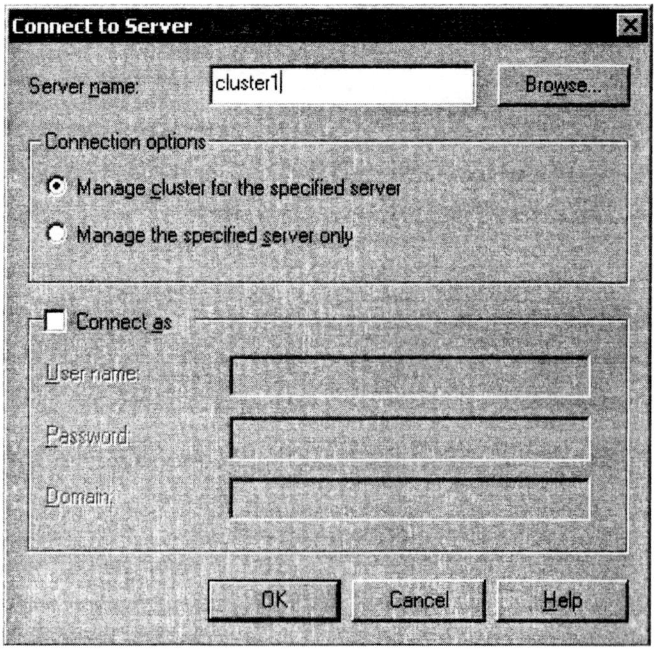

Figure 6-12
Creating a new cluster.

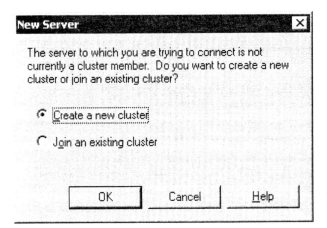

Figure 6-13
Creating a new cluster.

Selecting the **Create a new cluster** option will start the **New Cluster** wizard (see Figure 6-14). This wizard will walk you through the creation of a new cluster. Click **Next** to continue.

The wizard will then connect to the machine you specified (in this case, the local machine), search for all present network adapters, and collect the

Figure 6-14
Creating a new cluster.

necessary information (see Figure 6-15). If your machine does not have two network adapters present, or the machine is not running the Microsoft network client, the server analysis will fail. If you have configured everything right, the server analysis will complete. Click **Next** to continue.

Next, the wizard will ask that you name the cluster and then assign a description (Figure 6-16). If you manage multiple clusters, it is important that you have descriptive names. The description *Cluster3* is not as descriptive as *Atlanta cluster for mydomain.com Web site*. Once you have typed in a name and description, click **Next** to continue.

Next, the wizard will ask you the type of cluster you would like to create (see Figure 6-17). This decision is essential, for the cluster will be configured differently, depending on which selection you make. The General/Web cluster is a traditional cluster with an Internet Information Server Web server that serves up Web pages to clients. A COM+ application cluster is a cluster that load balances requests for COM+ components only. This type of cluster is helpful for building three-tier (or four-tier) Web applications. The COM+ routing cluster is a cluster of machines that does nothing but route requests to another cluster for the processing of COM+ components. Select **General/Web cluster** and then click **Next** to continue.

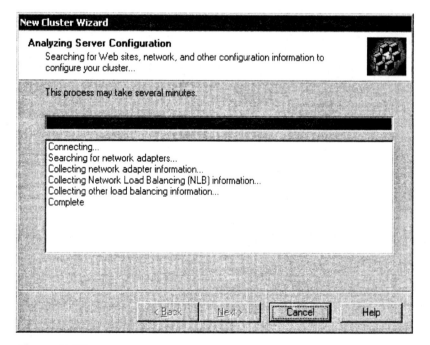

Figure 6-15
Analyzing server configuration.

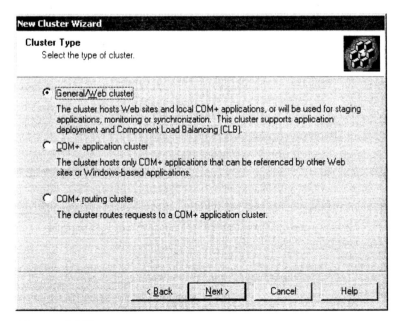

Figure 6-16
Naming the cluster.

Figure 6-17
Specifying cluster type.

Next, the wizard will show you the adapters that it has found on the server specified and will assign each adapter to a specific function (see Figure 6-18), either Management traffic network adapter or Load-balanced network adapter. The management traffic adapter should be the adapter that is currently connected to the private network and is not accessible by clients. The load-balanced network adapter is the adapter that is plugged into the public network and is accessible to clients. You will need to view these adapters and verify that they are correct. A common mistake is not realizing that the adapters are switched. This can be disastrous if not detected early, so be sure to inspect the adapters selected carefully. Once you have verified that the adapters are correct, select **Next** to continue.

Next, the wizard will ask you to specify an email address and email server name so that notifications can be sent to a designated party (see Figure 6-19). This email address should be the email address of the administrator and should be in the form of *user@domain.com.* The email server should be a server on your network that is running SMTP, and is accessible via name resolution. This can be a NetBIOS name or a fully qualified domain name. Once you have entered the information, select **Next** to continue.

This completes the New Cluster Wizard. You can select **Finish** to continue the new cluster configuration (see Figure 6-20).

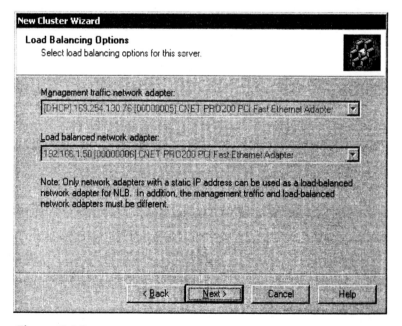

Figure 6-18
Specifying adapters.

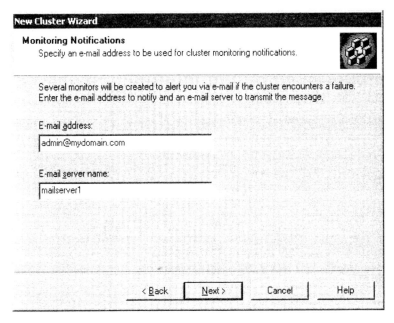

Figure 6-19
Configuring notifications.

Figure 6-20
Completing the New Cluster Wizard.

To review, let's list the things we have done so far. We have

- Prepared a server for AC 2000.
- Configured the network adapters.
- Installed AC 2000 tools.
- Created a new cluster by adding the local server to the cluster.

Now that you have one cluster running with one member, you can add other members to the cluster. The requirements for adding the node to the cluster are the same. You should have one network adapter in each node configured with a static IP address and all secondary adapters set to DHCP. You must also have the AC 2000 server component installed on each server you wish to add to the cluster. If you have completed these steps, then you are ready to add members to your cluster.

Within the AC 2000 administrative tool, right-click on the name of your new cluster and select **All Tasks** and then **Add Cluster Member...** (see Figure 6-21). This will start the Add Cluster Member wizard.

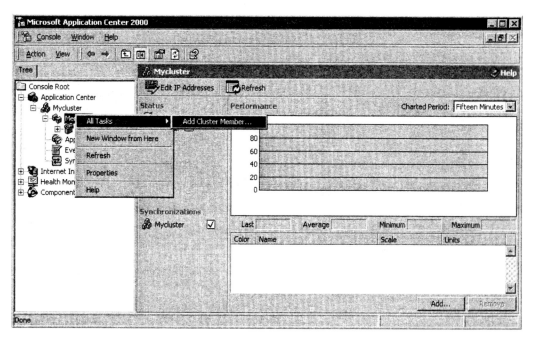

Figure 6-21
Adding a cluster member.

Once you begin the Add Cluster Member wizard, it reminds you that every node must have two network adapters for NLB to work correctly (see Figure 6-22). It also warns that you may overwrite Web data by adding the server to the cluster. This is because the first node that was added to the cluster is considered the cluster controller. As you add more machines to the cluster, the AC 2000 software will seek to wipe out the Web configuration and data to prepare for synchronization with the cluster controller. Once the Web configuration and files are deleted, the software will synchronize the cluster controller's Web site and configuration information to the new member. For this reason, always make sure the data you wish to publish to all other servers is present on your cluster controller prior to adding members to the cluster. Click **Next** to continue.

The next screen asks you to specify the server you wish to connect to as well as the username and password necessary to connect to the server and configure it (see Figure 6-23). Type in the name of the server you wish to add as a member of the cluster. Type a username and password of a user account

Figure 6-22
Add Cluster Member wizard.

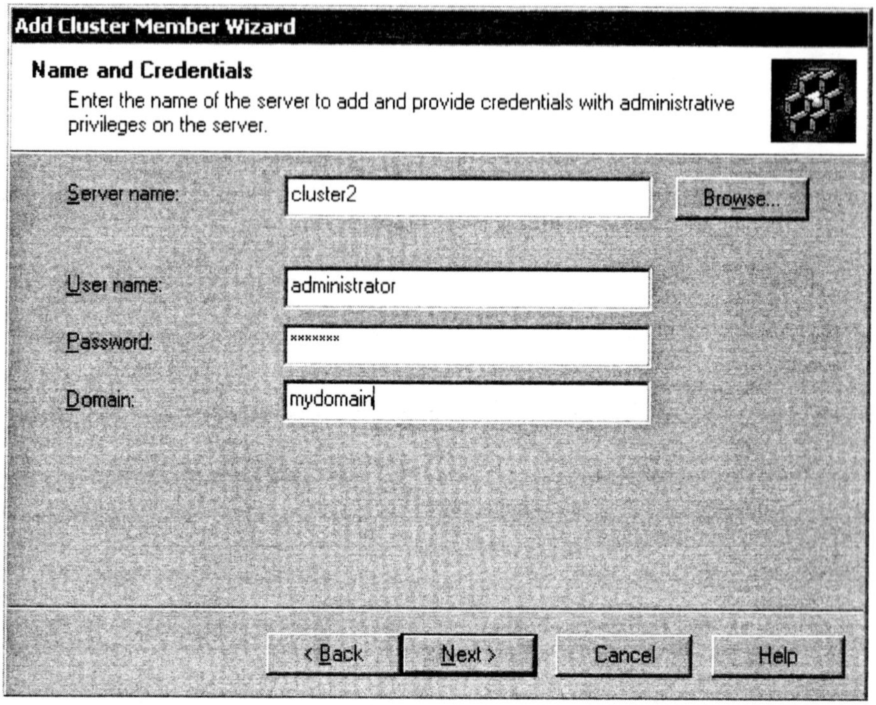

Figure 6-23
Connecting to new server.

that has administrative privileges on the remote machine. If the remote machine is a workgroup server, just leave the Domain field blank. Click **Next** to continue.

The next screen displays the network adapter information that the wizard has discovered (see Figure 6-24). You will see that the wizard will automatically assign an adapter to a particular function, designating one for management traffic and one for load balancing. Verify that these adapters are correct before continuing. There are also two other options: one to bring the cluster member online after creation and one to automatically synchronize the cluster member upon creation. Select the options you wish, for they can be changed after the member is created. These are just options that apply to the initial creation of the object within the cluster. Click **Next** to continue.

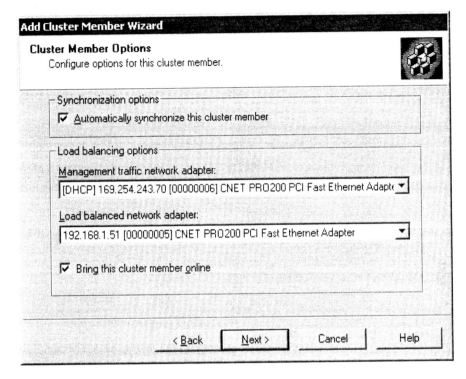

Figure 6-24
Cluster member options.

Note

It is never possible to apply the load-balancing component to more than one network adapter at a time within a single machine. If you attempt to manually apply the network load-balancing component to a second adapter, the load balancing that was previously applied to the first adapter will be disabled automatically.

The next screen informs you that you have completed the Add Cluster Member wizard (see Figure 6-25). Click **Finish** to continue.

Congratulations. You have now completed adding a member to your cluster. You can now repeat the process for up to 32 nodes.

Note

Even though you can theoretically add 32 machines to a network load-balanced cluster managed by AC 2000, the recommended number is 12. Any more than that can be counterproductive.

213

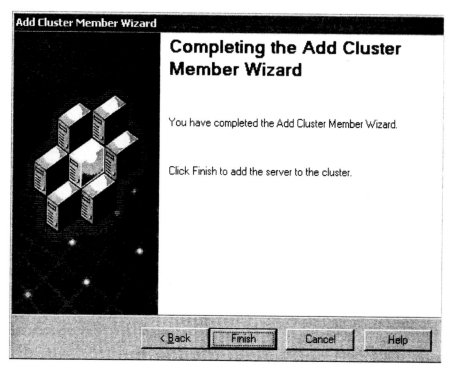

Figure 6-25
Finishing the Cluster Member wizard.

6.4 Component Load Balancing: Three-Tiered Clusters

Included within the AC 2000 product suite is the ability to load balance servers dedicated to responding to COM+ component requests. This valuable configuration allows systems designers to deploy Web applications in multiple tiers, extending the scalability of their applications. A *tier* is any component necessary for the processing of a particular application that is served by a dedicated server or group of servers. A cluster of servers that run a single static Web site would be considered a single-tiered application.

Not too long ago, designers decided to split the processing of an application between the client requests and the database access. To do this, designers configured a server to run the Web site application and stored data for that application in a database server separate from the Web server. This is an example of a two-tiered application, for one tier responds to client requests while the other tier provides data storage.

Applications are advancing, though, and programmers have begun writing applications that use COM+ components separate from the Web site code or the data access. These COM+ components are .dll (dynamic-linked library) files that are typically written in C++ and provide for the processing of business logic or rules within an application. User authentication is a good example of a process that can be provided through a COM+ component. Can't you provide authentication through an Active Server Pages (ASP) script within the Web site? you may ask. Well, yes, you can, but designers of large applications and server enterprise environments choose to streamline every process to make the application perform as efficiently as possible. Writing the authentication procedures within a COM+ component offloads the processing of this task so that the Web server does not have to process uncompiled code for every authentication request. The bottom line is COM+ is faster.

As the need for system scalability grows, applications are clustered to provide fault tolerance, reliability, and performance. The Web site can be clustered through NLB, creating the front end for the application. The database storage can also be clustered through the Microsoft Cluster Service, providing a reliable backend tier for the application. And now, through the tools within AC 2000, system designers can create clusters dedicated to the processing of COM+ components. This is called *component load balancing* and provides the third tier within the application.

In a typical application, a user would request a Web page from the Web server. The Web server would run ASP code, activating business logic located in a COM+ component that is stored on a component load-balancing (CLB) server. The CLB server runs the COM+ component, which accesses the data storage on the backend and returns data to the Web server, which in turn returns the data to the client. It may seem that this is a long process and that hosting all applications on a single machine would be faster. This may be true for a handful of users, but when your user count reaches several hundred per minute, your single server would fail to perform, whereas the three-tiered Web application discussed here would not have broken a sweat. The name of the game is scalability and fault tolerance. Building applications in such a way provides the fault tolerance, performance, and scalability needed for today's enterprise Web sites and applications.

Another tool built into the AC 2000 product suite is the ability to create a COM+ routing cluster. A COM+ routing cluster is a cluster of servers that direct requests for COM+ components to a COM+ cluster. This extends the architecture of the application into a fourth tier. A routing cluster sits between the Web server and the COM+ cluster and load balances requests for the COM+ cluster components, forwarding them as needed.

To build a CLB cluster or COM+ routing cluster, you simply need to follow the steps for creating a Web cluster (in the previous section) and select COM+ application cluster or COM+ routing cluster when prompted for application type (see Figure 6-17). COM+ application clusters and routing clusters can exist to complement an existing Web server cluster or apart from one to load balance COM+ application requests. Using these tools, systems designers can build an infrastructure suitable for any size environment, meeting the needs of today and providing scalability for the future.

6.5 Managing AC 2000

Managing AC 2000 is one of the joys of the product, for all administration can be done through a single interface. Regardless of which machine you wish to administer, any node within the cluster can be a host for the AC 2000 administrative console. Using the AC 2000 management application, you can

- View instant cluster status and status of all nodes.
- View performance statistics for individual nodes or the cluster as a whole.
- View events from the event log of any machine within the cluster.
- Configure and deploy application binaries and content to all nodes within the cluster.
- Synchronize all configuration and data between all nodes within the cluster.
- View the cluster health.
- Configure cluster properties, including affinity settings and requests forwarding.

AC 2000 allows you the convenience not only of one console, but also of a Web-based console. The Web-based AC 2000 management tool is a streamlined version of the MMC snap-in, but is still very powerful, allowing you to perform most of the functions available through the MMC console. This is useful for administrators who wish to manage clusters remotely through a Web browser. In addition to the console and the Web-based administration, there is also a variety of command-line options available.

6.5.1 Cluster Status

You will find the AC 2000 console snap-in in the Administrative Tools section of the Start menu. Once you open the console, ensure that the cluster you created earlier is listed under the Application Center icon in the left pane.

The AC 2000 console allows quick access to the status of the cluster through status icons located in the top left hand corner of the right pane. You will notice three icons for each server in your cluster. The first icon (going from left to right) indicates the status of the load balancing. The icon you see now (see Figure 6-26) represents normal load-balancing operations. A yellow caution symbol over the icon indicates a warning threshold has been reached and the cluster member is not receiving further client requests. A red stop sign with a down arrow indicates that a cluster member is offline. A question mark

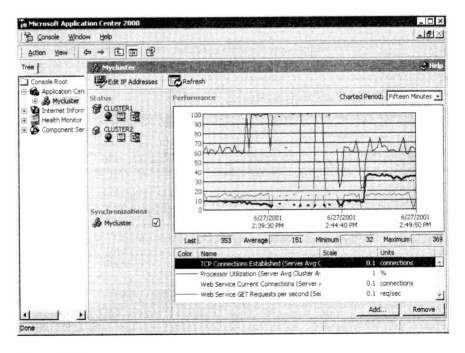

Figure 6-26
Viewing cluster status.

indicates an unknown condition that seeks your attention. If you see an hourglass, then the cluster member is draining connections.

The next icon is similar and refers to the health of the cluster member. A red exclamation point indicates a warning condition, but the cluster member would still be servicing requests. A red X indicates that a critical threshold has been exceeded and the cluster member is offline or is going offline. A question mark represents an unknown error. This can be related to service conflicts or a loss of network connectivity.

The next icon is the synchronize icon and indicates the synchronization status of the cluster members. An hourglass indicates that synchronization is in progress. A red arrow pointing down indicates that a user-requested synchronization session is taking place. And again, the question mark reflects an unknown condition that must be investigated.

6.5.2 Cluster Statistics

In addition to the effective status symbols, the AC 2000 console is tightly integrated with the performance monitor, allowing you to view statistics related to the cluster as a whole or to view individual machines within the cluster. This allows you to see which servers are working harder than others so that you can adjust the percentage of load assigned to each server.

To view statistics related to the cluster as a whole, click the **Add** button on the main screen (see Figure 6-26) and select the counters that you wish to add to the monitor. These statistics include many of the counters you are familiar with from the performance monitor, as well as a few specifically designed for cluster servers. If you wish to view statistics for particular servers, you will need to expand the cluster icon and then expand the member you want to monitor. As you select each member server, you will have the same opportunity to add counters and view their statistics.

6.5.3 Cluster Events

For any application, it is important to know what operations are taking place. From the inception of Windows NT, Microsoft has provided a mechanism for fielding application warnings and errors. This mechanism, called the event viewer, is a vital part of any troubleshooting process. AC 2000 has gone beyond the traditional event viewer by providing the observation of events directly from the application.

To view events generated by the cluster, expand the cluster icon and select the **Events** icon (see Figure 6-27). On the right pane, you will be able to view a collective list of events that have been generated by the machines within the cluster. The event viewer allows you to filter events by type, severity, source, and event ID. This is a valuable asset to the AC 2000 administrative console.

6.5.4 Cluster Application Management

In AC 2000 an application is a group of resources that are deployed and synchronized together across multiple nodes within the cluster. This could include Web site files, COM+ components, ISAPI filters, Data Source Names (DSNs), file and directory permissions, and registry settings. When you installed AC 2000, the installation took all existing Web sites and virtual Web

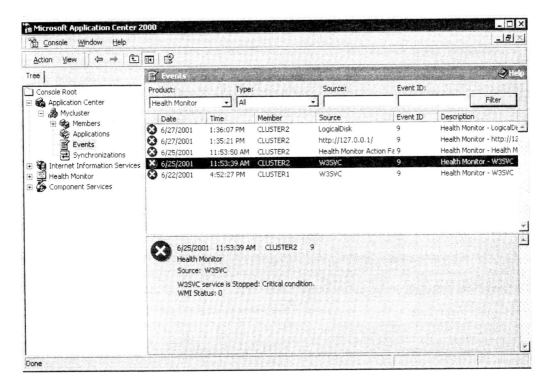

Figure 6-27
Viewing cluster events.

sites and made each one of them an application to be synchronized across all nodes in the cluster. Even though these Web sites are small and contain only static files, they are still considered an application based upon the meaning we have defined.

Using AC 2000, you can define and deploy your own Web applications seamlessly to all nodes within a cluster. If you expand the cluster icon and click on the **Applications** symbol, you will see the existing applications that are running (and synchronizing) within your cluster (see Figure 6-28).

Through this console, you can create new applications for deployment, rename existing applications, perform manual synchronization, or delete the existing applications. This unified console allows you to manage all application deployment on the cluster.

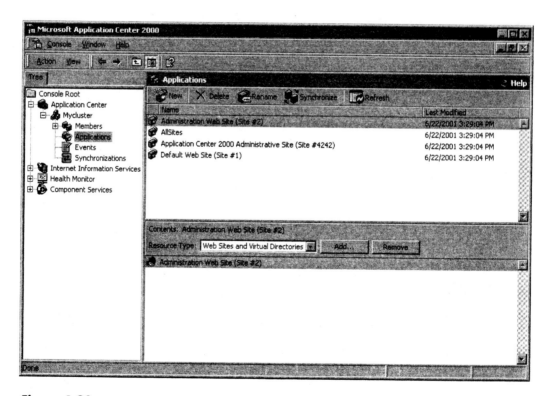

Figure 6-28
Viewing cluster applications.

6.5.5 Cluster Synchronization

Cluster synchronization is almost as important as the creation of the cluster itself. Many administrators who worked with network load balancing in its early days, prior to AC 2000, were frustrated by the inability of the application to synchronize content, and they spent many resources trying to write sophisticated scripts that would keep the data, components, and applications synchronized.

AC 2000 offers the automatic synchronization of all data, configurations, registry entries, components, and binaries. Through application deployment, even COM+ objects that require a registration and a reboot can be deployed without causing an interruption in service.

To view the current configuration and status of synchronization within your cluster, click on the **Synchronization** icon located under the Cluster icon (see Figure 6-29). The left pane reveals all synchronizations that are configured for the server. Configurations are added automatically when applications are deployed. By clicking the **Events** tab, you can also view errors that may have caused your application not to synchronize.

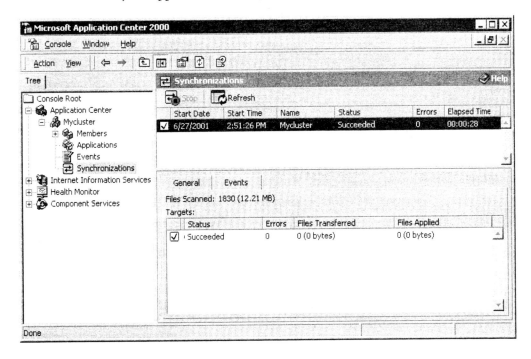

Figure 6-29
Viewing cluster synchronization.

6.5.6 Cluster Health

The health monitor is the cluster detective. It works through background components to monitor all operations within a cluster, making note of what it sees and reporting it to administrators through the console.

The health monitor uses *monitors* to keep track of information such as CPU utilization and TCP connections. Using either built-in thresholds or thresholds designed by an administrator, the health monitor records violations of the set policies, alerting administrators to the events via email or other specified alerts.

There are two types of monitors you can use within the health monitor. One is a synchronized (global) monitor that applies to all nodes within the cluster. The other is a nonsynchronized (local) monitor, which applies only to a single node within the cluster.

To access the health monitor, select the **Health Monitor** icon from within the AC 2000 console (see Figure 6-30). The first view gives you a comprehensive

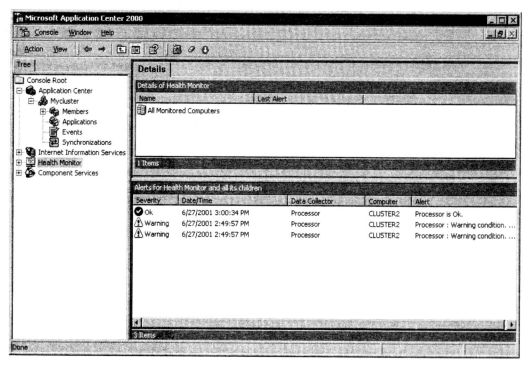

Figure 6-30
Viewing cluster health.

view of all alerts and error conditions presently listed for your cluster. If you wish, you can drill down within the health monitor icon and set alerts or monitors for specific servers as well as thresholds for certain conditions. If you chose to install the sample monitors, they will be listed as well for you to choose from.

6.5.7 Configuring Cluster Properties

If you are used to working with NLB as a manual administrative process, then you are probably wondering where the NLB settings that you are used to are. Well, don't worry; you can still configure your load-balancing thresholds and affinity settings to your liking.

If you right-click on the cluster (this will be whatever you named the cluster during setup) and click **Properties**, you will see a dialogue screen similar to that in Figure 6-31. This allows you to apply configuration settings to the cluster as a whole—meaning all nodes within the cluster will operate based on these configuration settings.

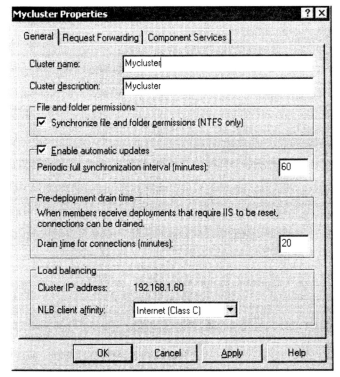

Figure 6-31
Viewing cluster properties.

The first options are Cluster name and Cluster description. These are for labeling and administration purposes only and can be changed without fear of reprisal. The next option asks if you would like to synchronize file and folder permissions (NTFS only) during synchronization. For instance, if you had a Web site that used specific permissions settings on a particular directory that contained sensitive data, you would want to synchronize the NTFS permissions you assign to this directory. Selecting the checkbox ensures that NTFS permissions changes are synchronized with all members of the cluster.

The next option dictates whether the cluster controller performs synchronization with other cluster nodes. It also allows you to specify the timing for such updates. It is recommended that you leave the default of 60 minutes. Shorting this time will only increase traffic on the network and could slow your application.

The next option is the Pre-deployment drain time. Drain time is a duration of time when a cluster member refuses to respond to client requests. The object is to drain the current connections so that you work a cluster member out of active duty without abruptly killing current connections. A 20-minute drain time should be plenty of time for all connections to finish their sessions. Drain times are typically used for deployment. When you deploy an application that contains an ISAPI filter or COM+ object that requires the service to be restarted, connections are drained until all connections are gone. Then the application is installed and the service is restarted—at which time the server is available for new connections once again.

The last option is the affinity setting. If you have used NLB in the past, then you should understand the use of affinity. The affinity setting defines the relationship between a client IP address and the cluster host that serves it. Affinity is used to manage state within a load-balanced cluster. Many applications manage session state as a client moves within the application. If you have used the Internet to navigate a dynamic Web site portal or to buy a book online, then you have experienced session state. Although you did not know it, the server was keeping track of your actions—the buttons you clicked and the information you entered. These bits of information are called session variables and are used in most Web sites today.

This presents a problem to the load-balanced cluster, for session variables are stored in server memory, a piece of storage that is not shared across several machines. Affinity is a way for the load-balanced cluster to deal with the session state issue. By understanding and correctly configuring affinity, you can correctly manage state across multiple machines. There are three possible affinity settings: none, single, or class C. For more information related to these affinity settings, please see Chapter 5.

The next screen presents an option that is closely related to affinity (see Figure 6-32). Unlike the other three options, however, request forwarding does not use the IP address of a client to determine its status. Request forwarding, an option found only within AC 2000, makes use of cookies to determine where a machine has been serviced during any particular session. Cookies are small text files that the server writes to the client's machine. These small files contain information that the other cluster hosts will use to determine if they are able to service the request. Cookies are not permanent, but last only for the duration of the standard session (about 20 minutes), after which they expire automatically, allowing any server to respond once again to the client's request.

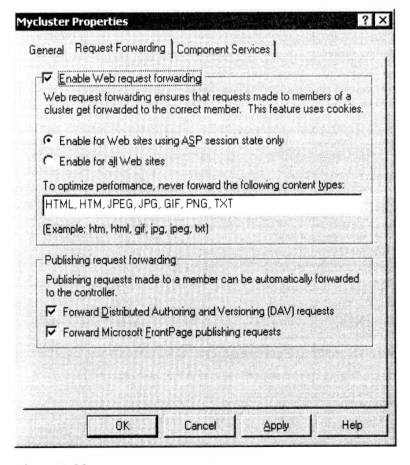

Figure 6-32
Request forwarding configuration.

Once you enable request forwarding, you have the option of enabling request forwarding for all Web sites or just for Web sites that manage state using ASP. You may ask, Why would I want to use request forwarding on non-ASP sites? Well, believe it or not, there are other programming languages besides ASP that manage state. If you run one of these languages on your server, you will need to select the All Web sites option to ensure that your state is managed effectively.

The next configuration option deals with the publishing of content using applications such as Microsoft FrontPage. If these options are checked, any cluster member that receives a publishing request from a FrontPage client will forward the request to the current cluster controller, ensuring that the publication takes place on the correct server. If you operate in a secure environment and you know that all Web publishers that publish content to the servers will publish to the cluster controller, then you may want to clear these options. Clearing them will not keep someone from publishing content to a cluster server member if they have the appropriate permissions, but once the synchronization occurs, all changes they have made will be overwritten.

The next configuration tab, **Component Services**, allows you to configure which servers on your network are configured as COM+ component-hosting servers (see Figure 6-33). The servers listed will receive all requests by the Web cluster for COM+ components. If the components you are using are local to each machine, make sure that this section does not contain any servers. If this were a CLB server, you would also want to make sure the field is blank.

In addition to configuring the cluster as a whole, it is possible to configure individual servers within the cluster. To configure a single server, right-click on the server within the administrative console and select **Properties**. The screen that this displays (see Figure 6-34) presents information about the cluster member and allows you to change three different options related to the cluster member.

The first is the synchronization of the member with the cluster controller. If you are viewing the properties of the cluster controller, then the synchronization section is grayed out, but if it is not the cluster controller, you have the option of enabling or disabling the synchronization.

The second option is the dedicated IP address. If you need to change the IP address of a host within the cluster, you will need to change the IP address here first, and then change the IP address on the server itself. After a reboot, the server should join the cluster without error.

The last configuration option is the amount of load that you request for this server based upon the total load balanced between all cluster nodes. This option is helpful for installations that include hardware that is less than desirable. Hardware that does not perform as well as other machines within the cluster should be given a smaller load within the cluster so that performance

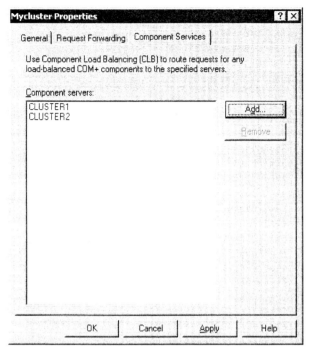

Figure 6-33
Configuring component services forwarding.

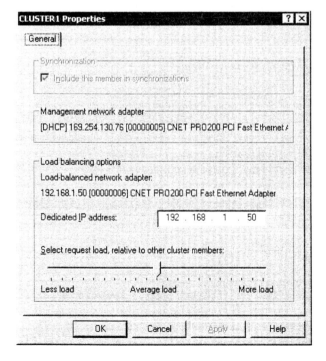

Figure 6-34
Viewing cluster member properties.

does not suffer when the server is loaded. The reverse of that premise is true as well. If you have one machine that is much more powerful than others within the cluster, you will want to set this machine to handle a higher percentage of the load than the other servers.

6.5.8 Command-Line Administration

In addition to the robust GUI interface provided with AC 2000, there are many command-line options that allow you to manage the cluster through a command prompt. The command-line utility *(AC.EXE)* can be used to perform management, configuration, and reporting of cluster nodes for direct administration or batch file transactions.

AC.EXE uses six separate functions that are listed in Table 6-1. There is a variety of options that can be used in conjunction with these functions, all of which can be found through online help.

Table 6-1   AC.EXE Functions

APPLICATION	Allows you to manage applications
CLB	Allows you to update a component services list on a Web cluster or COM+ routing cluster.
CLUSTER	Allows you to create or disband a cluster, list cluster members, and add/delete new cluster members.
DEPLOY	Allows the deployment and synchronization of applications.
LOADBALANCE	Allows you to query for load balance status information, modify load, drain connections, and enable/disable load balancing on a particular node.
HELP	Provides help for all AC.EXE command-line commands.

The syntax of the command is as follows:

```
AC function /option:value
```

Using these command-line options, you can perform just about any operation possible, including the creation and deletion of new clusters and applications. For more information related to the AC.EXE application, consult the online help or type *AC /?*

Chapter 7

CLUSTERING MICROSOFT SQL SERVER

If you are planning to build any type of ERP (Enterprise Resource Planning), CRM (Customer Relationship Manager), or e-commerce application, you will most likely need a database. To ensure that the database is always available, you should consider utilizing a failover cluster. The Microsoft Windows 2000 Advanced Server and Datacenter Server clustering services are designed to provide failover services for mission-critical databases—specifically, SQL Server. Although you could run other databases on a Microsoft Cluster Server (MSCS), it is recommended that you utilize SQL Server 7.0 or SQL Server 2000 for your implementation. Using SQL Server in conjunction with the MSCS, you can build high performance, fault-tolerant database systems.

In this chapter, you will learn how to plan, design, and install SQL Server 2000 on a Windows 2000 Cluster Server. Like the installation of the cluster service, a successful implementation takes careful planning and meticulous attention to detail.

7.1 Overview of SQL Clustering

Anyone who has run earlier versions of SQL Server on a cluster will be happy with the upgrade. SQL Server 2000 contains many new features, including support for up to 32 processors, up to 64 GB of RAM, XML elements, and synchronized standby servers. In addition, SQL Server 2000 has made great strides in improving the failover cluster features. SQL Server 2000 allows failover clusters to host multiple instances of the program, which is ideal for Application Service Providers (ASP) and hosted environments. The SQL Server 2000 installation program is also cluster-aware, allowing you to automatically create virtual servers through the setup program without affecting existing installations. After a long wait, SQL Server 2000 now supports up to 4-node failover clusters (using Datacenter Server). That means you can have databases fail over to three different machines in the event of a failure.

From a thousand feet view, running SQL Server on a cluster is not much different than running it on a single server, but a closer look will reveal some large differences. If you have worked with SQL Server in the past, then you understand how SQL Server utilized devices, maintained security, and executed stored procedures. But don't allow your previous experience with SQL Server fool you into believing that you can install SQL Server on a cluster without direction. The process is not the same as a standard installation.

In a standard (single server) SQL Server installation, three services control the SQL program, and the program is divided into binaries (program files) and data files (database storage). The SQL Executive service controls the execution of scheduled tasks, the SQL Server service manages client access, while the Microsoft Distributed Transaction Coordinator (MS DTC) service maintains replication, data translation, and transaction processing.

On one machine, the processes are very simple. The database and the binaries are stored within a set of files on the local hard disk. On an SQL Server 2000 clustered server, the program files run local to each cluster node, but the database is stored on the shared disk array. In earlier versions of SQL Server, both the program files and the database would fail over to a node as a result of a failure. In SQL 2000, only the database fails over. This provides a more efficient failover process.

When SQL Server installs on a cluster, a virtual server name (the network name resource) and an *instance* is created along with the disk and IP address resource and other components native to the SQL Server. This is significant, for it allows you to run multiple instances of the SQL Server program on the same server. You are allowed to have one virtual server for each disk group on the shared disk array. Within any given virtual server, you can install multiple instances of the SQL Server program. This isolates the databases into separately running occurrences on the shared disk array—a vast improvement on the limitations of earlier versions of SQL Server.

Note

The clustering capabilities of SQL Server 2000 are available only through the Enterprise version. The standard version will not install correctly on a cluster. Further references to SQL Server 2000 through this chapter, unless specifically stated, imply SQL Server 2000 Enterprise Edition.

7.2 Designing an SQL Cluster

As you design your SQL cluster, keep in mind that each disk group can have only one virtual server and that during a failure, all resources within a disk group will fail to another node within the cluster; they cannot be configured to fail over independently. For this reason, it is logical to group application resources together. For example, if you are hosting an ASP (application service provider) based application that utilizes a database, it is good design to create a disk group for each separate database that you seek to host rather than add multiple client databases to the same disk group. This allows a failure in one database to trigger a failover that would not affect the other client databases.

7.2.1 Active/Passive Configuration

If you are building a database that will be utilizing a single instance within a single virtual server, it is recommended that you employ an *active/passive* configuration. In a four-node cluster it would be termed an *active/passive/passive/passive* configuration. This simply means to install one virtual server with one instance of SQL Server on one node within a cluster, while the other servers provide service only for the database during a failover.

During the SQL Server 2000 installation process, the program will recognize that the MSCS is installed and will install the necessary binaries on all machines within the cluster you designate as a possible failover partner. This prevents you from having to run the install on each node within the cluster.

7.2.2 Active/Active Configuration

If you plan to host multiple virtual servers or instances of SQL Server, then you will most likely employ the *active/active* configuration. In larger environments, you may choose to apply the same technology to a four-node cluster, creating an *active/active/active/active* cluster.

This configuration simply means each server within the cluster hosts its own virtual server (or multiple virtual servers) and manages the disk group that contains the resources allocated to that virtual server. In the event of a failure on one machine, one of the other three machines in the cluster will pick up ownership of the disk group and begin to service requests and database transactions.

This allows a type of load balancing, for not any one server sits idle, but all are busy processing database requests for a particular virtual server. The only problem with this configuration is the resource load that it puts upon a server (or servers) when a failure (or multiple failures) occurs. If you choose to use this configuration, make sure that your hardware resources on any given machine are adequate enough to run all four (or more) virtual servers.

7.2.3 Multiple Instances

One of the greatest advantages to running SQL Server 2000 over an older version of SQL Server is the ability to install multiple instances of the database engine to run simultaneously on the same computer. This provides great flexibility to organizations that wish to run multiple databases across several different installations. ISPs and ASPs will find this feature beneficial to their service offerings.

There are two types of instances that can be installed on an SQL Server: a default instance and a named instance. The default instance is a standard installation of SQL Server, and clients connect to the server in the same way they always have. There can be only one default instance per server. Because a clustered SQL Server allows an installation of SQL Server to fail over, you must make sure that if all installations run on one machine, there is only one default instance. If you install a default instance on one server node in a cluster and then choose to install SQL Server on the second node (to create an active/active configuration), you must use a named instance for the second install, not a default instance.

A named instance is an installation that has a particular name within the context of a running SQL Server. Clients must connect to named instances by name. For example, if you create an instance named SQL1 on a server named CSATL1, you will need to use the name CSATL1\SQL1 to connect to the server.

When you install multiple instances, each instance gets its own

- System and user databases
- SQL Server and SQL Server Agent

- Independent registry keys associated with the services and databases
- Network addresses

Although separate instances create separate sets of services and databases, each machine will retain a single copy of

- Database utilities and administration tools
- Application registry entries
- MSSearch service for full text indexing
- English query and SQL 2000 Analysis services
- Development libraries and sample applications

A good clustered SQL Server design will contain one instance of SQL Server for each disk group. If you are limited to five disk groups within your cluster, then you logically would be limited to five instances of SQL Server. The word *logically* is used because it is possible to install more than one instance of SQL Server to the same disk group, but it is not recommended. Regardless of how you split your instances across a server, the maximum number of instances you can have on any one server is 16.

7.2.4 Client Connectivity

The client connectivity to SQL Server running under a cluster is not much different than a traditional SQL Server, with the exception of the following items:

- Named pipes and TCP/IP are the only supported protocols.
- You must use the clustered name resource or virtual IP address to connect to a clustered SQL Server, not the name of the individual nodes.
- You must use the full name of a particular instance when connecting to an SQL Server that is not a default installation (i.e., *servername\ instancename*).

7.2.5 Using Max Server Memory Option

The Windows NT operating system is a 32-bit system and is limited to a maximum of 4 GB of total RAM (random access memory). By default, Windows 2000 (because it is also 32 bit) reserves 2 GB of RAM for the operating system and allows applications to share the other 2 GB of memory. All memory in excess of 4 GB would be ignored. Through the use of some command line switches and configuration options, these settings can be overwritten, and the use of a memory address space over 4 GB is allowed.

AWE (Address Windowing Extensions) is an API included with Windows 2000 Advanced Server and Windows 2000 Datacenter Server that allows a 32-bit system to use address spaces larger than 4 GB. To use AWE on large systems, keep the following items in mind.

- Use the /3GB switch in the *boot.ini* file to force the operating system to use only 1 GB of memory, freeing up 2 GB of memory for applications. (Don't use this switch for systems with more than 16 GB of memory.)
- To enable AWE in Windows 2000 Advanced Server and Windows 2000 Datacenter, add the */pae* switch to the *boot.ini* file.

To enable SQL Server 2000 to make use of memory spaces above 4 GB (when AWE is enabled within the operating system), you must use the sp_configure stored procedure with an awe enabled option to modify the configuration. Although the sp_configure will enable large memory support, it will allow the application to use too much memory and could cause the operating system or other processes on that machine to suffer. To manage the memory effectively, you must use the max server memory option in conjunction with the awe enabled option.

Because the AWE option is an advanced option within SQL Server, you will also need to enable the show advanced options parameter within your script. The following script is an example demonstrating how to enable AWE support and limit the maximum memory used to 6 GB.

```
Sp_configure 'show advanced options',1
RECONFIGURE
GO
Sp_configure 'awe enabled',1
RECONFIGURE
GO
Sp_configure 'max server memory',6144
RECONFIGURE
GO
```

7.3 Installing SQL Server 2000 on a Cluster

Prior to installing the SQL Server 2000 software, you must be aware of several dependencies. Please review and make sure you have met the following requirements:

- MSCS is installed on all nodes within the cluster.
- The event logs in all nodes are not producing errors related to the cluster.
- The node that will host the installation owns the shared disks that will support the Windows 2000 installation.
- NetBIOS is disabled on all private network adapters.
- The disk drive letters for all shared disks are identical for all hosts.

If you have followed the instructions within Chapter 3, "Clustering Design Issues," then you should have most of these requirements met. Be sure to check your event log on all servers within the cluster to ensure there are no error messages being logged.

Prior to installing the SQL Server 2000 database software, you must configure the MS DTC resource. Luckily, Microsoft has decided to include a utility within the MSCS installation that will create and configure the MS DTC resource on all nodes within the cluster.

To install and configure the MS DTC resource on cluster node 1, click **Start**, **Programs**, **Accessories**, then **Command Prompt**. At a command prompt, type *comclust.exe* and hit **Enter** (see Figure 7-1). This will run the MS DTC Cluster Configuration wizard and add the MS DTC resource to the default (or quorum) disk group. It is safe to ignore the error message you receive that indicates that the server you are installing on is not a component load-balancing server. This is a feature you will learn to install in a separate chapter. Once the installation completes, repeat the process on all nodes within the cluster.

Once you have repeated the process on all nodes within the cluster, open the Cluster Administrator on one of the cluster nodes and click on the **Cluster Group**. Verify that the cluster group contains a resource called **MS DTC** and that it is online.

Once you have installed the MS DTC resource, you are ready to begin the SQL Server installation. Make sure that the cluster node that you wish to use for the SQL Server host is online and that it has ownership of the disk resource

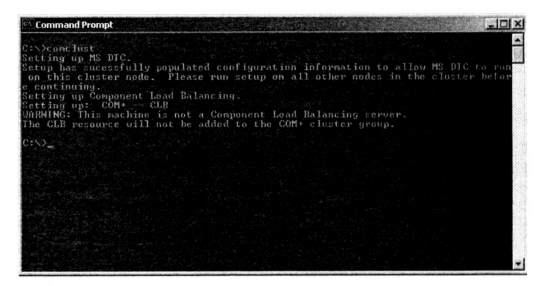

Figure 7-1
Installing the MS DTC resource.

you have reserved for the SQL Server. Place the SQL Server 2000 Enterprise Server into the CD-ROM drive and allow it to auto start. You should see a screen like that in Figure 7-2. If the CD-ROM does not auto start, click **Start**, **run**, **browse**, and navigate to the drive containing the CD-ROM. Locate the *autorun.exe* file on the CD-ROM and run it.

Click the **SQL Server 2000 Components** option. On the next screen (see Figure 7-3) select **Install Database Server** from the menu.

The SQL Server 2000 Installation wizard will start and inform you that it will allow you to install a new instance of SQL Server 2000 or modify an existing instance of SQL Server 2000 (see Figure 7-4). Click **Next** to continue.

The next screen allows you to specify the name of the server that you wish to install SQL Server 2000 on. There is a Local Computer option, a Remote Computer option, and a Virtual Server option. Because you are performing the installation of a server that has the MSCS installed, the installation defaults to the Virtual Server option. The name you type for the server name should be the network name you wish to assign to your new SQL Server instance. If you were adding an instance to an existing virtual server, you would enter that name here (see Figure 7-5). Enter the name of the virtual server you would like to create, make sure that **Virtual Server** is checked, and press **Next**.

Figure 7-2
SQL Server setup.

Figure 7-3
Selecting database install.

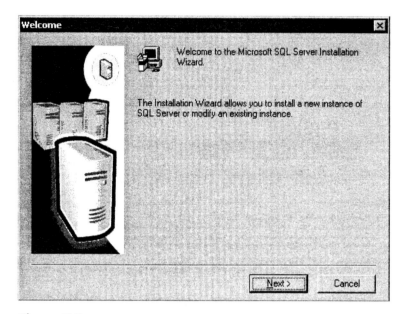

Figure 7-4
SQL Server Installation wizard.

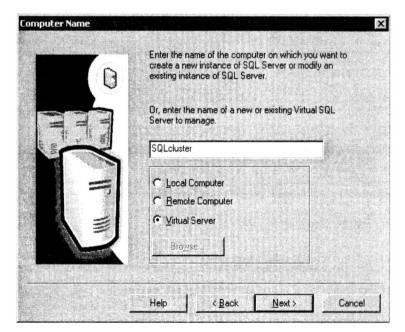

Figure 7-5
Naming the virtual server.

The next screen requests a username and company name for product registration purposes (see Figure 7-6). The user screen is required but does not have to be associated with an actual username. Any name will do. The company name is optional. Enter a username and company name (if desired) and press **Next** to continue.

The next screen displays the licensing agreement for SQL Server 2000 (see Figure 7-7). Please read the licensing agreement before proceeding. You can page down to display the complete agreement. Once you have read the license agreement in its entirety, click **Yes** to proceed.

The next screen represents your virtual server information sheet. This screen allows you to assign a virtual IP address to all networks connected to your server (see Figure 7-8). Although you could assign an IP address to the private network card, it is not logical to do so, for there are no clients that connect via that interface. Type in the IP address of the virtual server you would like to use for the selected network. The wizard will assign the subnet based on the existing network properties of that network adapter. Click **Add** to add the virtual IP address for the selected network. The IP address you assign in

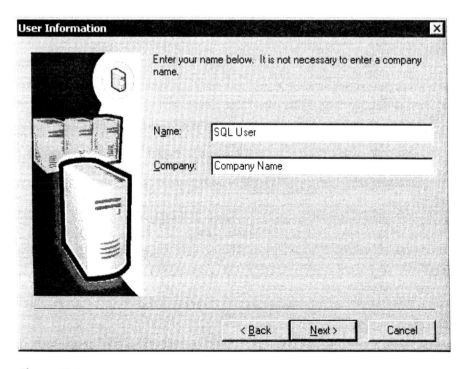

Figure 7-6
Entering the user information.

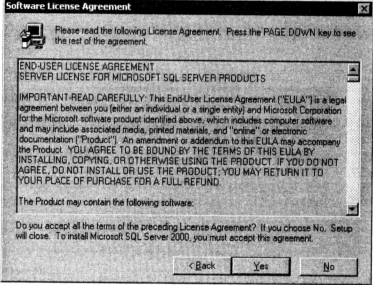

Figure 7-7
SQL Server Software License Agreement.

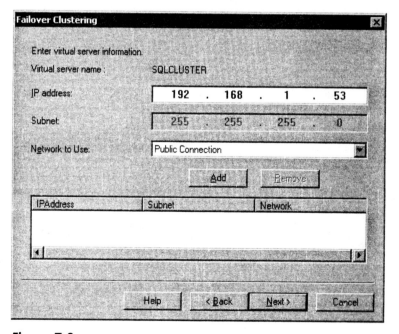

Figure 7-8
Creating a virtual IP address.

this section will be associated with the network name you assigned to the SQL Server virtual server and registered through WINS and DNS.

The cluster disk selection dialogue allows you to select which disk within your shared disk array will host the SQL Server virtual server (see Figure 7-9). Although it is possible to run other applications within the same disk group, it is not recommended. You will notice that each disk available is categorized under the group it has been assigned to by the Cluster wizard. Select the disk you wish to use for your virtual server and select **Next**.

The Cluster Definition screen allows you to define which servers within the cluster will participate as failover candidates for SQL Server (see Figure 7-10). By default, all nodes configured for clustering will be listed under Configured Nodes. You can add and remove nodes as you desire. You may wish to limit the failover within a four-node cluster to two particular machines, due to hardware limitations or applications running on other nodes that may conflict. Select any nodes you do not wish to host the SQL Server application during failover and select **Remove**, then press **Next** to continue.

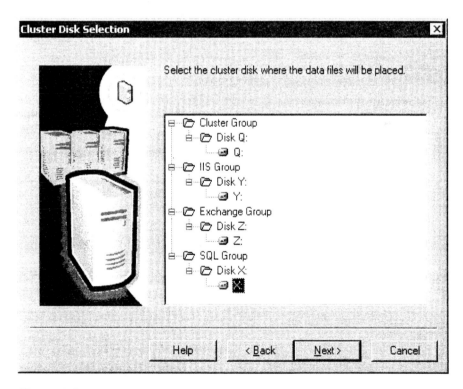

Figure 7-9
Selecting the physical disk resource.

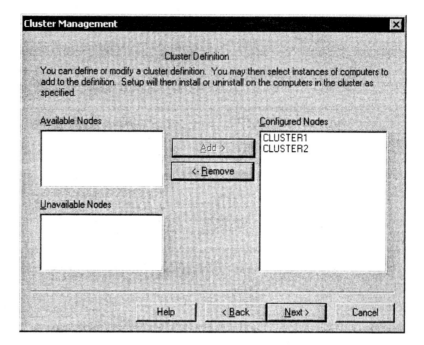

Figure 7-10
Defining the cluster nodes.

The remote information dialogue prompts the user for credentials neces-sary to connect to remote nodes within the cluster (see Figure 7-11). Unlike previous versions of SQL Server, you do not have to visit each machine with the installation media to set it up as a failover node. The installation is now able to connect to all nodes within a cluster and install the necessary software remotely. To accomplish this, a username and password with the administra-tive rights to the remote machines must be submitted. This login must be a domain account. It is safe to use an administrator account for this purpose, for the submitted account will not be assigned to a particular service, but will only be used to connect to remote machines for software installation. Enter the username you wish to use, along with a password and domain name, and then select **Next**.

The next screen allows users to specify the type of installation they wish to apply (see Figure 7-12). Using the provided radio buttons, the user may select a Typical, Minimum, or Custom install. These options are no different than a standard installation of SQL Server 2000. Most users will select Typical, while if you have limited disk space or specific software needs, you may wish to select Minimum or Custom. The minimum install will give you a basic installation

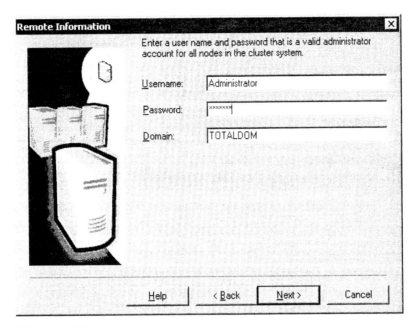

Figure 7-11
Assigning remote access to cluster nodes.

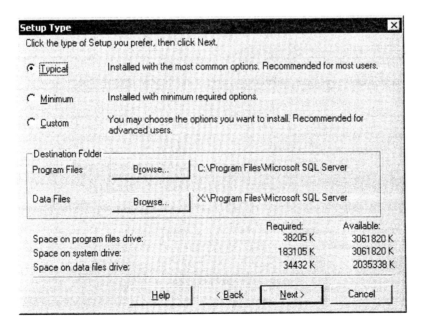

Figure 7-12
Selecting installation type.

without any options that may take up vital space, while a custom install will allow you to select the specific options you wish to install.

In the destination folder section you will notice that the wizard has chosen to install the program files on the local disk and the database files on the shared disk. This is not only for the local machine, but also for all machines within the cluster. The default settings are typically suitable. Select the **Next** button when you are ready to continue.

Note

*When you select **Next** to continue, you may receive an error that says, "The drive chosen for the program files installation path C: is not valid on all nodes of the cluster. Choose another drive to install the program files." This message appears if the cluster node you are using for installation cannot contact other nodes within the cluster through an RPC (remote procedure call) connection. This is typically caused by a missing file and print sharing component on one of the nodes within the cluster. To correct this error, enable file and print sharing on all nodes within the cluster. This can be done through the network properties of each machine.*

The Services Account dialogue asks for the service account that will be assigned to the virtual server (see Figure 7-13). This account must be a domain account. This is the account that will start the SQL Server service on the cluster server. It is important that this service account have administrator privileges on the domain. Make sure that the account is not the administrator account and that the password is difficult to guess. Type in the username for the service account (this account should have already been created). Once you have typed the password and domain name, click **Next** to continue to the next screen.

The Authentication Mode dialogue is used to configure the authentication that the instance of SQL Server you are installing will use when receiving client requests (see Figure 7-14). Windows authentication mode will fully integrate SQL Server with the Active Directory (or SAM Security) database and will allow you to assign users to databases from the Active Directory. This means that all new users will need to be created on the domain prior to assigning them access to databases within SQL Server. If you are in a corporate environment and the only users that will be accessing the SQL Server database(s) will be internal employees that already have an account within Active Directory, then Windows Authentication Mode may be the best choice for you.

If the application you are hosting is an Internet-based application, or if you need the ability to assign usernames to databases outside of Active Directory, then the Mixed Mode will most likely be the right choice. The Mixed Mode is

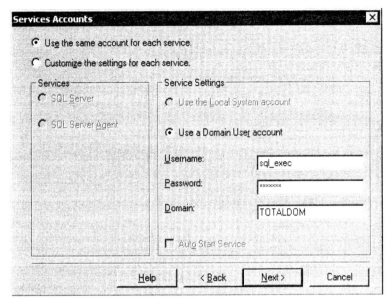

Figure 7-13
Setting up service account.

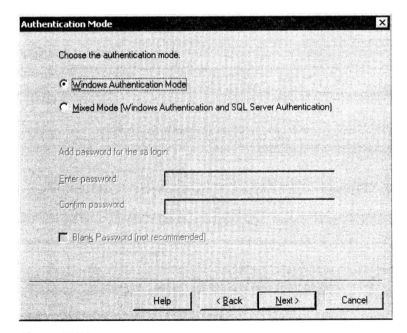

Figure 7-14
Choosing Authentication Mode.

recommended because of the flexibility it gives. Through this mode, you can assign rights to users within Active Directory or assign rights to users that you create within SQL Server. The benefit is the ability to allow access to the SQL Server without granting access to the domain. If you do choose Mixed Mode, you will need to assign an SA password. The SA account is the default system administrator account for SQL Server. If your system is for testing only or is not accessible through the Internet, you may wish to select the Blank Password option. This will allow any client to connect to the server with administrative privileges using the SA username and a blank password. Once you have made your selection, press **Next** to continue.

The Start Copying Files dialogue informs you that setup is about to prompt you for licensing information and gives you the ability to change any settings you may have selected up to this point in the setup (see Figure 7-15). There is no turning back after this point, so be sure that you have selected the desired settings, then click **Next** to continue.

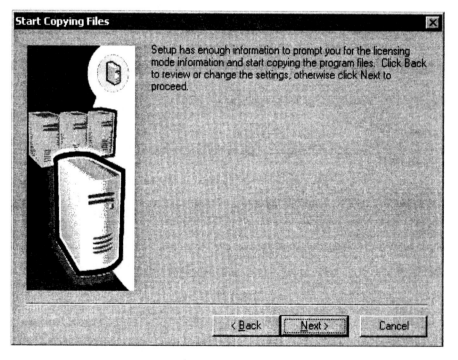

Figure 7-15
Copying files.

One of the many changes that you will notice in SQL Server 2000 is the licensing mode. There are two licensing modes available for any given server (see Figure 7-16). You must choose one of these options during setup and the decision cannot be reversed.

- Per Seat—The per seat requirement mandates that you have one Client Access License for each device that connects to the SQL Server.
- Processor License—Under this mode, each processor in the server must have a license.

The difference in the licensing typically is a matter of function. The Per Seat licensing mode is used for internal applications where connectivity to the database can be controlled and a specific number of clients need to connect.

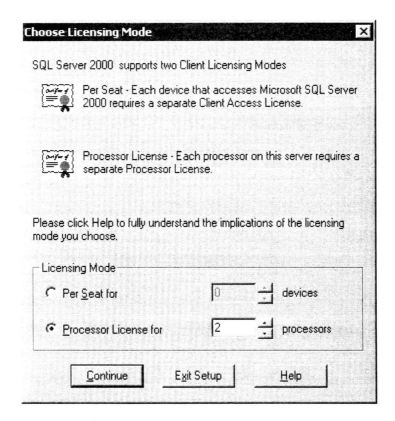

Figure 7-16
Choosing Licensing Mode.

The Processor License mode is for Internet-based applications where the client access may be in the thousands, or hundreds of thousands, per day. If you select processor mode, make sure you increase the license number for each processor you have in a server that may have to run the SQL Server database. For instance, if you have a two-node cluster and one node is a dual processor machine and the other is a quad-processor machine, you will need to set the processor license to four.

Once you have completed your licensing choice, select **Continue** to begin copying files (see Figure 7-17). Setup will then inform you that it is performing several required operations and that it may take several minutes for it to complete. During this phase, the cluster server is installing SQL Server on all nodes within the cluster. This may take an extensive amount of time, depending upon the speed of your server. Do not restart your server during this process or you may corrupt your installation.

Once the process is complete, setup informs you that it has successfully created virtual server resources for the cluster (see Figure 7-18). Press **Finish** to complete the SQL Server 2000 cluster setup.

Once setup is complete, open the Cluster Administrator and select the disk group that contains the cluster resources (see Figure 7-19). Verify that the following resources are present and online:

- SQL IP Address
- SQL Network Name
- SQL Server
- SQL Server Agent
- SQL Server Fulltext

If all of these resources are online, then you have successfully installed SQL Server 2000 to the cluster server.

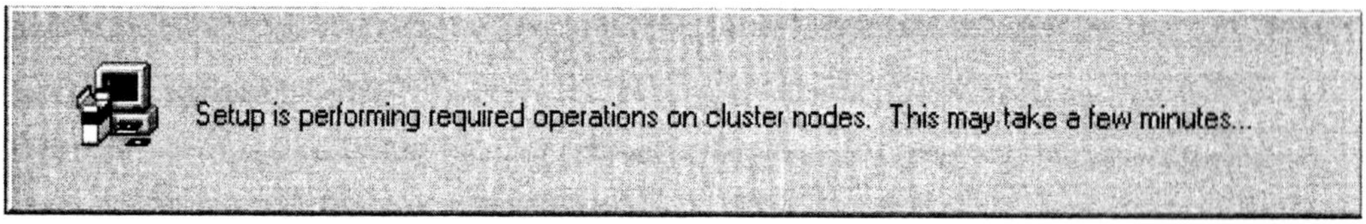

Setup is performing required operations on cluster nodes. This may take a few minutes...

Figure 7-17
Performing required operations.

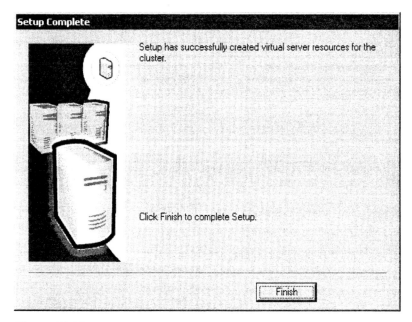

Figure 7-18
Finishing SQL Server setup.

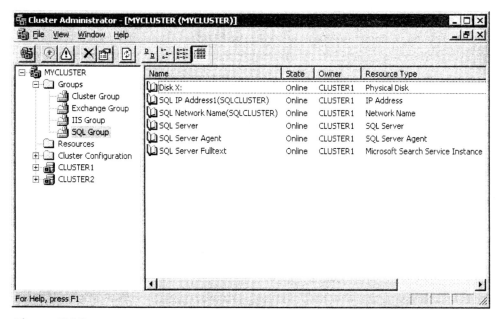

Figure 7-19
Verifying the installation.

7.3.1 Installing SQL Server 2000 to Multiple Nodes

If you choose to configure your cluster as an active/active SQL Server—meaning you have two separate instances of SQL Server running on each node within the cluster—you must run the setup for SQL Server 2000 from the CD-ROM on the second node after completing the installation on the first node.

There is not much difference between installing SQL Server 2000 to the first node and installing it to the second node, but there are a few things you should know about. First, you must create a named instance of SQL Server on the second machine. You cannot create a default server installation on the second node. To do so would cause failure on one node after a failover occurs, because one server cannot host two default instances.

When asked which disk you wish to install the SQL Server 2000 instance on, you must choose a shared disk that is different than the disk chosen in the first installation. Two installations on two separate machines cannot share the same hard disk.

Also, once installation is complete on the second node, be sure to configure your groups with a preferred owner, and select the Allow Failback option so that you can be sure that both databases do not run on the same machine indefinitely following a failure.

7.4 Managing an SQL Server Cluster

Learning to manage an SQL Server cluster is in many ways as important as building it. You may be familiar with SQL Server administration, but an SQL Server running on a cluster is a different type of installation that requires a better understanding of the features.

7.4.1 SQL Tools

If you are familiar with previous version of SQL Server, then the coverage of the following tools will make sense. If you are new to SQL Server, it is recommended that you pick up a book on SQL Server 2000 to become more familiar with the Database Administration Tools before proceeding through this section.

7.4.1.1 Enterprise Manager

Using Enterprise Manager to manage a clustered SQL Server is not much different than using it on a standalone server. However, there are a few items to be aware of.

When you are registering a server within Enterprise Manager, it important that you specify the virtual cluster name, not the name of the local node. To register your server, open Enterprise Manager and right-click on the **SQL Server Group**, then click **New SQL Server Registration...** If the SQL Server Registration wizard pops up, click the box that will allow you to register your SQL Server manually, and then click **Next**.

In the Registered SQL Server Properties dialogue (see Figure 7-20), type the name of the virtual server you wish to manage. If it is a particular instance

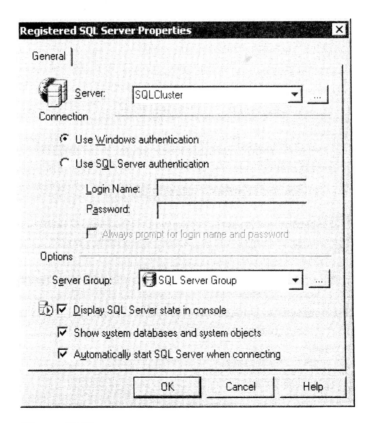

Figure 7-20
SQL Server registration.

of SQL Server, make sure to type the name and the instance (i.e., *server-name\instance*). Click the **Use Windows authentication** option (you should be logged in as administrator). Then click **OK** to add the server.

It is important that all SQL Server instances hosted on the cluster server share the same service account. Failover, full text searches, and other options will not work properly if these accounts are not the same. If you find that you must change the service account password, be sure to change the password through Enterprise Manager rather than through the Control Panel | Services option. Using the Control Panel option will corrupt your SQL configuration.

Creating databases within Enterprise Manager will be consistent with non-clustered SQL Server administration, but will not allow you to view nonshared disks drives. The server you are managing is a virtual server and therefore will not allow databases to be created on the local drives.

If you encounter an SQL Server failover while administering a table or database through Enterprise Manager, you will receive a communication link failure. You will need to press Esc to exit from the Table/Database Design dialogue. This allows you to exit and undo the changes you were making to the table. If you try to run a query or save your table, you will receive only errors. Using the Esc key allows you to exit the interface and then re-enter it after authenticating to the new server.

Also be advised that when you stop the SQL service through Enterprise Manager, the cluster server will shut down the full text and SQL Agent resources as well. Unfortunately, it will not bring these resources online once the SQL service is online, so a manual start of those services is required.

7.4.1.2 Full Text Queries

Full text queries in a clustered server environment are not much different than in a standard SQL Server installation, with the following exceptions:

- An instance of SQL Server 2000 must run on the identical system account on all nodes within the cluster.

- You must make service account changes through Enterprise Manager, not through the Control Panel.

If you followed the instructions noted earlier with regard to installing SQL Server 2000 on a cluster, then you most likely chose a domain account as your SQL Server service account. This account must be the same on all nodes for the full text queries to operate correctly.

If you ever need to change the service account for any reason, be sure to change the account through Enterprise Manager, rather than through the

Control Panel | Services applet. The Enterprise Manager application is cluster-aware and will make the change to all nodes, while the Control Panel applet is not.

7.4.1.3 Service Control Manager

If you are familiar with SQL Server, then you have used the Service Control Manager. The SCM is the small icon at the bottom right of the task bar that allows you to start and stop SQL Server services. In previous versions of SQL Server, a cluster installation will remove the applet from the taskbar and require you to start and stop SQL Server services from the Cluster Administrator program only.

In SQL Server 2000, the applications used for the management of SQL Server are cluster-aware and will operate correctly on the cluster, so starting and stopping the cluster services, as shown in Figure 7-21, are consistent with standard SQL Server practices.

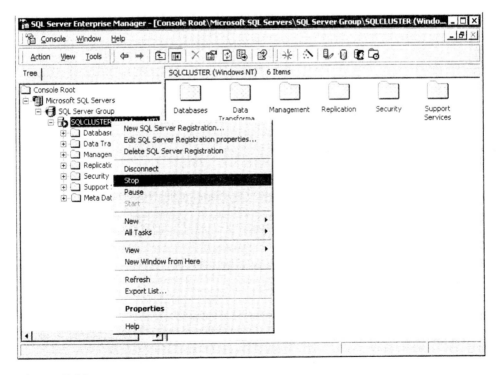

Figure 7-21
Starting and stopping the SQL Server service.

7.4.1.4 SQL Profiler and SQL Query Analyzer

Running SQL Profiler and Query Analyzer on a clustered server is consistent with standard SQL installations; just keep in mind the following items:

- Both applications require that you connect to the server using the virtual network name, not the individual server names.
- Interruption of service due to a failover while a trace or query is being executed will require the trace or query to be rerun when the new server is online.

7.4.1.5 SQL Mail

Configuring SQL Mail for SQL Server has always been a difficult task due to its reliance upon the local Messaging Applications Programming Interface (MAPI) profiles (which often are not even installed on a server). To configure SQL Mail for a clustered server, the same requirements apply.

- Make sure that all instances of SQL Server are running the same service account for service startup.
- Configure a MAPI profile on each node within the cluster that shares an identical profile name and settings.

7.4.2 Cluster Administrator

The Cluster Administrator is the tool used within Windows 2000 to manage cluster groups and resources. On the previous version of SQL Server, all administration of the SQL Server services had to be done through the Cluster Administrator. Due to great enhancements to the SQL Server 2000 product line, all SQL Server administration tools, such as Enterprise Manager, Service Manager, and Query Analyzer, are now cluster-aware and can be used to manage the SQL services. However, if you still wish to use the Cluster Administrator to start and stop services, you are more than able to do so.

The Cluster Administrator can be used to take resources offline (thus stopping the service). To do so, navigate within the Cluster Administrator to the resource you wish to shut down, right-click on the resource, and select **Take offline**. This will shut down the service. To bring the service back online, right-click the resource and select **Bring online**.

Note

If you shut down the SQL Server service, the Cluster Administrator will shut down the SQL Server Agent and SQL Server Full Text Search services due to dependencies that exist between the services. Once you bring the SQL Server service online, you will have to bring the other two services online in like manner. The Cluster Administrator will not start the services automatically.

7.4.3 Command-Line Options

If you manage your servers remotely, it is likely that you use terminal server or telnet to manage the server. Using terminal server is not any different than managing the server from the console, but if you use telnet, you need to be aware of some of the restrictions.

Telnet offers a command-line interface to the server; however, you are not working on a virtual server, but on a node within the cluster. Commands you use to start and stop the SQL Server services must be cluster-aware. To ensure you do not corrupt your configuration, you must use the *cluster.exe* commands to start and stop the SQL Server services. cluster.exe is a command line administration tool included with the cluster installation.

The syntax for the *cluster.exe* command is as follows:

```
CLUSTER [clustername] RESOURCE [resourcename] /option
```

You can use the `/online` and `/offline` options to start and stop the SQL Server service from the command prompt. For instance, to stop a running instance of SQL Server you would use

```
CLUSTER "sqlcluster" RESOURCE "sqlserver" /offline
```

Do not under any circumstance use the `net start` and `net stop` options for starting or stopping SQL services running on a cluster server. These commands are not cluster-aware and may corrupt your installation.

7.5 Summary

SQL Server 2000 is a powerful relational database system that provides enterprise class data storage for applications. Used in conjunction with the MSCS found within the Windows 2000 Advanced Server and Windows 2000 Datacenter Server operating systems, SQL Server 2000 can provide high reliability and fault tolerance suitable for any enterprise application.

Chapter 8

CLUSTERING EXCHANGE SERVER 2000

The Internet was started in an effort to share information between geographically separated sites. There is no one application more responsible for the Internet than email—or electronic mail. What started as electronic mail—short text messages sent from one computer to another—has grown into an industry known as messaging. Messaging now includes message transfer, scheduling, calendars, meeting planning, video mail, instant messaging, and workgroup collaboration. Although Microsoft came late to the table with Microsoft Mail, it has more than made up for the tardiness through the advent of Exchange Server. Over the past few years, Exchange Server has managed to supplant the gods of messaging from their thrones and gain an ever-increasing market share of the messaging pie.

Microsoft Exchange Server 2000 includes a vast array of functionality that has rocketed Microsoft even further toward its goal of complete market domination, with more and more companies migrating from Lotus Notes-based and Novell Groupwise-based email systems. To accent the previous Exchange service offering of advanced messaging and robust protocol support, Exchange Server 2000 adds a conference server as well as an instant messaging server to its arsenal of power-packed features.

As companies begin to migrate their email environment to Microsoft Exchange, more and more they are seeking ways to ensure its fault tolerance and stability for their enterprise. Previous versions of Exchange Server have sought to meet this need through clustering, but have fallen short of the vision. The new implementation of Exchange Server 2000, however, is more consistent with that vision and is built with clustering in mind. Not only does Exchange Server 2000 install and configure easier than ever on a cluster server, but it allows better administration through integrated tools and smoother failover.

8.1 Overview of Exchange Server Clustering

Prior to installing Exchange Server 2000 Enterprise Edition on any system, there are a few prerequisites that must be met. Exchange Server 2000 requires the NNTP (Network News Transport Protocol) service and the SMTP (Simple Mail Transfer Protocol) service. The SMTP service is typically installed by default, but the NNTP service is only installed as an option within the IIS (Internet Information Server) installation. You can view your installed services by clicking **Start**, **Settings**, **Control Panel**, **Administrative Tools**, and then **Services**.

Exchange Server 2000 clustering has been reengineered to run on Windows 2000 Advanced Server clusters more efficiently and problem-free than ever. As you may remember about earlier versions of Exchange, the setup routine installed a full set of binaries and data files to the shared drive storage and a subset of the Exchange utilities to the failover node.

The new installation takes advantage of locally stored binaries, utilizing the cluster nodes' ability to fail over to a locally installed program on either node. The setup routine is now cluster-aware and installs only binaries (executables) during the installation. Once setup is complete on one server, the other server runs through the same setup routine. This installs a local copy of the executable files on each server.

Note

Because the binaries are stored locally now, it is imperative that the path to the binaries is identical on both nodes. It is recommended that you do not change the default path, to ensure consistency, but if you must change the path, make sure you change the path on both installations.

The database files, contrary to how they were installed on previous versions, are not placed on the shared disk array during setup. The setup program installs binaries only during installation. To setup the database, you must create several cluster resources within the cluster disk group allotted for the Exchange install. After creating several resources (which you will do later in this chapter), you will create the Microsoft Exchange System Attendant. Once you start the created resource, the Microsoft Exchange System Attendant will automatically create the Exchange datastore and necessary transaction logs to host the clustered database.

8.2 Designing an Exchange Server 2000 Cluster

Before you launch into a complete cluster implementation of Exchange Server 2000, take a moment to review your plan. You should look at the following questions to make sure you know exactly how you will be implementing Exchange 2000 in your enterprise:

- Is your Exchange cluster a new server within an existing organization?
- Will your Exchange server need to communicate with other Exchange servers?
- Will users on the Internet need to access your Exchange server?
- What type of clients will connect to your Exchange server?
- How much space will you need to store your company's mail?
- Will you utilize multiple data stores?

In addition to these general questions, you will need to decide the following technical issues:

- What IP address will be used for the virtual Exchange server?
- What network name will be used for the virtual Exchange server?
- What will the Exchange organization be called?
- How will you integrate the clustered Exchange server into an existing Exchange organization?

All of these questions should be answered before undertaking a clustered Exchange server project, not because you cannot select these names as you go along, but more because the building of an Exchange cluster is sometimes tedious and you want to be able to concentrate completely upon the implementation. Hunting for unused IP addresses or server names should be done prior to the install, not during.

The most important requirement, however, is that you have the proper software. To build an Exchange Server cluster, you will need the Windows 2000 Advanced Server (or Windows 2000 Datacenter Server) operating system installed on all nodes within the cluster. You will need clustering to be installed and fully functional. Be sure to check the event viewer for error messages that may need to be resolved prior to the installation. If your cluster is not functioning correctly, there is a good chance your Exchange cluster will not either.

Note

Although Windows 2000 Datacenter Server now supports up to four nodes within a cluster server, Exchange 2000 Enterprise edition supports only two node clusters. Expanding this to a multiple node cluster scenario is planned for future releases.

You will need one available disk group to install your databases on, as well as the Exchange Server 2000 Enterprise Edition CD-ROM. If you made notes in a previous chapter detailing IP addresses and network names, be sure to have them handy.

Note

Only the Exchange Server 2000 Enterprise Edition supports clustering. The Exchange Server 2000 standard version will not run on a clustered server. Further references to Exchange Server 2000 within this chapter signify Exchange Server 2000 Enterprise Edition unless noted otherwise.

8.3 Installing Exchange Server 2000

Installing Exchange Server 2000 on a cluster is a five-step process. First you must install required components. Then you must configure Active Directory using the ForestPrep and DomainPrep configuration options. Once the Active Directory has been configured, you must install the cluster-aware Exchange

Server 2000 on both nodes within your cluster. Finally, you must configure all of the cluster resources, enabling them to create and configure the Microsoft Exchange datastore.

8.3.1 Installing IIS Components

To install the necessary IIS components, select **Start**, **Settings**, **Control Panel**, then **Add/Remove Programs**. Click on the **Windows Components** button on the left to access the Windows Components dialogue (see Figure 8-1). Scroll down to the **Internet Information Services (IIS)** option, click on it, and select **Details**.

Within the Internet Information Services options, scroll down and ensure that the **SMTP Service** is checked, along with the **NNTP Service** (see Figure 8-2), then click **OK**.

If you have installed terminal services in the past, you may need to verify the type of terminal server installation mode you wish to use (see Figure 8-3). Click the appropriate selection and click **Next**.

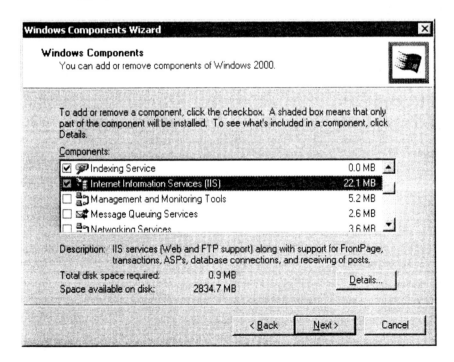

Figure 8-1
Installing IIS components.

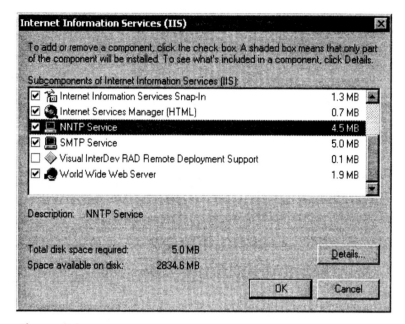

Figure 8-2
Installing NNTP and SMTP.

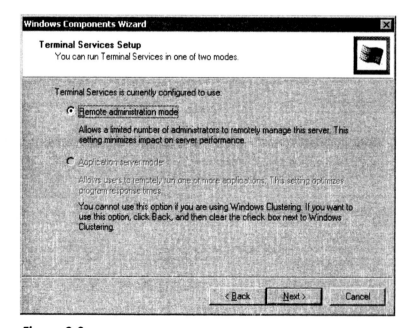

Figure 8-3
Configuring terminal services.

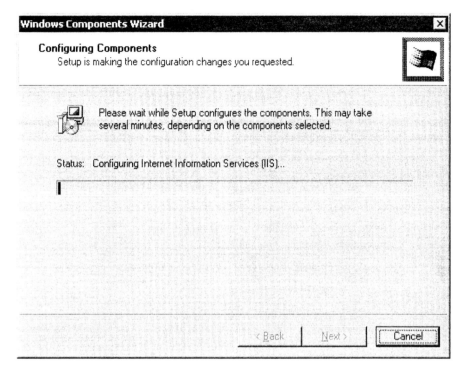

Figure 8-4
Configuring components.

Windows will begin installing the selected components (see Figure 8-4). This could take several minutes, depending on the options you have selected.

Once the setup has completed, the Windows Component wizard will notify you that you have successfully completed the installation (see Figure 8-5). If for any reason your installation fails, uninstall the entire IIS package, restart your computer, and then reinstall the selected components. The Exchange XML/HTML components are dependent upon a clean installation of IIS so that the necessary components can be installed and configured.

Once the wizard has completed, click **Finish** (see Figure 8-5). Although a restart is not required, it is recommended before moving to the next step.

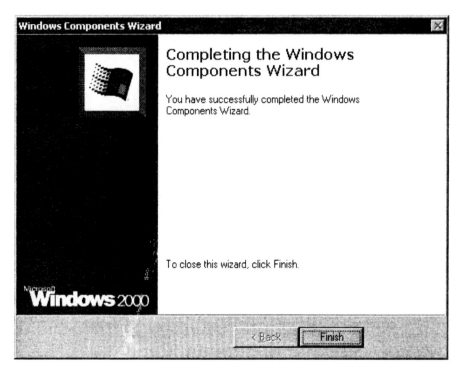

Figure 8-5
Completing the Windows Components wizard.

8.3.2 Exchange ForestPrep Installation

The next part of the Exchange 2000 installation is called the ForestPrep. This process allows the Exchange Server 2000 Wizard to modify the existing Active Directory forest configuration, preparing it to host the Exchange 2000 objects and properties. Remember Exchange 2000 is fully integrated with Active Directory, and therefore it is critical that the ForestPrep installation be run prior to installing it.

To run the ForestPrep installation, place your Exchange 2000 CD-ROM in the CD-ROM drive and click **Start**, then **Run**, and type the following command:

```
CD_Drive_Letter:\setup\i386\setup.exe /forestprep
```

This will begin the ForestPrep installation (see Figure 8-6). The wizard that appears will lead you to believe that you are installing Exchange 2000, but if

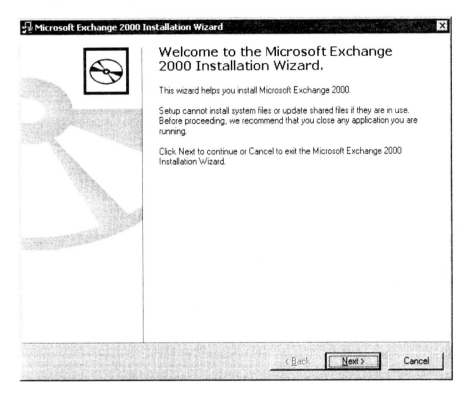

Figure 8-6
Beginning forestprep install.

you used the /forestprep switch correctly, then you are doing a Forest-Prep install only, which actually does not install files to the local drive.

Click **Next** to continue. You will then be presented with an end-user license agreement (see Figure 8-7). Read the license agreement in its entirety and then select the **I Agree** option. Then click **Next** to continue.

The next screen prompts you for a product information key (see Figure 8-8). Obtain the key from your software media or license and type it in the space provided. Click **Next** when you are finished.

The next screen will show you the Component Selection dialogue (see Figure 8-9). In most installations of this kind, this is where you would make changes to the installed components by selecting what you want and deselecting what you don't want. Because this is a ForestPrep installation and not the Exchange install, you must accept the default. You should notice that to the left of the Microsoft Exchange 2000 component listing, there is an option that

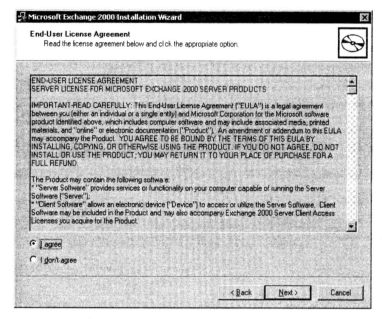

Figure 8-7
Microsoft Exchange Licensing Agreement.

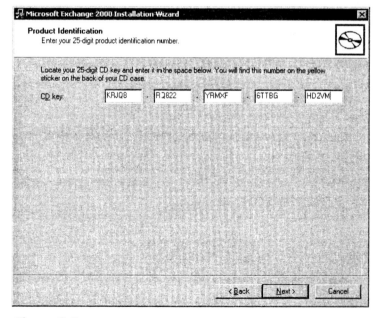

Figure 8-8
Entering product information key.

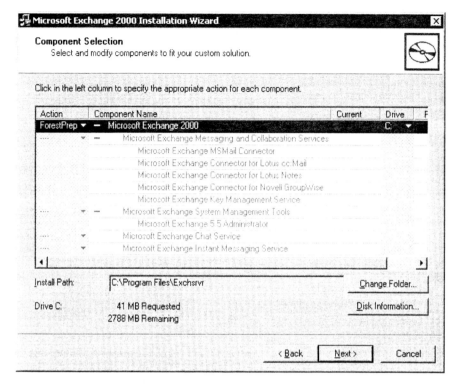

Figure 8-9
Selecting components.

says ForestPrep. If this option does not say ForestPrep, then you are not performing a ForestPrep install and you must exit the program and follow the earlier instructions to begin a ForestPrep install.

Click **Next** to continue the installation. If this is the first Exchange 2000 Server to be placed within your domain, a dialogue will ask you to choose whether you want a new organization or you want to join an existing Exchange 5.5 organization. If you already have Exchange 2000 Server running within this domain, the setup will skip this step, assuming that you want to add the new server to the existing organization.

Warning

If you have an existing Exchange 2000 organization within the same domain as the cluster servers, the wizard will automatically make the new server part of the same organization. For the cluster configuration of Exchange 2000 (which will be done later) to succeed, you must add the cluster service account to the existing Exchange 2000 organization as an administrator. If the cluster service account does not have this privilege, you will receive an error message that says, "An unknown error has occurred. Facility: Win32 ID no: c0075000 Microsoft Exchange Cluster Administrator Extension" during the cluster configuration.

Select **Create a new Exchange Organization** if you do not have an existing Exchange 5.5 organization (see Figure 8-10). This will allow you to create a new Exchange organization.

On the next screen, type in a name for your organization (see Figure 8-11). It is imperative that you remember this name for later reference. It is not as important to the Exchange installation or administration of the Exchange Server as it is to the recovery options that would be necessary in the event of a catastrophic failure. Many administrators do not document these items because they know they have easy access to them through the Active Directory or Exchange System Manager. However, if the server is down or failed in some

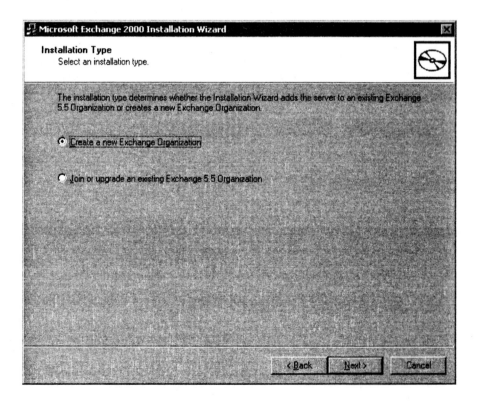

Figure 8-10
Creating a new organization.

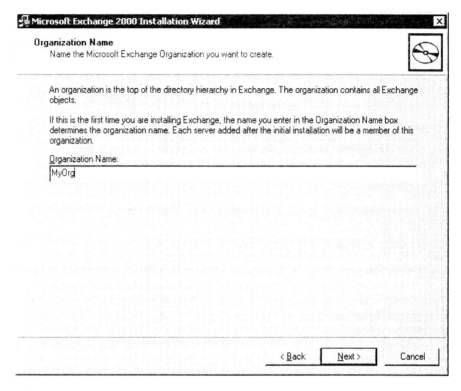

Figure 8-11
Naming/joining the organization.

way, access to this information will be restricted, and it may be needed to rebuild your Exchange database from a backup. Be sure to document your configuration prior to bringing the Exchange Server online. Once you have named the organization, select **Next** to continue.

The Exchange administrator account is the account within the domain that is assigned full administrative rights to the Exchange Server configuration. This account will be the user that assigns rights to other users within the organization. It is recommended that if your organization uses Enterprise Admins for delegation of network privileges, this account be a part of the Enterprise Admin group. Type in the domain and username of the administrator to whom you would like to assign complete rights to the Exchange organization (see Figure 8-12) and select **Next** to continue.

As the install begins, you will be notified that Exchange has recognized that you are running setup on a cluster server and that it will run the cluster-aware version of Microsoft Exchange (see Figure 8-13). Click **OK** to begin the installation.

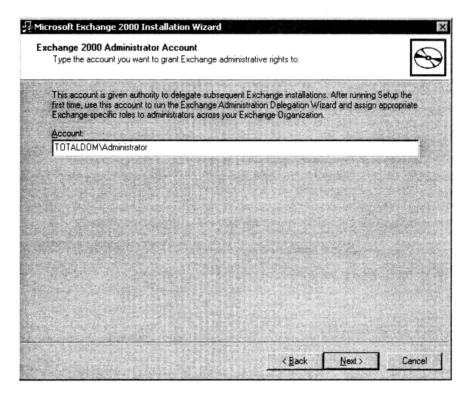

Figure 8-12
Assigning the Exchange Administrator.

As the installation begins (see Figure 8-14) you will see the progress bar as well as the operations that the install is performing. During this process, the installation will configure registry entries, modify schema attributes of the Active Directory, and prepare the forest to host Exchange Server 2000.

The wizard will inform you when installation is complete (see Figure 8-15). Click **Finish** to continue.

Figure 8-13
Cluster-aware notification.

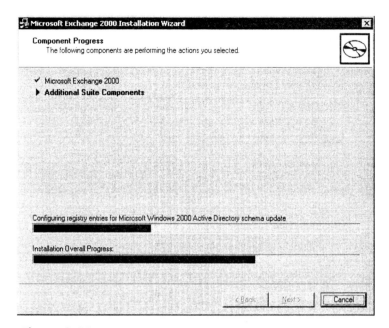

Figure 8-14
Installing components.

Figure 8-15
Completing the Exchange 2000 Installation wizard.

8.3.3 Exchange DomainPrep Install

The next step towards an Exchange Server 2000 cluster is to modify the current domain to prepare it for the Exchange installation. This is accomplished by running the same setup you did in the last section, but omitting the /forestprep option and adding a /domainprep option. This tells the Exchange Server 2000 installation that you have completed the forest preparation and you are ready to install Exchange Server 2000 within the domain. To begin the install, click **Start**, **Run**, and type the following command:

```
CD_Drive_Letter:\setup\i386\setup.exe /domainprep
```

This will begin the DomainPrep installation. Once the Exchange 2000 Installation wizard begins, click **Next** to continue (see Figure 8-16).

The next screen reveals the Microsoft license agreement for Exchange Server (see Figure 8-17). Read the license agreement in its entirety and select the **I agree** option. Then click **Next**.

The wizard requests a product identification key to continue (see Figure 8-18). Enter the product identification key included with your software and click **Next** to continue.

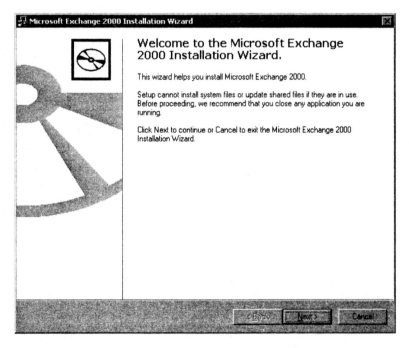

Figure 8-16
Beginning DomainPrep install.

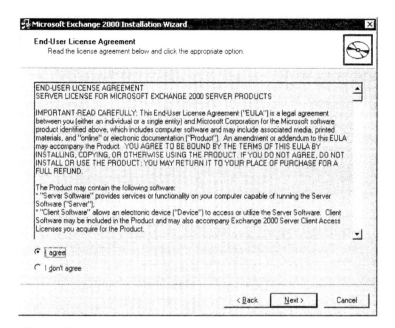

Figure 8-17
Microsoft license agreement.

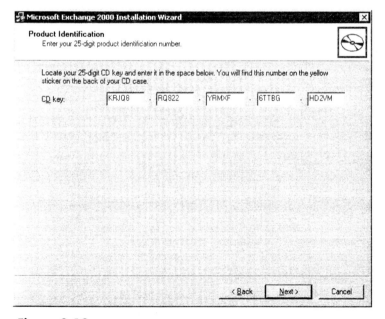

Figure 8-18
Entering product information key.

In the Component Selection dialogue (see Figure 8-19), verify that the action listed for the Microsoft Exchange 2000 component is DomainPrep. If it is not, then the command line used to start the installation was typed incorrectly. If this is the case, cancel setup and start it again using the command line specified earlier. If the action does say DomainPrep, then you can continue the installation. Press **Next** to continue.

The Exchange 2000 installation will detect that you are running the installation on a cluster and will notify you that it will install the cluster-aware version of Microsoft Exchange (see Figure 8-20).

The security warning that pops up will inform you that allowing members to reside within the pre-Windows 2000 servers and applications group is insecure, and all users should be removed from this group to secure your mailboxes (see Figure 8-21). If you did a full install of Windows 2000 on the server that hosts the Active Directory, chances are there are no members within this group and this message can be ignored. If you upgraded from a previous version of

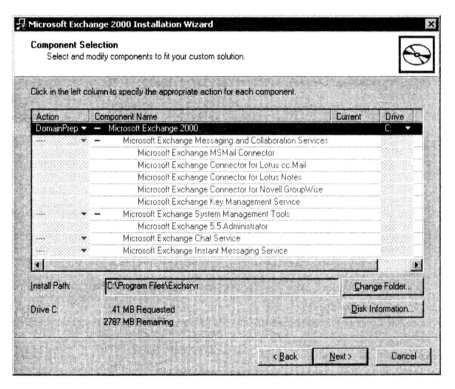

Figure 8-19
Component selection.

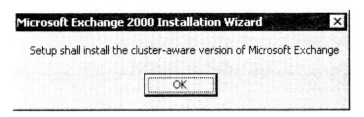

Figure 8-20
Cluster-aware notification.

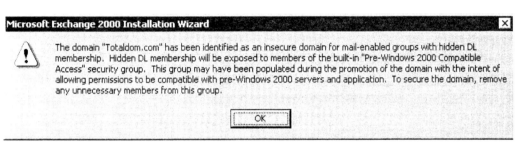

Figure 8-21
Domain security warning.

Windows NT, then you may want to check the group to ensure that the membership is empty. Click **OK** to continue.

The Exchange 2000 Component Progress dialogue reveals the installation process (see Figure 8-22). Much like the ForestPrep install, files are not being copied to the disk at this time. The DomainPrep installation is preparing the domain for the installation of Exchange Server 2000 by modifying permissions on certain objects within the directory. This install should take significantly less time that the ForestPrep install.

When the DomainPrep install finishes, the wizard will inform you that the installation is complete (see Figure 8-23). Press **Finish** to proceed.

8.3.4 Installing Exchange Server

Now that you have completed the ForestPrep and DomainPrep installations, you are ready to install Exchange Server on all nodes within the cluster. Place the CD-ROM in the first node and click **Start**, and then **Run**. Type the following command to begin the Exchange 2000 installation:

```
CD_Drive_Letter:\setup\i386\setup.exe
```

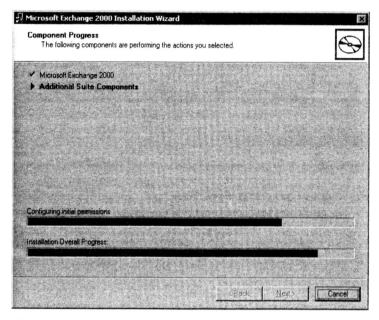

Figure 8-22
Component installation.

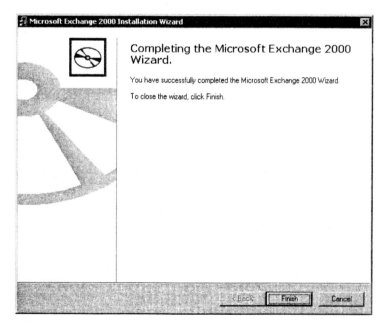

Figure 8-23
Completing the Exchange 2000 Installation wizard.

This will begin the Exchange 2000 Installation wizard. Click **Next** at the startup screen to begin the installation (see Figure 8-24).

Review the license agreement (see Figure 8-25). Assuming you have already read this twice (due to the previous DomainPrep and ForestPrep installs), click the **I agree** option and then **Next** to continue the installation.

In the Product Identification dialogue, locate and enter the key number into the fields presented (see Figure 8-26). Then click **Next** to continue.

In the Exchange 2000 Component Selection dialogue, click the down arrow next to Microsoft Exchange 2000 and select **Typical** (see Figure 8-27). This will enable the Microsoft Exchange Messaging and Collaboration Services as well as the Microsoft Exchange System Management Tools. If you need to select tools or components outside of the typical install, such as the Chat service or the Connector for Lotus Notes, click **Custom** instead of **Typical** and modify the action next to those components to **Install**. If you do select alternate components, make sure that you install the identical set of components on the other nodes within the cluster.

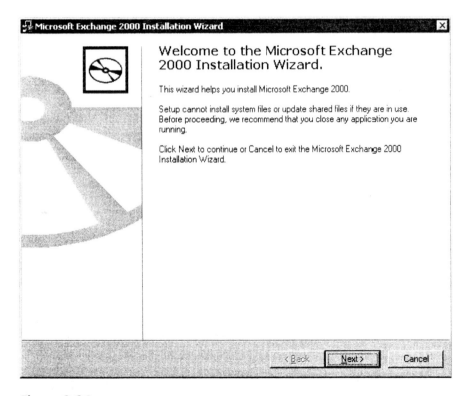

Figure 8-24
Installing Microsoft Exchange 2000.

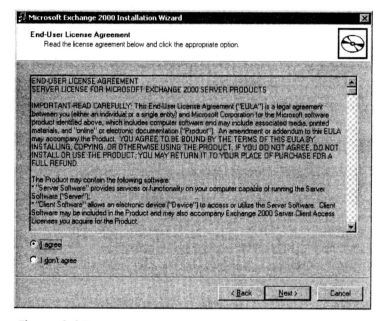

Figure 8-25
Exchange 2000 licensing agreement.

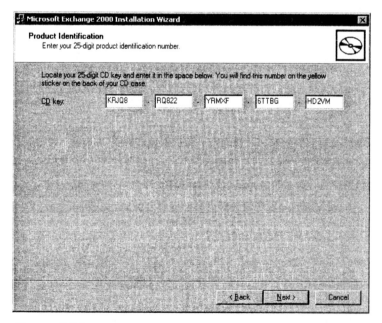

Figure 8-26
Entering product identification key.

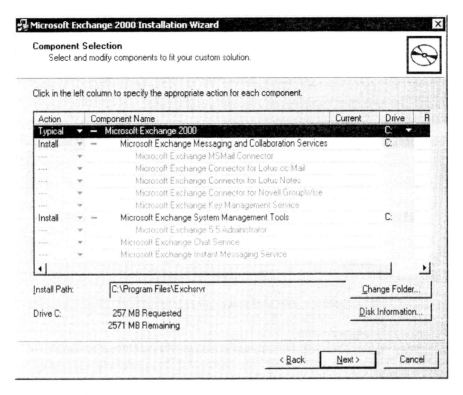

Figure 8-27
Exchange 2000 Component Selection.

The drive for all components should be set to the C: drive. As a cluster-aware installation, the wizard will not install database files, only binaries, which in Exchange Server 2000 are stored locally to each machine. The database files will be created later in the configuration.

Click **Next** to continue the installation.

The next screen presents a license agreement (see Figure 8-28). This agreement is different from the previous agreement, for it specifies that Exchange Server 2000 is licensed based on per seat licensing only. It is required that you purchases a client access license for every client that connects to the Exchange Server. Select the **I agree that I have read and agree to be bound by the license agreements for this product** option and select **Next**.

The Component Summary (see Figure 8-29) lists the components that you have selected for your installation. If the summary is incorrect, select the **Back** key to change your settings; otherwise, press the **Next** key to continue.

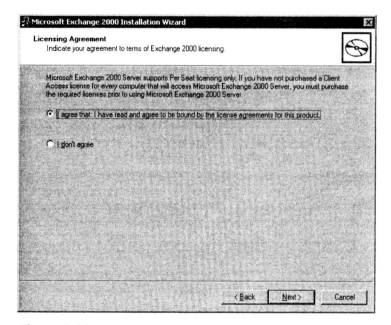

Figure 8-28
Per Seat Licensing Agreement.

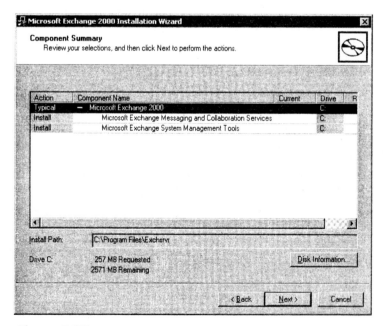

Figure 8-29
Exchange 2000 Component Summary.

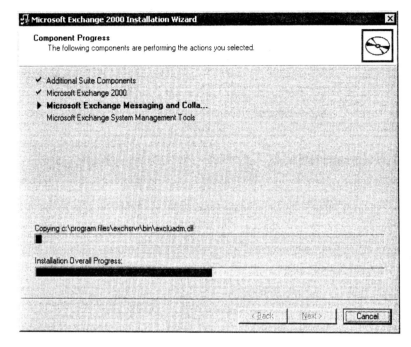

Figure 8-30
Installing Exchange 2000 components.

The Exchange 2000 Installation wizard copies all of the files necessary to run Exchange Server 2000 on the local computer (see Figure 8-30). No database files or message stores are copied at this time.

The wizard will request that you reboot your computer after the installation of Exchange Server and proceed to the cluster administrator to complete the configuration of Exchange Server (see Figure 8-31). Click **OK** to continue.

Once the installation is complete (see Figure 8-32), select **Finish** to continue.

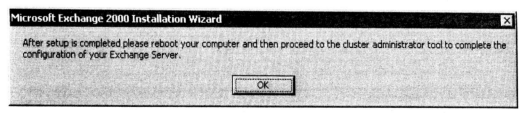

Figure 8-31
Reboot notification.

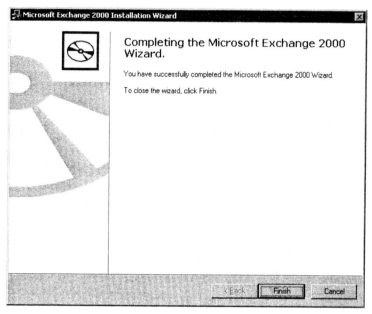

Figure 8-32
Completing the Exchange 2000 installation.

8.3.5 Installing Exchange Server 2000 to the Second Node

Once the installation of Exchange Server is complete on node 1, you need to repeat the process on the node 2. You do not, however, need to go through the ForestPrep or DomainPrep installs again. Just run the basic installation and configure the server identically to the previous node. Once installation is complete, reboot both nodes, one at a time.

8.3.6 Configuring Cluster Resources

Once you have Exchange Server installed on both nodes within the cluster, you have to create the necessary group and resources to host the Exchange services. Remember the Exchange installation was cluster-aware and therefore did not install database services to the machine. This step does not take place until the resources are correctly created and configured through the cluster administrator.

Make sure that both nodes have the Exchange Server software installed and that both have been restarted since the installation. If this is not the first Exchange Server in your organization, make sure that the user account that the cluster services use is assigned administrator privileges to the existing Exchange organization. The creation of Exchange databases will not work without this privilege in place.

To begin configuring the cluster resources for Microsoft Exchange, open cluster administrator, right-click on the **Groups** folder, and select **New**, then **Group** (see Figure 8-33).

In the New Group dialogue box (see Figure 8-34), type in the name of the new group and a description. This will be the group that will contain all of the Exchange cluster resources, so name the group Exchange Group or something similar. The description is only for labeling purposes and is an optional field.

Click **Next** to continue. The next dialogue asks you to select a preferred owner for the resource group (see Figure 8-35). This will be the server that you wish to run the services on in most situations. During a failure, the other nodes will be available but will not serve as a primary host for the application.

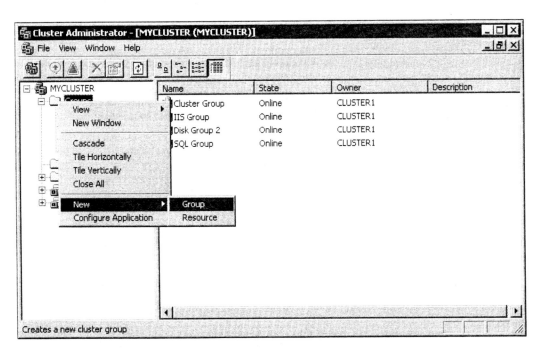

Figure 8-33
Creating an Exchange group.

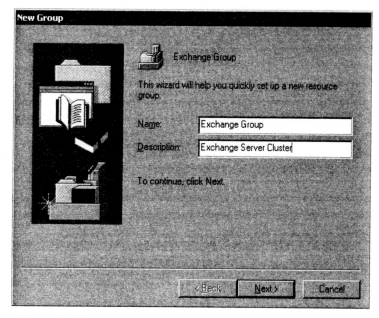

Figure 8-34
Naming the Exchange group.

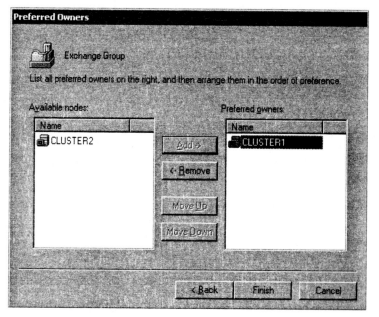

Figure 8-35
Selecting a preferred owner.

Click the server you would like to become the preferred server, select **Add** to add it to the preferred owners list, and click **Finish** to continue.

The next step is to create an IP address resource for the cluster. Each application should be contained within a disk group, and each disk group should house its own IP address. The IP address resource you create here will be the address of the Exchange virtual server you will create later.

To create an IP address resource, right-click on the disk group you created and select **New**, then **Resource** from the menu. In the New Resource dialogue, enter the name you wish to use to refer to the IP address resource you are creating (see Figure 8-36). It is recommended that your resources be named in a way that is descriptive of their function. For instance, you would not want to name a resource "resource1," for that is not very descriptive and would not allow you to recognize it for what it is. The suggested name is "Exchange IP Address."

Type a description for the resource to help you identify it in a list of resources. In the **Resource type:** field, select **IP Address** from the

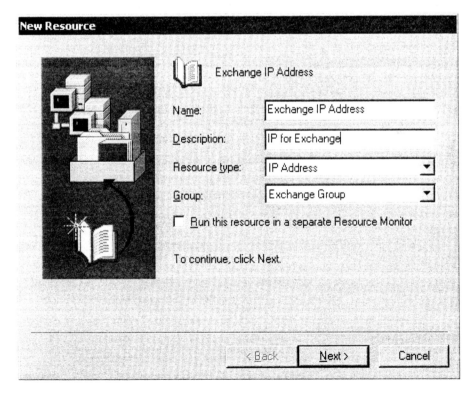

Figure 8-36
Configuring Exchange IP Address resource.

drop-down list. In the **Group:** field, make sure that the disk group you created is listed.

All resources you create can be run in a separate resource monitor if you choose, but this option is resource-intensive and should only be used when troubleshooting resource failures. Select **Next** to continue.

In the Possible Owners dialogue (see Figure 8-37), select the nodes within your cluster that may need to run the application you are creating in the event of a failure. Typically, this will include all nodes within your cluster; however, you may have a four-node cluster and choose to run Exchange on two nodes. In this case you would select the two nodes that you wish to be possible owners and select **Add** to add them to the list of possible owners. Click **Next** to continue.

The Dependencies dialogue is used to specify which resources must be brought online before the resource you are creating can be started (see Figure 8-38). Because this is an IP address resource, it has no dependencies and you can select **Next** to continue.

In the Parameter dialogue (see Figure 8-39), you are asked to supply an IP address to be used for the resource. Type in the IP address you choose to use. The subnet will be populated for you. Make sure the network connection that

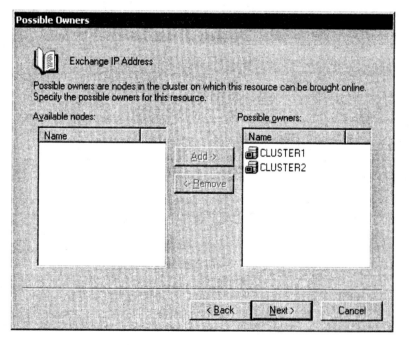

Figure 8-37
Selecting possible owners.

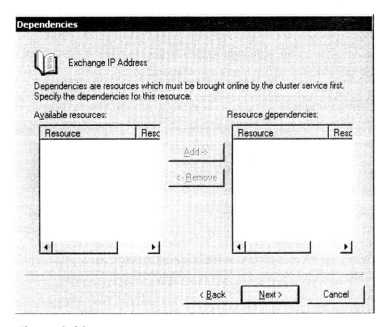

Figure 8-38
Citing dependencies.

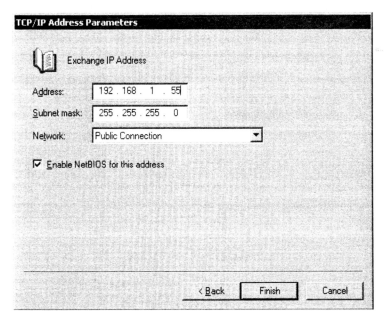

Figure 8-39
Setting IP address for Exchange virtual server.

allows connectivity to the clients is selected, and enable the **Enable NetBIOS for this address** option. Then click **Finish** to create the resource.

The next resource you need to create is the network name resource. This will be the NetBIOS name assigned to the IP address you created in the previous step. In the New Resource dialogue (see Figure 8-40), type in a name for the resource. This is only the name used within cluster administrator, not the actual network name to be used. Also type a description for your resource. Select **Network Name** as the resource type and make sure the group is set to the Exchange group you created earlier. Click **Next** to continue.

In the Possible Owners screen (see Figure 8-41), select the same nodes you selected for the IP address resource. Once you have selected the possible owners, click **Next** to continue.

In the Dependencies dialogue (see Figure 8-42), select the IP address resource you created earlier and then click **Add**. Obviously, you cannot bring a network name online without an IP address, so the IP address resource is a dependency of the network name resource. Click **Next** to continue.

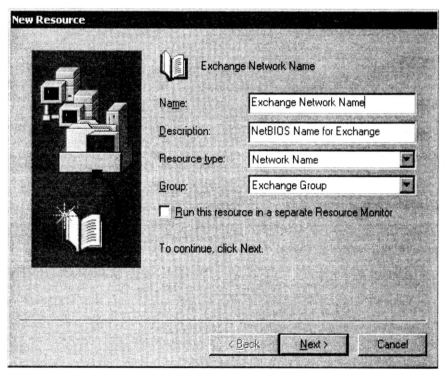

Figure 8-40
Creating the Exchange Network name resource.

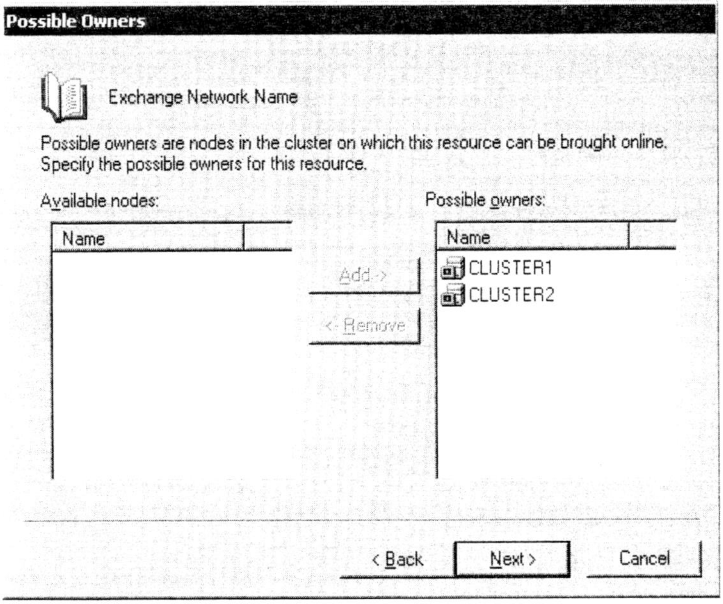

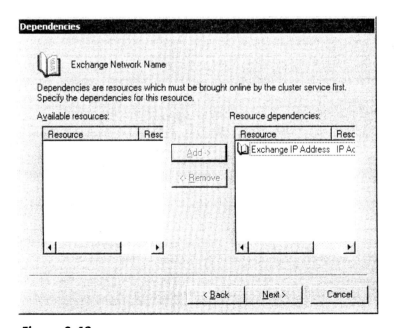

Figure 8-41
Selecting possible owners.

Figure 8-42
Citing dependencies.

In the Network Name Parameters dialogue (see Figure 8-43), type in a name that you would like to use for this resource. This will be the network name registered within DNS and WINS. This name should be no more than 14 characters long and should conform to the NetBIOS naming standards. Click **Finish** to complete the creation of the network name resource.

The next step is to move the shared disk resource from the default group to the new group you have created. When the cluster was built, the service should have assigned every shared disk to a disk group. At this time, locate the disk group that contains the disk resource you would like to use for the Exchange databases and transaction logs. With your mouse, left-click and drag the disk resource to the new group (see Figure 8-44).

Once you drop the disk resource onto the new group, you will be given a warning asking you to confirm the move from one disk group to another (see Figure 8-45). Select **Yes** to continue.

Once you have confirmed the move, another confirmation screen will pop up asking you to confirm the move once again (see Figure 8-46). Why there are two confirmations is a mystery, but obviously, moving disks from one group

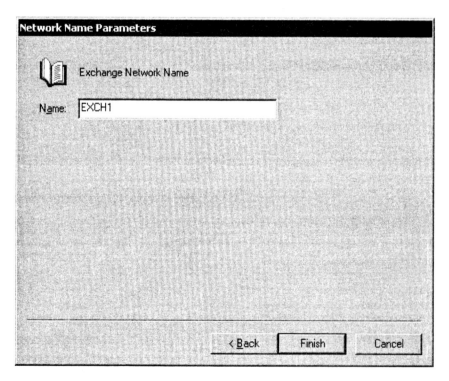

Figure 8-43
Naming the resource.

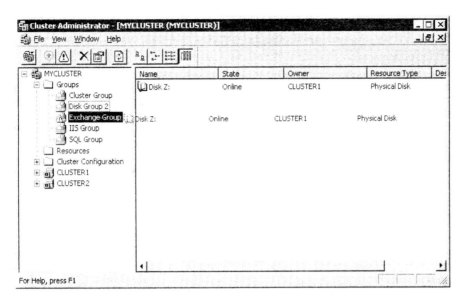

Figure 8-44
Moving the disk resource.

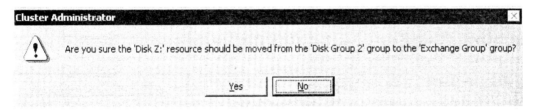

Figure 8-45
Disk move confirmation.

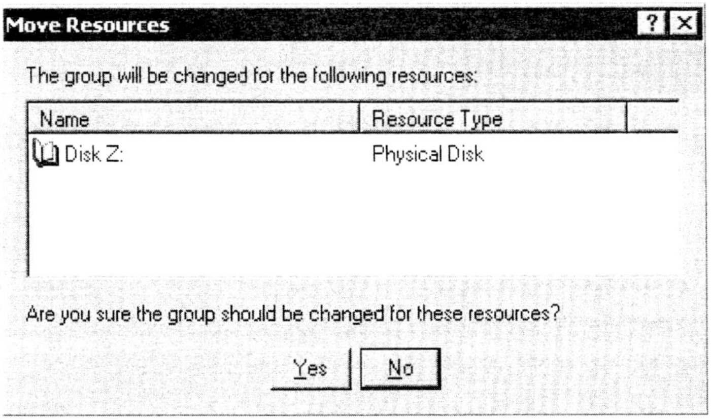

Figure 8-46
Disk move confirmation.

to another is not something to be taken lightly. Click **Yes** to confirm the move once again.

Now that the disk has been moved and you have created the IP address and network name resources, right-click on each resource and select **Bring Online**. The disk resource is most likely already online, but if it isn't, make sure to bring it online first. The IP address and network name resources should be brought online beginning with the IP address, then the network name resource.

The next resource to create is the Exchange System Attendant resource. This resource is unique because it will automate the creation of all the other resources necessary to run Exchange Server on your cluster.

Right-click the group once again and select **New**, then **Resource**. In the New Resource dialogue (see Figure 8-47) type the name of the new resource. It is recommended that you use "Exchange System Attendant" for the name

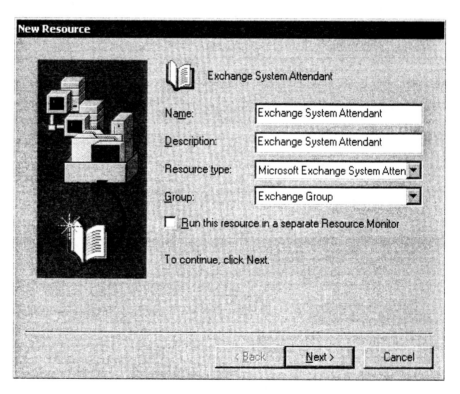

Figure 8-47
Creating the Exchange System Attendant resource.

to help keep all of the resources straight once they are created. Type in a description, select **Microsoft Exchange System Attendant** as the resource, and make sure the group selected is the Exchange group you created earlier. Click **Next** to continue.

In the Possible Owners dialogue (see Figure 8-48), select the nodes that you selected for the IP address and network name resource and click **Add** to add them to the list of possible owners. Click **Next** to continue.

In the Dependencies dialogue (see Figure 8-49), select the disk resource and the network name resource and click **Add** to add them to the dependencies lists. You do not need to add the IP address resource, for the network name resource already has an IP address dependency. Click **Next** to continue.

On the next screen, the path to the Exchange Server database files should default to *driveletter:\EXCHSRVR* (see Figure 8-50). If you wish to change this, feel free to do so, but be advised that the drive letter must reference the shared disk that is a part of the Exchange group. In other words, if the disk resource that you added to the resource group refers to Z:, then you cannot install the system attendant onto the X: drive.

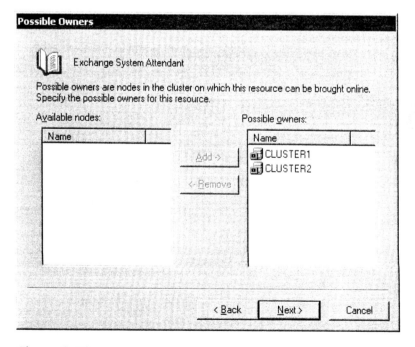

Figure 8-48
Selecting possible owners.

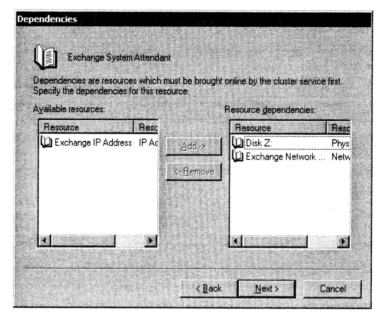

Figure 8-49
Citing dependencies.

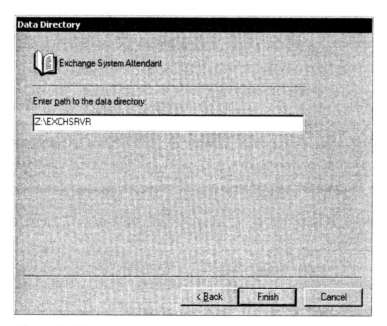

Figure 8-50
Entering data directory path.

Click **Finish** to complete the resource configuration. As the resource is created, it will immediately begin creating other resources and adding them to the group. The following resources should be created at this time:

- Exchange Information Store instance
- Exchange Message Transfer Agent instance
- Exchange Routing Service instance
- Exchange HTTP Virtual Server instance
- Exchange POP3 Virtual Server instance
- Exchange IMAP4 Virtual Server instance
- SMTP Virtual Server instance

Once the resources have been created, right-click on each resource, one at a time, and select **Bring Online** to start the Exchange services.

8.4 Managing Exchange Server 2000

Like other applications that run on a cluster, management of the Exchange Server is not much different than on a typical install. The following section recognizes the slight differences that may be present in the management of a clustered Exchange Server.

8.4.1 Active Directory Users and Computers

As part of the Exchange Server installation, Active Directory Users and Computers is installed on all nodes within the cluster. You can use Active Directory Users and Computers to add users and mailboxes to the new server.

One great advantage to this implementation of Exchange Server is that you do not have to run Active Directory Users and Computers on the machine that is hosting the shared disk for the application to create the user account and mailbox. Either node within the cluster can be used to add users.

Running Active Directory Users and Computers on other nodes besides the cluster nodes where Exchange Server is installed will not dynamically create the necessary mailboxes for each user created. If you run Active Directory

Users and Computers on a workstation or server where Exchange has not been installed, be sure to install the Microsoft Exchange System Management Tools.

8.4.2 System Manager

In most cases, the Exchange System Manager operates on an Exchange cluster in the same way it does on a nonclustered server. There are just a few things that you should consider.

- Do not create new virtual servers within System Manager.
- SMTP logging defaults to a local path.

Because Exchange 2000 uses HTTP virtual servers for Outlook Web Access, the creation of new virtual servers will cause the Outlook Web Access function to fail. As a general rule, do not create virtual servers on an Exchange Server.

Also, by default, the SMTP service logs activity to the *c:\winnt\system32\ logfiles* directory. For logging to work correctly on a clustered server, the logging must be done to a shared disk. Using the System Manager, you can change this value.

8.4.3 Using Outlook on Cluster Nodes

There are many occasions when an administrator might choose to install the Outlook client on a clustered Exchange Server 2000 node. Although it is safe to do so, there is one configuration that you should be aware of. According to Microsoft, installing Outlook on a cluster node will incorrectly modify the following registry key:

```
HKEY_LOCAL_MACHINE\SOFTWARE\Microsoft\Exchange\
Exchange Provider\Rpc_Binding_Order
```

The Outlook install changes the registry key value to `ncalrpc`, which causes the Schedule+ Free/Busy to stop working. To fix this problem, modify the registry key value to

```
ncacn_ip_tcp,ncacn_spx,ncacn_np,NetBIOS
```

Once this value is changed, the Schedule+ Free/Busy will work.

8.4.4 Command-Line Options

If you manage your servers remotely, it is likely that you use terminal server or telnet to manage the server. Using terminal server is not any different than managing the server from the console, but if you use telnet, you need to be aware of some of the restrictions.

Telnet offers a command line interface to the server; however, you are not working on a virtual server, but on a node within the cluster. Commands you use to start and stop the Exchange Server services must be cluster-aware. To ensure you do not corrupt your configuration, you must use the *cluster.exe* commands to start and stop the Exchange Server services. *Cluster.exe* is a command-line administration tool included with the cluster installation.

The syntax for the *cluster.exe* command is as follows:

```
CLUSTER [clustername] RESOURCE [resourcename] /option
```

You can use the `/online` and `/offline` options to start and stop the Exchange Server services from the command prompt. For instance, to stop a running instance of the Exchange SMTP virtual server instance, you would use

```
CLUSTER "mycluster" RESOURCE "SMTP Virtual Server" /offline
```

Do not under any circumstance use the `net start` and `net stop` options for starting or stopping service running on a cluster server. These commands are not cluster-aware and may corrupt your installation.

Chapter 9

CLUSTERING INTERNET INFORMATION SERVER

There are not many companies these days that are not running some type of Web site. Although not every company hosts its own Web site, they are all concerned about the Web sites' uptime and reliability. Guaranteeing uptime of WWW Servers has always been a problem for Web Hosting Providers (WHP), for fault tolerance is hard to achieve when hosting a $20 per month Web site—certainly a cost prohibitive endeavor. Many WHPs tout statistics such as 99.999 percent uptime, but in reality, this is just marketing. This type of fault tolerance requires not only fault-tolerant equipment within each server, but additional servers that can be used to replace a defunct server at any time.

This may be changing, for the advent of services like network load balancing and clustering are becoming more and more cost effective. Systems that used to cost several hundred thousands of dollars to implement can now be brought online for only a fraction of the cost. High availability is now available to anyone who chooses to put up a server. These tools provide low-cost alternatives to hardware-based clustering and load-balancing solutions. WHPs may choose not to use them, but it is not because these solutions lack the power or flexibility of their hardware-based cousins.

In this chapter we will take a look at Internet Information Server (IIS), a package of Internet-based services that is included with all Windows 2000 operating systems. The package includes a World Wide Web (WWW) Server,

299

a Network News Transfer Protocol (NNTP) server, a File Transfer Protocol (FTP) server, as well as a Simple Mail Transfer Protocol (SMTP) server. Using the Microsoft Clustering Service (MSCS), these applications can offer highly available Internet services.

9.1 IIS Overview

IIS was originally released by Microsoft as an add-on product for the Windows NT server operating system. It included several services that were used to provide Internet-based services such as WWW services and FTP services. IIS has grown quite a bit since its original implementation and has shown itself as a worthy opponent within the WWW Server market share battle. To date, IIS's market share is still growing daily, replacing many UNIX-based alternatives.

As a clustered application (or set of applications), IIS excels, allowing administrators to add a significant amount of fault tolerance to their implementations. Much like other clustered applications, IIS follows the binary-local/data-shared model, keeping local copies of the binaries that run the application and storing the data itself on the shared disk. Through the IIS resources created within the cluster administrator, service of a particular Web site can failover from one server to another.

Many people choose to load-balance applications like IIS due to the traffic they receive on their Web sites. That is a viable solution (which was discussed in Chapter 5, "Building a Load-Balanced Cluster"), but clustering is also a good solution. The choice of load balancing or clustering depends upon the circumstances. If you run a large Web site and you need to maintain millions of hits per day on a Web site that is mostly static (or static on the front end), then load balancing is a good choice for you. However, if your Web site does not have that volume of traffic and you wish to ensure that it never goes down, clustering is a good choice for you. Both solutions provide fault tolerance, but they are managed differently. Clusters share disk space with other nodes in the cluster, and therefore negate the need for synchronization between servers for Web content. If you have a site that is constantly being updated by programmers, then clustering may be the best choice. Otherwise, you have to figure out how to synchronize changes made on one server to all other servers in the load-balanced cluster.

In addition to the WWW service included with IIS is the FTP service. This service allows the transfer of files through file transfer protocol. FTP is widely used on the Internet for file storage, document indexes, and a system-independent way of transferring files from one place to another. All that is needed to connect to an FTP server is an FTP client, which is included with most operating systems. Clustering allows organizations that provide large amounts of files (like the Microsoft FTP site) to the masses in a way that is fault-tolerant.

SMTP is the standard language that mail servers speak to transfer mail from one domain to another. IIS includes an SMTP service for a couple of reasons. First, it allows Web sites created for the WWW service to send email through scripts. Second, SMTP can be used as a mail relay for existing domains to add some security to their networks. Email is critical to most organizations and has become more important than the fax machine in most offices. The SMTP server allows you to provide a secondary mail server for your domain so that if your mail server is not available for any reason, the secondary server will receive and queue your mail until your server is back online. Used in conjunction with MSCS, the SMTP relay service can be a valuable asset.

Through the next section you will learn how to cluster the WWW, FTP, and SMTP services. You have the choice of clustering one or all of the services to meet your needs.

9.2 Clustering the WWW Service

The WWW service is included with the IIS family. IIS used to be an add-on for Windows NT 4.0 and earlier operating systems, but has been included with the operating system installation since Windows 2000 Server was released. The WWW Server is a powerful way to host Internet, intranet, and extranet Web applications, for it supports ASP (Active Server Pages), XML, and CGI (Common Gateway Interface) scripting by default, and can easily be configured to support PERL, Cold Fusion, and other third-party products.

By clustering the WWW service, you run two separate physical instances of a Web site, which appear to the users as one site. Unlike load balancing you may have learned about in an earlier chapter, clustering stores the data in one place on the shared disk array, so synchronization of data is not necessary. You do, however, have to synchronize the configuration of the WWW Server between all nodes, but this can be done manually or through an automated tool.

Before installing your Web cluster, there are a few prerequisites that you should meet. First, the Microsoft Distributed Transaction Coordinator (MS DTC) service must be running as a cluster resource if you choose to support transactions within your Web site. Second, the Web directory must be created on the shared disk. The next section will walk you through this process.

9.2.1 Prerequisites for the WWW Server

If you choose to support transactions through your Web site, then you will need the MS DTC service, an application that allows programmers to code transactions within their applications. Luckily, Microsoft has included a tool with the cluster installation that automates the installation of MS DTC within your cluster.

To install MS DTC in your cluster, open a command prompt and type *comclust.exe* (see Figure 9-1). This will install the MS DTC resource into the same group as the Quorum resource. You will receive an error stating that the server is not a component load-balancing server. This error can safely be ignored.

Once the *comclust.exe* program completes, run the program on every node within the cluster. This will ensure that the proper registry entries are made within each node.

Note

If you need to uninstall the MS DTC for any reason, you can run the com-clust.exe program with the -r attribute. This will uninstall the application.

Once you have completed configuring the MS DTC on each machine, open Windows Explorer and create a Web directory on the shared disk that you wish to use for your Web site. You can use any name you wish; just make sure it does not contain invalid characters (see Figure 9-2).

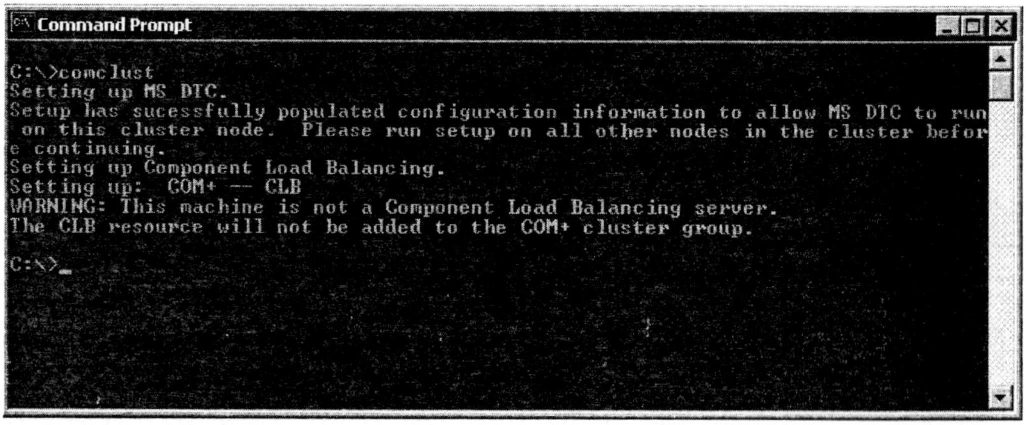

Figure 9-1
Installing MS DTC.

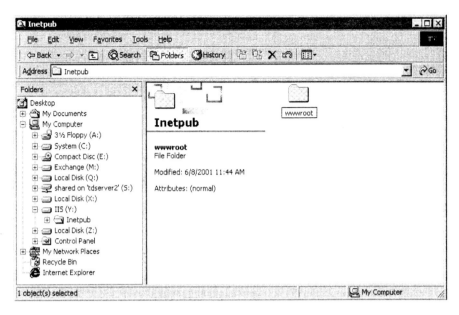

Figure 9-2
Creating the Web directory.

Once the directory is created, add two new documents to the directory by right-clicking in the right window and clicking **New**, and then **Text Document**. Name the files *default.htm* and *default.asp* (see Figure 9-3).

Once the directory and default documents are created, you are ready to proceed with the cluster resource installation and configuration.

9.2.2 Installing the Virtual WWW Server

Open the cluster administrator and select the disk group you wish to use for the virtual WWW Server. Right-click on the disk group and select **New** then **Resource**. Type in the name you would like to use for the TCP/IP resource, along with a description (see Figure 9-4). Under Resource type, select **IP Address** and select **Next**.

The next screen is the Possible Owners screen. By default, all nodes within the cluster are listed under Possible Owners. If there are any nodes that you do not want to host the resource in the event of a failure, click on that node and select **Remove** to have it removed from the list (see Figure 9-5). Click **Next** to continue.

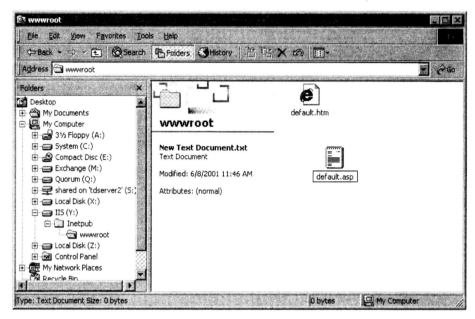

Figure 9-3
Creating default documents.

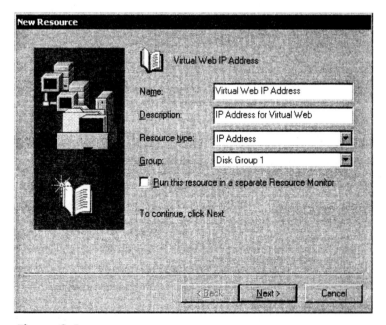

Figure 9-4
Adding TCP/IP resource.

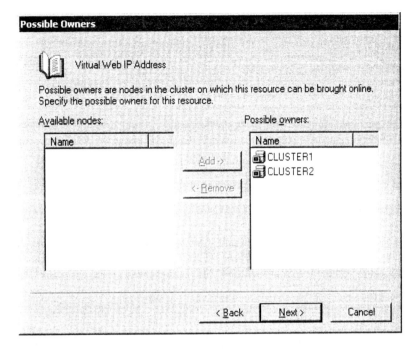

Figure 9-5
Configuring possible owners.

In the Dependencies dialogue, select the disk resource that is listed. In reality, the IP address is not dependent upon the disk, but you do want to bring the IP address online if the disk is not available, so making the IP address dependent upon the disk is a valid option. Click on the disk and select **Add** to have it added to the dependency list (see Figure 9-6). Click **Next** to continue.

The next screen allows you to assign an IP address to this resource (which makes sense, since it is an IP address resource). Type in the IP address you wish to use for your virtual WWW Server (see Figure 9-7). This address will be bound to the network card automatically as soon as the resource is brought online. It is not necessary to manually add it to the network configuration. The subnet will be populated automatically.

Make sure the **Public Connection** is the network that is selected, for advertising an IP address on the private network connection will not make much sense. The enable NetBIOS option allows the NetBIOS naming to be used for the address. If you are running this WWW Server to host an internal application and you need to access the server through a name resolved by

305

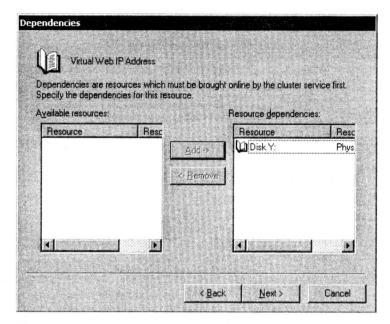

Figure 9-6
Citing dependencies.

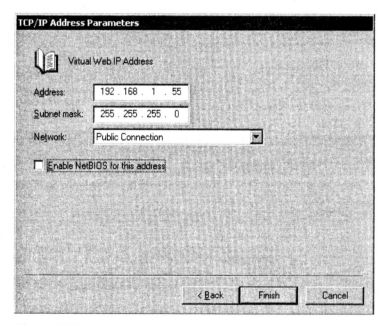

Figure 9-7
Assigning an IP address.

WINS, then you should check this option; otherwise, clear the box and select **Finish** to complete the IP address configuration.

Once the configuration is complete, right-click on the resource and select **Bring Online** to start the IP address resource (see Figure 9-8). You should be able to ping this address from another workstation once it is brought online.

As a next step, before creating the WWW Server resource, open the Internet Services Manager console. You will find this by clicking **Start**, **Programs**, then **Administrative Tools**. In the Internet Services Manager, right-click on the computer icon and select **New**, then **Web Site** from the menu (see Figure 9-9). This will start the Web Site Creation wizard.

At the Web Site Creation wizard startup screen (see Figure 9-10), select **Next** to continue.

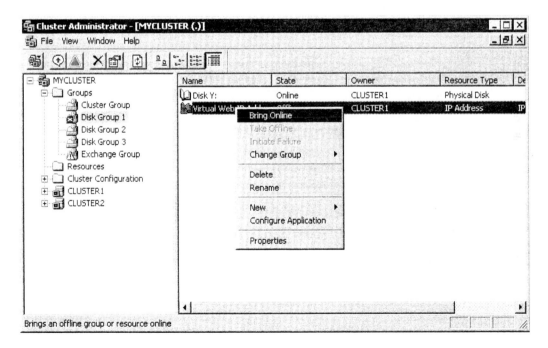

Figure 9-8
Bringing resources online.

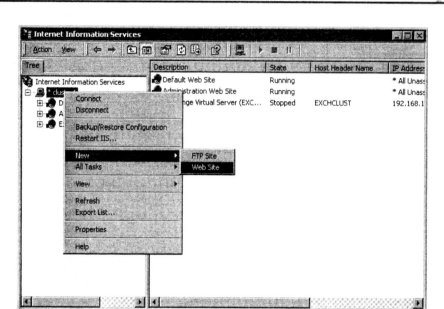

Figure 9-9
Creating a Web site.

Figure 9-10
Starting the Web Site Creation wizard.

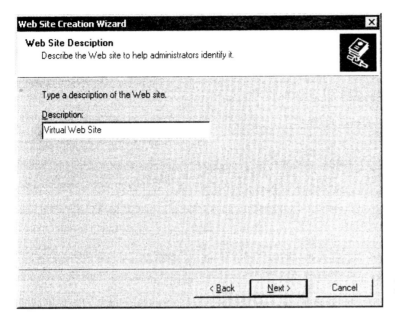

Figure 9-11
Web Site description.

In the Web Site Description dialogue, type the name of the site you are creating (see Figure 9-11). This name is used only for descriptive purposes.

The next screen asks for the IP address and port settings of the site you are creating (see Figure 9-12). Type in the IP address that you assigned to the IP address resource within cluster administrator. If you choose to use a host

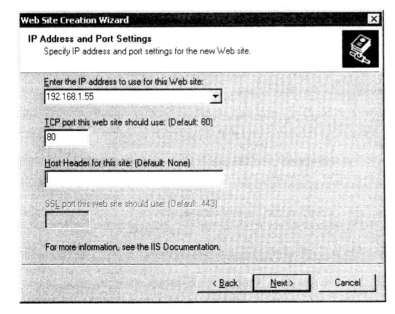

Figure 9-12
IP address and port settings.

309

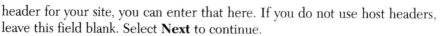

header for your site, you can enter that here. If you do not use host headers, leave this field blank. Select **Next** to continue.

In the Web Site Home Directory dialogue (see Figure 9-13), type in the path to the Web directory you created in Windows Explorer for the Web site. This directory must be located on the shared disk array.

The next screen allows you to set permissions on the Web directory (see Figure 9-14). If you do not require special permissions for your Web directory, leave the default and select **Next** to continue. If you would like to modify the default permissions, feel free to do so.

The final screen notifies you that you have created the virtual Web site (see Figure 9-15). This does not, however, indicate that you have successfully created a clustered Web site; you have simply configured IIS on one machine to respond to requests.

Once the virtual WWW Server is created within the Internet Services Manager, open cluster administrator once again. Right-click on the disk group that contains the IP address resource you created and select **New** then

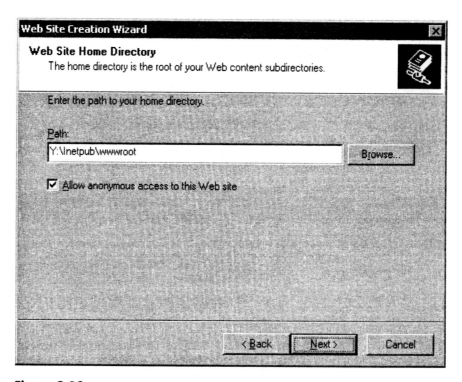

Figure 9-13
Setting home directory.

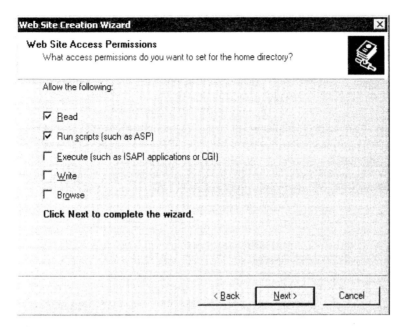

Figure 9-14
Setting permissions.

Figure 9-15
Completing the Web Site wizard.

Resource. In the New Resource dialogue, type the name you would like to assign to the virtual WWW Server (see Figure 9-16), a description for the server, and a resource type of "IIS Server Instance." Click **Next** to continue.

In the Possible Owner dialogue, select any nodes you do not want to host the virtual WWW Server in the event of a failure (see Figure 9-17). Click **Next** to continue.

In the Dependencies dialogue, select the disk resource and the IP address resource and select **Add** to add the resources to the Resource dependencies list (see Figure 9-18). Select **Next** to continue.

Next, select **WWW** from the parameters screen, and from the drop-down list, select the virtual WWW Server that corresponds to the virtual WWW Server you created in the Internet Services Manager (see Figure 9-19). Click **Finish** to complete the installation of the virtual WWW Server.

Right-click on the IIS resource and select **Bring Online** to make sure the resource starts correctly.

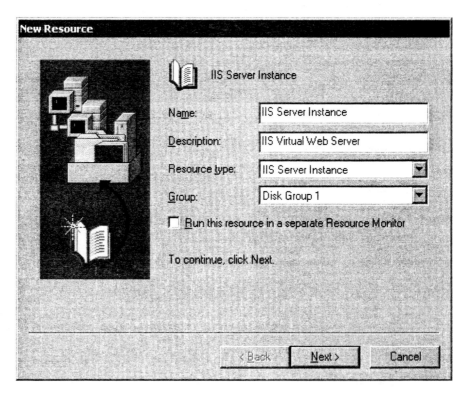

Figure 9-16
Creating the IIS resource.

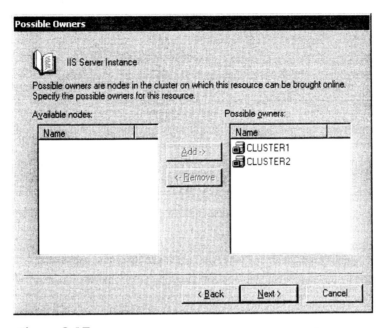

Figure 9-17
Assigning possible owners.

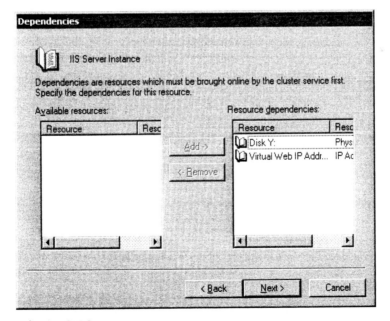

Figure 9-18
Citing dependencies.

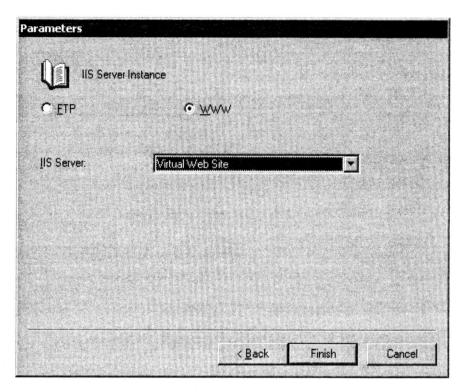

Figure 9-19
Setting the IIS server.

9.2.3 Synchronizing the Nodes

To successfully operate a WWW Server on a cluster server, you have to ensure that the configuration of the WWW Server is identical on every node. This synchronization can be done manually or through a utility called IISSYNC.

Prior to configuring the other nodes within your cluster or running the IIS-SYNC utility, you need to be sure that your login and authentication information is correct so that it will replicate correctly. If you have installed the clustering service on domain controllers, then your username and password will be a domain account, but if your cluster is installed on two member servers, then your anonymous account credentials will be local computer accounts and will not synchronize correctly.

To ensure that your WWW Servers synchronize their configuration correctly, open the Internet Services Manager and connect to the server you have configured (most likely node 1).

Right-click on the virtual Web site that you created for the cluster and select **Properties.** Select the **Directory Security** tab (see Figure 9-20). Click the **Edit** button to reveal the **Authentication Methods** dialogue (see Figure 9-21).

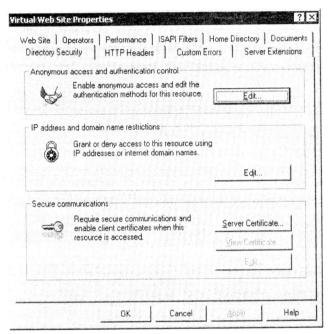

Figure 9-20
Viewing the virtual Web site directory security.

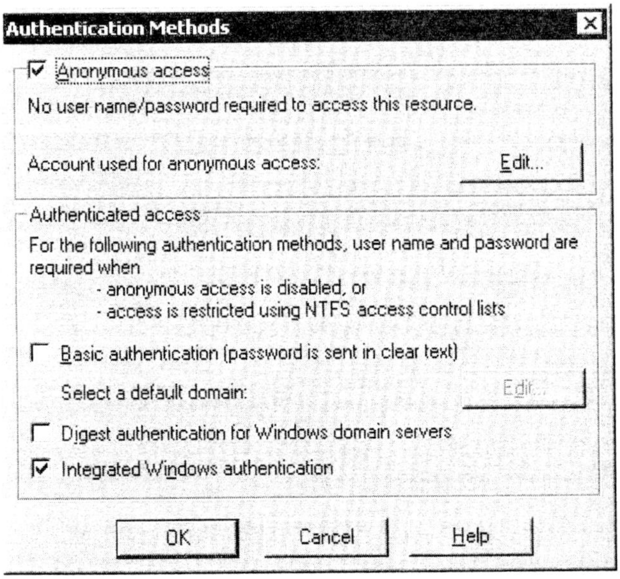

Figure 9-21
Viewing the Authentication Methods.

On your Authentication Methods screen, you should see Anonymous access and Integrated Windows authentication checked, while the other options are cleared. Select the **Edit** button to reveal the anonymous account credentials. For the clustering of the WWW Server to work correctly, the user listed in the Username field should be a domain account (see Figure 9-22). If it is not, you will need to create two new users through Active Directory Users and Computers. Name the first IUSR_*domainname* and the second IWAM_*domainname*. These users will be used by IIS for anonymous account authentication.

Once you have created those two users, click the **Browse** button on this screen and select the new IUSR_*domainname* user from the directory. Type in the password you have assigned to the user. Make sure to clear the Allow IIS to control password option and select **OK**. Select **OK** to save your settings.

Then open a command prompt on node 1 and navigate to the *c:\inetpub\adminscripts* directory. Run the following two commands:

```
Cscript adsutil.vbs SET W3SVC/WAMUserName WAM_domainname
Cscript adsutil.vbs SET W3SVC/WAMUserPass "userpassword"
```

If you receive an error prompting you to use Cscript as Vbscript, type *yes* and hit **Enter,** then run the scripts without the Cscript on the beginning of the string.

Once you have completed those two tasks, you must synchronize the configuration of node 1 (which you have already done by adding the virtual Web site in the previous section) with node 2 and so on. To do so, you can either fail the resources you have created within cluster administrator to the new

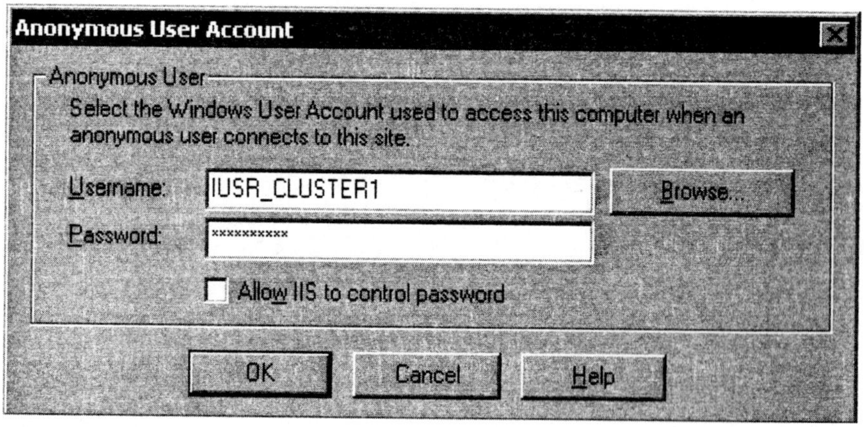

Figure 9-22
Anonymous account credentials.

node and then manually recreate the Web site through Internet Services Manager, or you can run the IISSYNC utility.

If you choose to configure each virtual Web manually, be sure to use exactly the same configuration you used previously so that the servers are consistent. Going forward, any change made to any server within the cluster will need to be done on the other servers as well.

If you choose to use IISSYNC, just open a command prompt, navigate to the *c:\winnt\system32\inetsrv* directory, and execute the following command:

```
IISSYNC node2_servername
```

This will synchronize the configuration between node 1 and node 2 (see Figure 9-23). If you need to configure multiple nodes, just use the command followed by a list of nodes, delimited by a space, as follows:

```
IISSYNC node2_servername node3_servername node4_servername
```

IISSYNC is not an automated script, so you will need to run the configuration command every time you change the configuration of any node within the cluster. This makes IISSYNC a good candidate for task scheduling. If you do schedule a task to run the IISSYNC utility, make sure that you are making changes only to the server that is being replicated; otherwise, you may overwrite what you have changed on other machines.

Figure 9-23
Executing IISSYNC.

If you choose to replicate a different node's changes, the syntax is different. If you want to replicate node 3's changes to the other nodes within the cluster, you would execute the command from node 3 and would include node 1, node 2, and node 4 in the string, as in the following example:

```
IISSYNC node1_servername node2_servername node4_servername
```

IISSYNC is not limited to the WWW service, but should be run after any configuration change to the WWW service, the FTP service, or the SMTP service.

9.3 Clustering the FTP Service

FTP is an Internet-standard language for transferring files; it is almost as old as the Internet itself. There are not many companies that do not host some type of FTP server to provide easy file access for clients. Take *ftp.microsoft.com*, for example. There are many files and utilities that are available at that FTP site, and you can be sure that the site receives several thousands of hits per hour.

To host mission-critical file storage on an FTP server, clustering the server is the only way to ensure fault tolerance and failover in the event of a failure. Fortunately, clustering the FTP service is not much different than clustering the Web service, for they are configured in the same way.

9.3.1 Prerequisites for the FTP Server

Contrary to the Web service, the FTP has only two prerequisites. The service must be installed, and the directory that will contain all of the files for the FTP server must be created. To verify that the FTP service is installed, you can open Internet Services Manager and see if there is a Default FTP Server listed. If this is the case, then you have FTP installed. You can also click **Start**, **Settings**, **Control Panel**, **Add/Remove Programs**, then **Add/Remove Windows Components**. Once you are in the Windows Components dialogue, click on **the Internet Information Server** option and select **Details**. There should be a selection called **File Transfer Protocol Service**. Ensure that this option is selected.

You must have a directory to serve as a root datastore for all of your FTP files that you wish to host on your server. Open Windows Explorer (see Figure 9-24) and select a drive letter that is shared by the cluster servers. From the

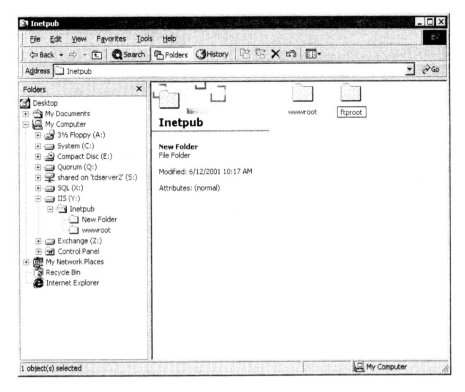

Figure 9-24
Creating the FTP directory.

menu, select **File**, **New**, then **Folder**. Name the folder whatever you wish, and hit **Enter** to create it.

Once this directory is created, you are ready to proceed with the cluster installation.

9.3.2 Installing the Virtual FTP Server

Installing the virtual FTP server is a process that involves the cluster administrator application and the Internet Services Manager application. It is a good idea to open both programs for the installation so that you will have easy access to each.

In cluster administrator, select the disk group that contains the disk that you used to host the directory you created. Right-click on the disk and select **New**, then **Resource**. In the New Resource dialogue (see Figure 9-25), type the

319

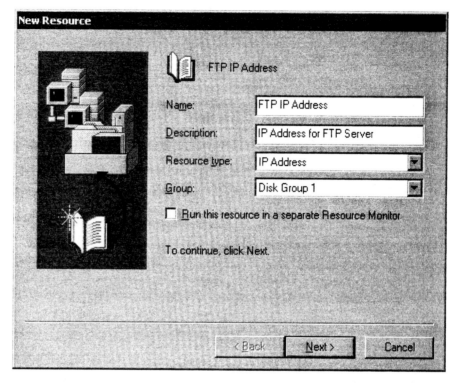

Figure 9-25
Creating the IP address resource.

name and description you would like to assign to the FTP service you are creating. Select **IP Address** as the resource type, and click **Next** to continue.

In the Possible Owners dialogue, you are prompted to select which servers
can run the application in the event of a failure (see Figure 9-26). By default,
all nodes within the cluster will be listed in the Possible Owners list. Select any
nodes you do not wish to host the service and select **Remove** to remove them
from the list. Click **Next** to continue.

On the next screen, you are prompted to cite which resources are dependencies of the one you are creating. Because the IP address is meaningless
without the disk that hosts the FTP files, select the disk resource and select
Add to add it to the list of resource dependencies (see Figure 9-27).

The TCP/IP Address Parameters screen allows you to assign which IP
address you would like to use for the resource you are creating. Type in the IP

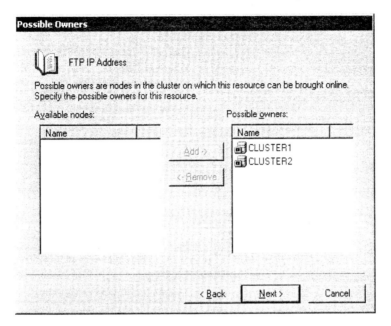

Figure 9-26
Assigning possible ownership.

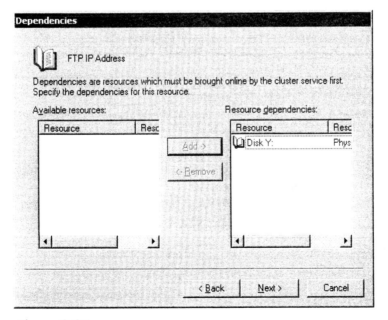

Figure 9-27
Citing dependencies.

321

address you would like to use (the subnet will be populated for you) and make sure the network selected is **Public Connection** (see Figure 9-28). Click **Finish** to complete the configuration of the IP address resource.

Once the IP address resource is created, right-click on the resource and select **Bring Online** to start the resource (see Figure 9-29). If you choose to, you can test the IP address at this time by pinging the address from another host on the network.

Switch over to the Internet Services Manager. Right-click on the computer icon and select **New**, then **FTP Site** to start the FTP Site Creation wizard (see Figure 9-30). If you receive an error stating that the service is not installed, you will have to go to the Add/Remove Programs applet to add the FTP service, as described in the section "Prerequisites for FTP Server".

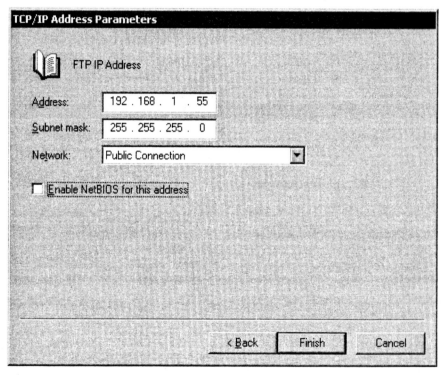

Figure 9-28
Assigning an IP address.

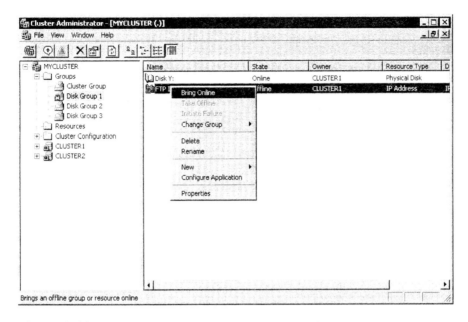

Figure 9-29
Starting IP address resource.

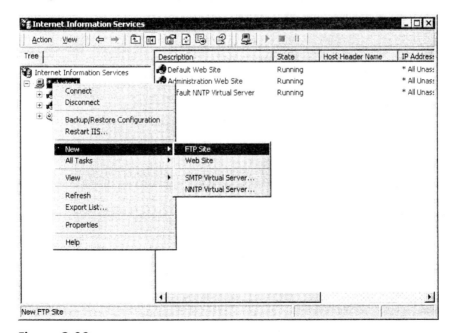

Figure 9-30
Creating the virtual FTP site.

323

The FTP Site Creation wizard will walk you through the creation of the virtual FTP server you wish to create (see Figure 9-31). Click **Next** to continue.

The next screen prompts you to assign a name or description to the new site (see Figure 9-32). Make sure this is a name that you can recognize, because you will need to pull it out of a list later in the installation. Type in the name you would like to use and select **Next** to continue.

The IP Address and Port Settings screen allows you to assign a particular address to the FTP server so that the server will respond only to requests made directly to the specified IP address. Type in the IP address of the IP address resource you created earlier in the cluster administrator (see Figure 9-33). You can change the TCP port used by the application, but it is not recommended. The default port of 21 is typically sufficient. Click **Next** to continue.

Figure 9-31
Starting the FTP Site Creation wizard.

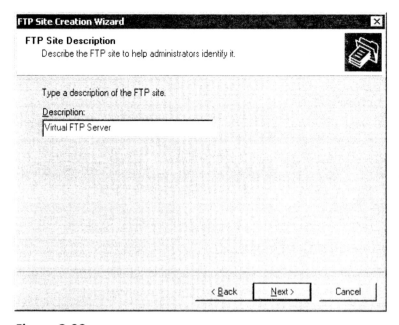

Figure 9-32
Naming the FTP site.

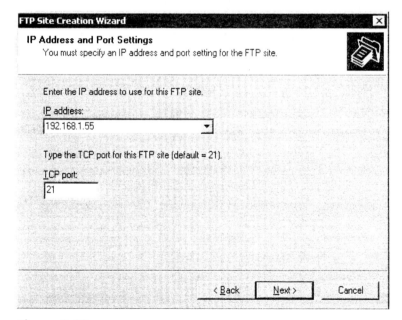

Figure 9-33
Assigning IP address and port settings.

325

The next screen prompts you for the home directory (see Figure 9-34). This will be the root storage folder for all files hosted on your FTP server. Click the **Browse** button and navigate to the directory you created earlier in Windows Explorer. This must be a directory located on the shared disk array. Once you have selected the folder, click **Next** to continue.

On the FTP Site Access Permissions screen, specify which permissions you would like the anonymous access account to have in the root folder of the FTP site (see Figure 9-35). You can modify this later if you need to. Depending on your situation, you may want to limit the access to read-only and assign specific permissions to alternate user accounts. Once you have selected the options you wish to apply, select **Next** to continue.

The wizard will then inform you that you have successfully completed the FTP site creation (see Figure 9-36). This does not mean that your site is clustered yet. Press the **Finish** button to continue the cluster configuration and move to the next step.

Switch over to the cluster administrator program once again. Select the disk group that contains the IP address resource you created earlier. Right-click on

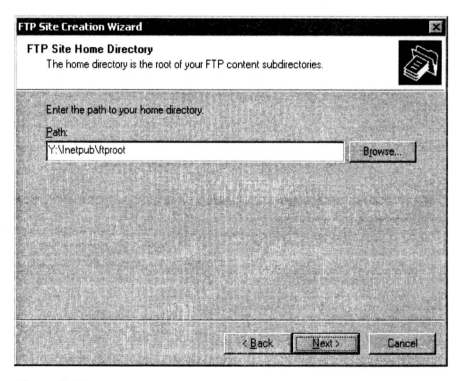

Figure 9-34
Entering path to FTP root directory.

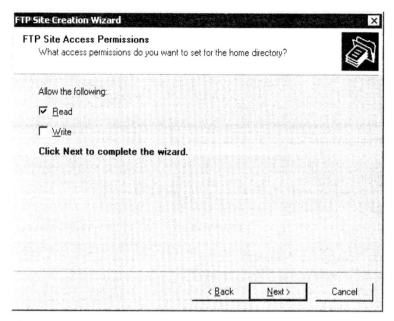

Figure 9-35
Setting access permissions.

Figure 9-36
Completing the FTP Site Creation wizard.

the disk group and select **New**, then **Resource**. In the New Resource dialogue, type the name and description you would like to assign to the virtual FTP server. Then select the **IIS Server Instance** as the resource type (see Figure 9-37). Click **Next** to continue.

In the Possible Owners dialogue, select the nodes you do not want to host the application and select **Remove** to move them to the Available nodes list (see Figure 9-38). This configuration should be consistent with the possible ownership of the IP address you configured earlier.

The FTP virtual server cannot run without the disk resource and the IP address resource. Select the disk resource and IP address resource on the Available resources list and click **Add** to move them to the Resource dependencies list (see Figure 9-39). This will prevent the FTP virtual server from starting unless the disk resource and IP address resource are online.

On the next screen, select **FTP** as the service option and use the drop-down list to select the name of the virtual server you created through the Internet

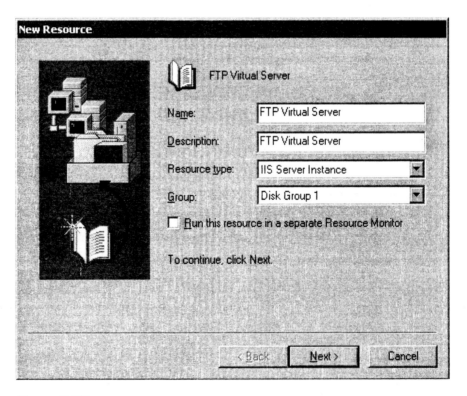

Figure 9-37
Creating the FTP cluster resource.

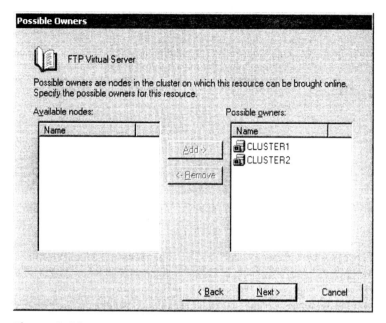

Figure 9-38
Assigning possible ownership.

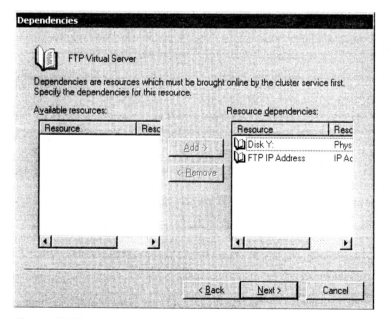

Figure 9-39
Citing dependencies.

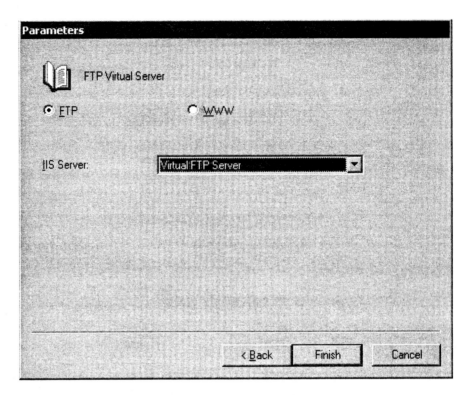

Figure 9-40
Assigning the resource to the virtual FTP server.

Services Manager program (see Figure 9-40). Press the **Finish** button to complete the installation and add the instance to the disk group.

Once the resource has been added, right-click on the resource and select **Bring Online** to start the resource, and ensure that it works properly. If the instance fails to start, check the event viewer or cluster log for direction on the cause of the failure.

9.3.3 Synchronizing the Nodes

In the same way the WWW Server configuration had to be replicated to the other nodes before the service would correctly fail over, the FTP server configuration must also be synchronized with the other nodes for proper failover to occur.

Again, you have two options: You can manually fail over the resources within the disk group to another node and then manually configure the Internet

Services Manager in the same way you configured node 1. Or, you can use the IISSYNC utility to synchronize the nodes.

Warning

Prior to using IISSYNC to synchronize the configuration of IIS servers, you should be sure that all servers are using the correct domain-based username and password for anonymous login accounts. If you are running your cluster on member servers, be sure to follow the instructions set forth under the WWW Server section for changing the username and password for member servers. If your cluster nodes are domain controllers, you can ignore this warning.

To use IISSYNC, open a command prompt on node 1 and navigate to the *c:\winnt\system32\inetsrv* directory and run the following command:

```
IISSYNC node2_servername
```

This will synchronize the configuration between node 1 and node 2 (see Figure 9-41). If you need to configure multiple nodes, just use the command followed by a list of nodes, delimited by a space, as follows:

```
IISSYNC node2_servername node3_servername node4_servername
```

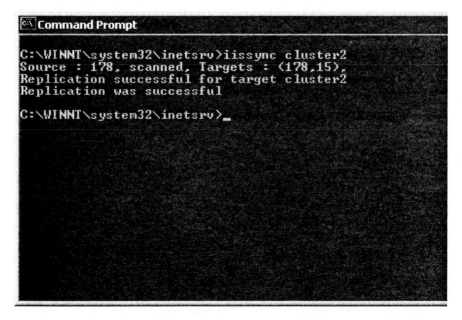

Figure 9-41
Synchronizing the IIS servers.

9.4 Clustering the SMTP Service

The SMTP is an industry standard protocol for the transfer of electronic mail. Mail servers such as Microsoft Exchange, Lotus Notes, and Eudora Mail use SMTP to send and receive electronic mail. Microsoft's IIS includes an SMTP service that can be used by other mail systems as a relay point for sending and receiving mail.

The advantages of using a mail relay include the following:

• Mail relays can be placed within demilitarized zones, keeping direct Internet connections from infiltrating your network.
• Mail relays can be used to offload the process of sending and receiving mail so that large mail systems can better serve local clients.
• Mail relays can be used to provide added security to the design of a mail system, allowing one for send-only and one for receive-only.
• Mail relays can be used as a secondary server, queuing mail intended for a specific server while the server is offline.

As you can see, there are many advantages to using a mail relay. With something as critical as email, it makes sense to place the service on a cluster server.

9.4.1 Prerequisites for the SMTP Server

There are a few prerequisites that you should cover before attempting to install the SMTP service on a cluster. The following sections will introduce you to the preliminary steps to take before configuring the SMTP service to run on a cluster.

The first thing you must do is confirm that the SMTP service is installed. To do this, click **Start**, **Settings**, **Control Panel**, **Add/Remove Programs**, then **Add/Remove Windows Components**. Locate the **Internet Information Server** option, select it, and click **Details**. If SMTP is installed, it should have a check mark next to it. If it does not, check the option and select **Next** to go through the installation procedure. Repeat this process on every node until you are sure that every node is running the SMTP service.

Once you are sure that the SMTP service is installed, right-click on **My Computer** and select **Manage**. Double-click **Services and Applications**, and then click on the **Services** icon. In the right pane, locate the service called **Simple Mail Transfer Protocol (SMTP)**. Double-click the service to view its properties. Change the startup type from Automatic to **Manual**, and then click the **Stop** button to stop the service. Click **OK** to save the changes. Repeat this step on every node within the cluster to ensure that the service is set to start up manually.

The remaining prerequisites can be done on node 1 only. Open Windows Explorer and navigate to the shared drive you wish to use to store your mail files. This should be a drive that is shared between all nodes in the cluster. Create a directory on the drive to store your mail files. The default is *mailroot,* but you can choose any name you like.

Open the Internet Services Manager and look to see if it shows a Default SMTP virtual server. If it does, then follow these steps:

1. Right-click on the default SMTP virtual server and select **Properties**.
2. Click the **General** tab and then click **Advanced.**
3. Under IP Address, select (**All Unassigned**).
4. In the Identification dialogue, change the TCP port setting from 25 to 20.
5. Click **OK.**

If you did not see the default SMTP virtual server within Internet Services Manager, then you do not need to follow the previous steps. This process changes the default port of the SMTP service so that when you create a new SMTP service within the cluster administrator, you will not have conflicting services.

9.4.2 Clustering the SMTP Service

The first step to configuring the SMTP service is the creation of an IP address resource within the disk group you choose to use for your cluster. Open cluster administrator and navigate to the group that contains the disk that holds your mail directory. Right-click on the group and select **New** and then **Resource** from the menu.

In the name and description fields, type in a name and description that you would like to use for your IP address resource. These are for administrative purposes only. Under Resource type, select **IP Address** (see Figure 9-42) and select **Next** to continue.

The next screen prompts you for possible ownership of this resource. Typically, all nodes within the cluster will be able to host the application, but you may have special circumstances that require you to exclude certain clus-

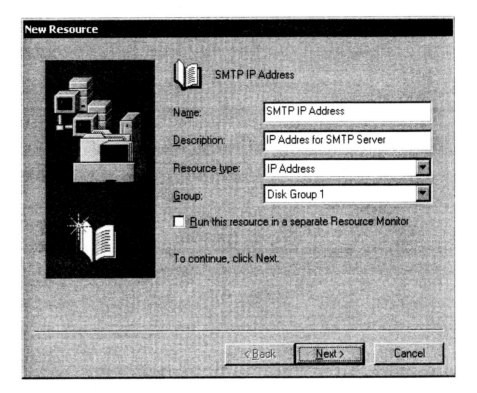

Figure 9-42
Creating the IP address resource.

ter nodes from the list. If so, select the nodes you want to exclude and select **Remove** to take them off of the list of possible owners (see Figure 9-43).

In the Dependencies dialogue, select the disk resource that is available and click **Add** to make it a part of the Resource dependencies list (see Figure 9-44). Click **Next** to continue.

On the next screen, you are asked to assign an IP address to the resource. Type in an IP address that is not in use on your network (the subnet will be provided for you), and select the **Public Connection** option under the **Network** field (see Figure 9-45). Select **Finish** to add the IP address resource to the disk group. Once added, right-click on the resource and select **Bring Online** to start the resource.

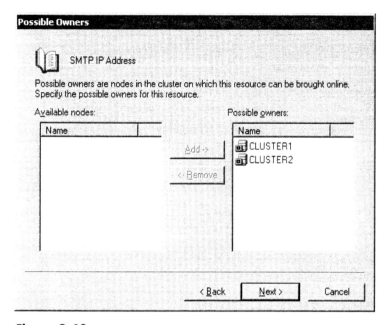

Figure 9-43
Assigning possible owners.

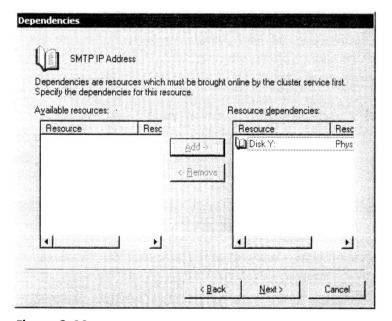

Figure 9-44
Citing dependencies.

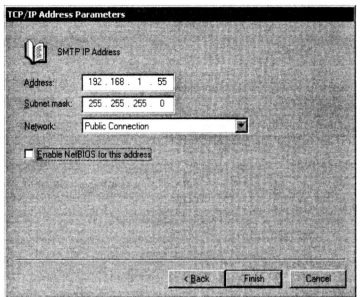

Figure 9-45
Assigning an IP address.

In the Internet Services Manager, right-click on the computer icon and select **New**, then **SMTP Virtual Server** (see Figure 9-46).

The New SMTP Virtual Server wizard will start and ask you for the SMTP virtual server description. You can use any description you would like; just make sure it is something that you can recognize (see Figure 9-47). Click **Next** to continue.

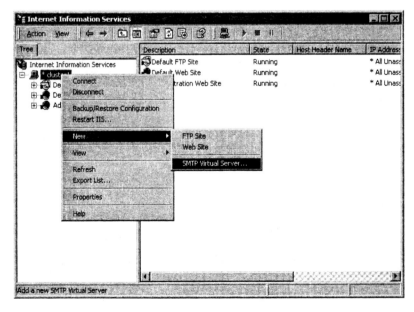

Figure 9-46
Creating the SMTP virtual server.

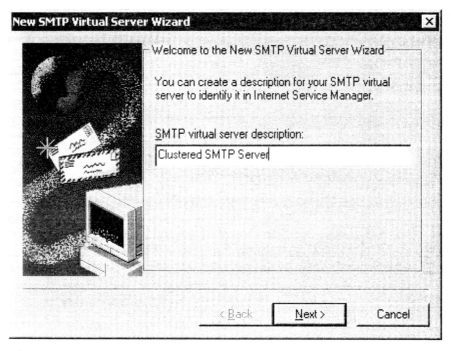

Figure 9-47
Naming the SMTP virtual server.

When asked to select an IP address, you will need to leave the default set-ting of (**All Unassigned**), for the SMTP Virtual Server wizard will not recog-nize the IP address you assigned to the disk group. Leave the default setting (see Figure 9-48) and click **Next** to continue.

The next screen prompts you for a path to your mail home directory. This is the directory you created in the section entitled, "Prerequisites for the SMTP Server." Click the **Browse** button, navigate to the directory you creat-ed, and select it (see Figure 9-49). Once complete, click the **Next** button to continue.

On the next screen, type the name of the default domain you would like to use. This will typically be the DNS domain name that your company uses to receive mail. You will have the ability to add more domains once the site is created; this domain is just the default. Type in a domain name (see Figure 9-50) and select **Next** to continue.

Switch back to the cluster administrator and locate the group that contains the IP address resource you created earlier. Right-click on the disk group and select **New**, then **Resource** from the menu. In the name and description field, type the name and description you would like to assign to the virtual

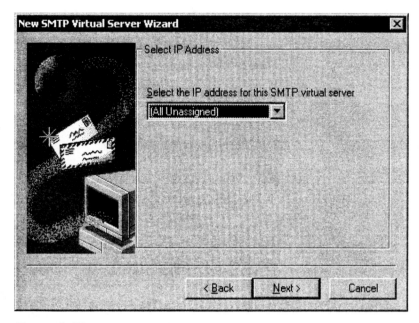

Figure 9-48
Assigning an IP address to the SMTP server.

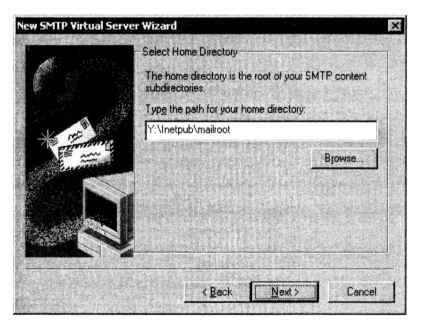

Figure 9-49
Selecting a path.

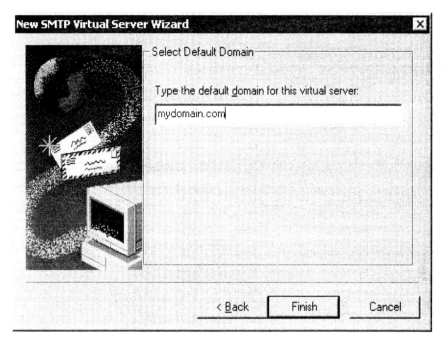

Figure 9-50
Specifying the default domain.

SMTP server. For resource type, select **SMTP Server Instance** from the drop-down menu (see Figure 9-51). Select **Next** to continue.

On the next screen, all nodes in the cluster should be listed in the Possible Owners list. If you have cluster nodes that you do not want to host the SMTP virtual server, click on that node and select the **Remove** button (see Figure 9-52). Click **Next** to continue.

In the Dependencies dialogue, select the disk resource and the IP address resource you created earlier. Press the **Add** button to add them to the list of dependencies (see Figure 9-53). Select **Next** to continue.

On the next screen, you are prompted to select which SMTP virtual server to associate this resource with. You should pick the server in the list that you created in the Internet Services Manager (see Figure 9-54). Make sure you do not select the Default SMTP virtual server.

Once the resource has been added to the group, right-click on the resource and click **Bring Online** to start the SMTP virtual server. If the SMTP server startup fails for any reason, reference the event viewer or the cluster log to determine the root cause.

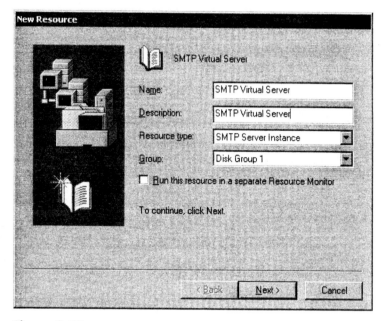

Figure 9-51
Creating the SMTP virtual server resource.

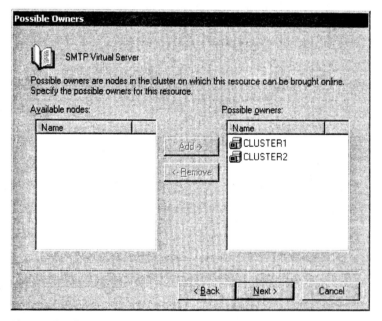

Figure 9-52
Assigning possible owners.

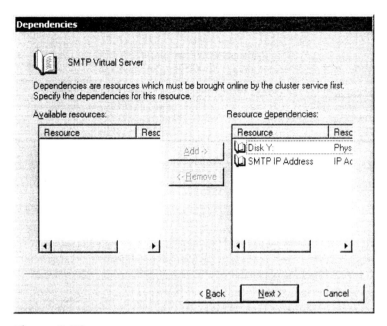

Figure 9-53
Citing dependencies.

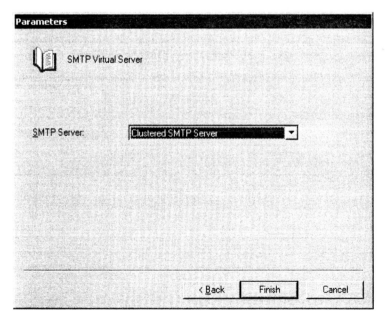

Figure 9-54
Selecting the SMTP virtual server.

9.4.3 Synchronizing the Nodes

Once the service has been installed and configured to run on the cluster, you must synchronize the configuration with all other nodes in the cluster. You can manually synchronize the SMTP virtual server by creating an SMTP virtual server with identical settings on the other nodes, or you can run the IISSYNC utility to automatically synchronize both machines.

To use IISSYNC, open a command prompt on node 1, navigate to the *c:\winnt\system32\inetsrv* directory, and run the following command:

```
IISSYNC node2_servername
```

This will synchronize the configuration between node 1 and node 2 (see Figure 9-55). If you need to configure multiple nodes, just use the command followed by a list of nodes, delimited by a space, as follows:

```
IISSYNC node2_servername node3_servername
node4_servername
```

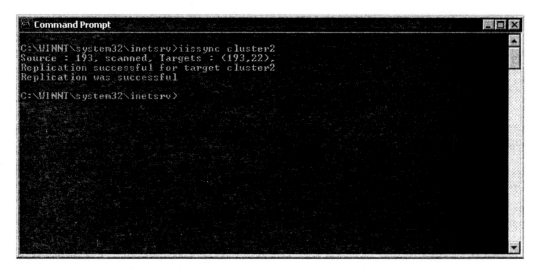

Figure 9-55
Synchronizing the nodes.

9.5 Summary

IIS is a powerful and robust platform for hosting Web pages, documents for file transfer, and a mail relay. Due to its stability alone, IIS is gaining ground on many other products that have, until recently, owned much of the market share. Used in combination with MSCS, IIS can employ the latest technology to build fault-tolerant, high-availability applications and services for the enterprise.

Chapter 10

CLUSTERING FILE AND PRINT SERVICES

Through the last few chapters you have learned how to implement advanced applications such as Microsoft SQL Server, Microsoft Exchange Server, and Microsoft Internet Information Server in a clustered environment. These applications meet very specific needs within the enterprise, providing highly available, fault-tolerant foundations for other applications and services that may run concurrently with them. But the Microsoft Clustering Service (MSCS) can be used to empower even the smallest, most insignificant network services that many of us take for granted.

Most, if not all, networks are originally installed to meet a basic need of file and print sharing. Even small networks thrive (and survive) based on these services. The MSCS can be used in conjunction with these services to provide fault tolerance for file shares and print shares within your network. Used in conjunction with Windows 2000 features, the MSCS can also apply fault tolerance to enterprise services such as DFS (distributed file service). In this chapter we will look at ways in which the MSCS can be used to enhance file sharing and print sharing within a network of any size.

10.1 Introduction

A file share is a centrally located directory that is accessible by machines on a network. File shares are used for the collaboration of workgroup users within a networked environment. By fully utilizing file shares, you can virtually eliminate the storage of vital data on a local machine.

Consider a typical network of 50 machines, all of which are used by people within the company for performing different functions. A few of them may store human resource documents, while another group stores programming code, while still another group utilizes a database to store purchase orders. If you allow all users to store their data on their local machines, you have the exact recipe for disaster. If you were to lose one machine, you would lose all the data on that machine.

Many people allow local storage, but set up backup routines so that users can back up their own files. This may be a good solution for companies that do not have users creating vital data, but it is not fit for a mission-critical environment due to the reliance you must put upon the end user to run the backup routine. Plus, you use twice the amount of storage necessary, for copies of the data will be stored locally and on the network. You may also run into a versioning problem, where one person is working on a document on the network while another person is working on the same document hosted on the local machine. Again, this is a messy situation.

Though the use of file shares, login scripts, and some informal training, you can redefine how your network storage takes place. A file share is a directory on a server that is "shared" so that others can see the directory and store data in its folders. Using a login script, you can map certain drive letters to certain network locations, making the network drive appear as a local drive to the user. By encouraging the users to store all of their data in a network drive, you centrally manage all of the data within your organization. This has many benefits.

- Data in a central place eliminates versioning issues.
- Data in a central place can be backed up nightly by the server.
- Data in a central place is not affected by the failure of one workstation.
- Users can move from machine to machine and still access their data.
- Data in a central place can be better secured.

Another great advantage of centralized storage is that file shares, combined with the MSCS, can be clustered, providing fault-tolerant data storage to end-users. This means that data is not affected by the failure of a workstation or by the failure of a server!

Printing is a similar issue. In most networks that are small, printers are attached to local machines, and as the network grows, they add more and more printers to the machines they purchase. In some companies, you find that every computer has its own printer. In some cases this may be warranted, but typically it is a waste of resources. Printers, like file shares, can be centrally located. By networking a printer, you can make the device independent of the local machine and available to all through the network. Because the printer is not attached to the local machine, it needs a server to serve as a storage container for jobs that are sent to the printer. This is called a *print queue*. Any workstation or server can serve as the print queue, but to pursue the vision of centralized computing, you should host all of your print queues on your servers. This centralizes management of the printers and allows you to add fault tolerance to the printers in your organization. Even greater than the fault tolerance you can add to a single machine, print servers (servers that host print queues) can be run on a cluster, making the printers impervious to workstation or server failure.

The next section describes how to set up file and print sharing on a cluster server. It also explores the clustering of DFS, which is a distributed file system used in many Windows NT/2000-based networks today.

10.2 Clustering File Shares

Clustering a file share is not a difficult process, but needs care to ensure that the share can be accessed through the network and that all of the proper resources are assigned as needed. To install a clustered file share, complete the following steps.

The first thing that is needed is a directory for the share. Open Windows Explorer and locate the (shared) drive you wish to create your share on. Once you have selected the drive, click **File**, then **New**, and select **Folder** from the list (see Figure 10-1). You can name your folder anything you would like, but make sure you remember it, for you will have to refer to it in a later step. If you were building a typical file share, the next step would be to create the share from within Windows Explorer, but a cluster share is different because it has to be recognized by all nodes within the cluster. To do so, the creation of the cluster must be through cluster administrator.

Open cluster administrator and right-click the disk group that contains the disk you desire to use for the file share (which should be the same as the drive

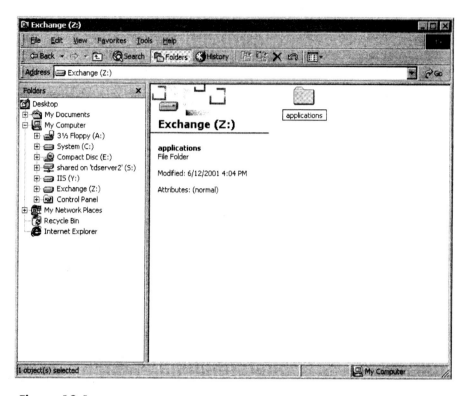

Figure 10-1
Creating the directory.

you used to create your directory). Right-click on the disk group and select **New**, then **Resource** from the menu. In the New Resource dialogue, type a name and description for the file share IP address resource. In Resource type, select **IP Address** from the menu (see Figure 10-2), then select **Next**.

On the next screen, select any nodes on the right side that you do not wish to host the application in the event of a failure (see Figure 10-3). Click **Remove** to move the nodes from the Possible Owner list. This will prevent the resource from failing over to the nodes you removed. Select **Next** to continue.

In the Dependencies dialogue, select the disk group that the file share will reside upon and click **Add** to add it to the Resource dependencies list (see Figure 10-4). The IP address will be dependent upon the disk group, for if the disk is not available, the file share is not available and there is no need for the IP address. Click **Next** to continue.

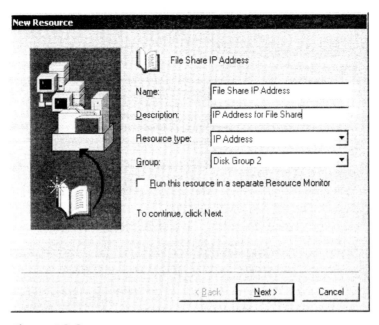

Figure 10-2
Creating the IP address resource.

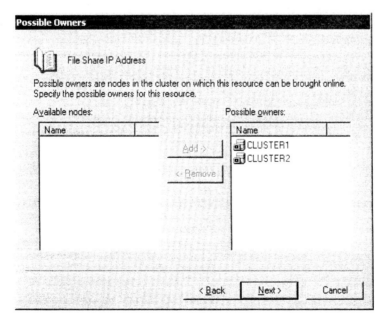

Figure 10-3
Assigning possible ownership.

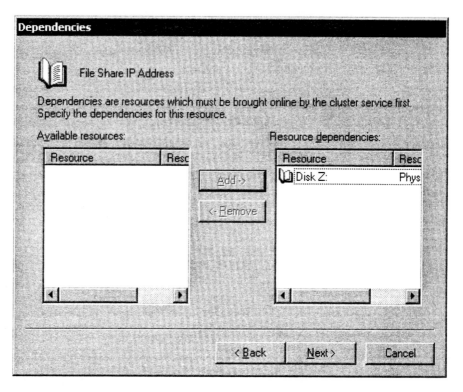

Figure 10-4
Citing dependencies.

On the next screen, you must assign an IP address to the IP address resource. This will be the address users access to work with the file share. Type in an address that is not in use by other devices on the network and make sure that **Public Connection** is selected (see Figure 10-5). For this address, make sure you enable NetBIOS. Windows networks utilize NetBIOS for connectivity to file shares, so NetBIOS is required. Click **Finish** to complete the creation of the IP address resource.

Once it has been created, right-click on the resource and select **Bring Online** to ensure that the IP address resource does not fail.

The next step is to create the network name resource you will use for the file share. Right-click on the disk group you are using; click **New**, then **Resource**. Type in a name and a description for the network name resource. Select **Network Name** from the Resource type list (see Figure 10-6) and select **Next** to continue.

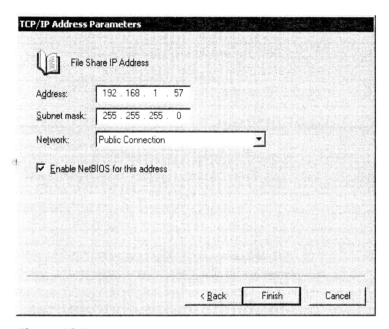

Figure 10-5
Assigning an IP address.

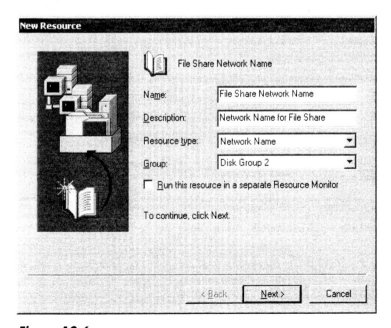

Figure 10-6
Creating the network name resource.

351

On the next screen, select any nodes on the right side that you do not wish to host the application in the event of a failure (see Figure 10-7). Click **Remove** to move the nodes from the Possible owners list. This will prevent the resource from failing over to the nodes you removed. These settings should be consistent with the IP address resource you created earlier. Select **Next** to continue.

In the Dependencies dialogue, select the IP address that you created earlier and click **Add** to add it to the Resource dependencies list (see Figure 10-8). The network name will be dependent upon the IP address, for if the IP address is not available, there will be nothing to bind the name to, and the network name will fail. Click **Next** to continue.

In the Network Name Parameters box, type in a name you would like to use for the network name resource (see Figure 10-9). This name should be consistent with NetBIOS naming conventions, for it will be registered within DNS (and possibly WINS) as part of the initiation of the resource. Once complete, click the **Finish** button to complete the creation of the network name resource. Once it has been created, right-click on the resource and select **Bring Online** to ensure that the network name does not fail.

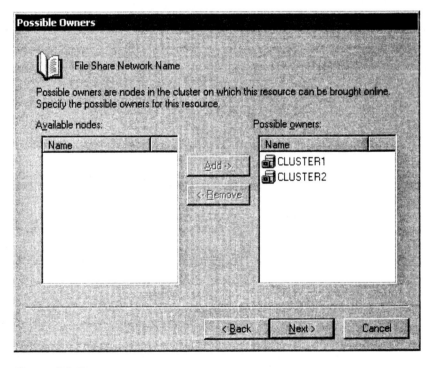

Figure 10-7
Assigning possible ownership.

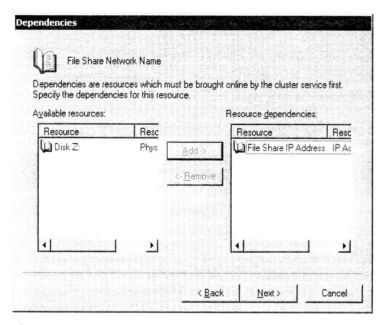

Figure 10-8
Citing dependencies.

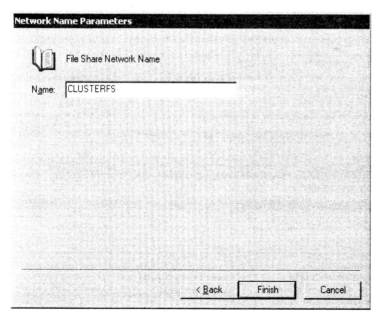

Figure 10-9
Assigning the network name.

Next, you must create the file share resource. This resource will actually create and control the parameters of the file share. Right-click the appropriate disk group (where you have created the IP address and network name) and select **New**, then **Resource.** In the New Resource dialogue, type the name and description of the file share you want to create. If you are going to create multiple file shares on this cluster server, it is recommended that you use descriptive names. In the Resource type field, select **File Share** (see Figure 10-10). Click **Next** to continue.

On the next screen, select any nodes on the right side that you do not wish to host the application in the event of a failure (see Figure 10-11). Click **Remove** to move the nodes from the Possible owners list. This will prevent the resource from failing over to the nodes you removed. These settings should be consistent with the other resources you created earlier. Select **Next** to continue.

In the Dependencies dialogue, select the network name that you created earlier and click **Add** to add it to the Resource dependencies list (see Figure 10-12). The file share resource will be dependent upon the network name resource, creating a daisy chain of dependencies from the disk group to the file share. Click **Next** to continue.

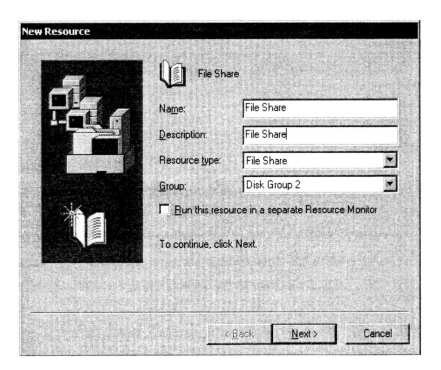

Figure 10-10
Creating the file share resource.

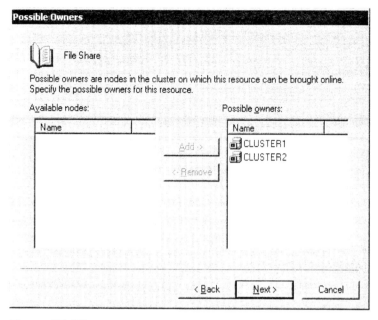

Figure 10-11
Assigning possible ownership.

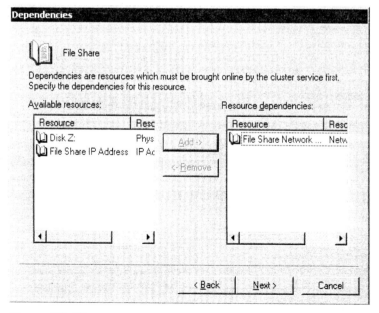

Figure 10-12
Citing dependencies.

355

In the File Share Parameters dialogue, type the name you would like to appear on the network to advertise the file share. Make sure the name does not conflict with any existing file shares on the cluster. Type the path to the directory you created for your file share. This should be a directory in a shared drive (see Figure 10-13). In the User Limit, you can specify the maximum amount of sessions to allow for this resource, or you can select **Maximum allowed**, which will not limit the sessions.

If you click the **Permissions...** button, you can assign the appropriate share permissions as you would with a traditional share. This allows you to secure the share from users that should not have access. Keep in mind that these permissions apply to the share, and not to the directory itself.

The **Advanced...** button presents some unique options (see Figure 10-14). The options include the creation of a normal share (which is the share we will be creating here), the creation of a DFS root share (which we will describe in the next section), and the option to share subdirectories.

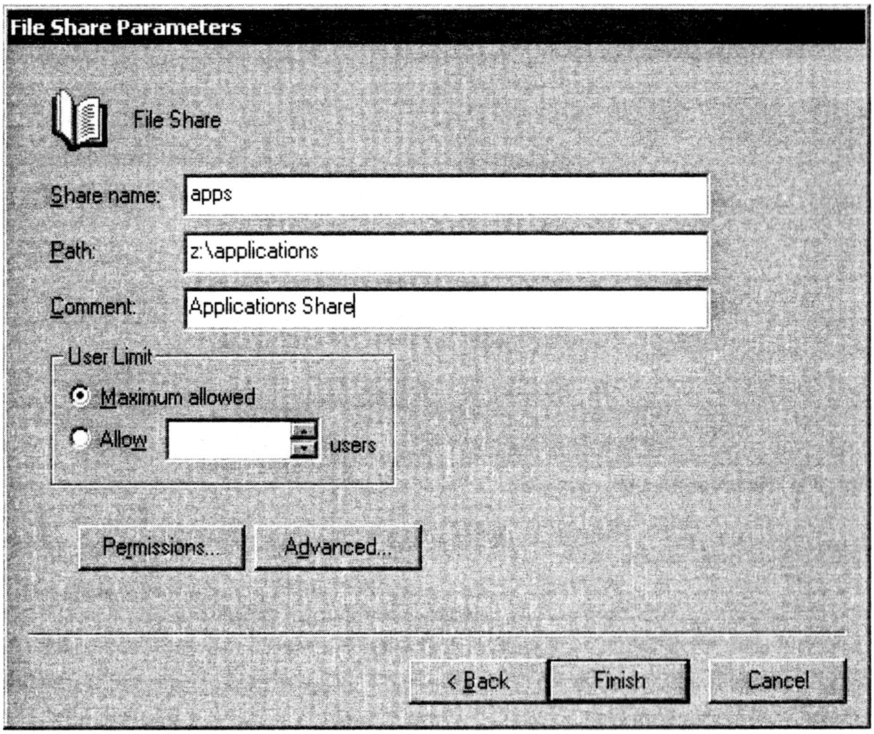

Figure 10-13
Configuring the file share.

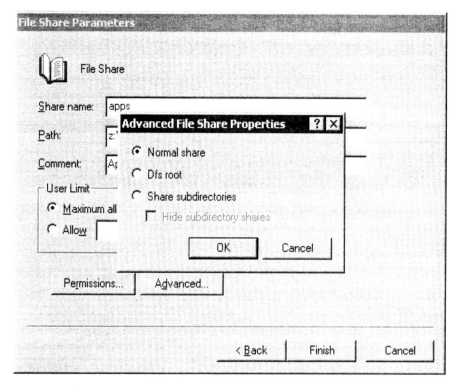

Figure 10-14
Configuring advanced properties.

The Share subdirectories option allows you to create one share that contains multiple directories, and the cluster will share every directory within the root directory as a separate share. Administrators who wish to cluster home or personal directories commonly use this type of structure. Many traditional administrators will create one user folder for home directories, and create a user directory specifically for each user under that one directory, and then share each directory on the network for the user to connect to. This can be tedious to manage, so the cluster administrator gives you the option of creating one directory and automatically sharing all directories beneath it. This is an outstanding feature that many wish were available within the Windows 2000 operating system itself. It would certainly make the administration of user home directories easier.

Select **Normal share** and then **OK** to exit the Advanced File Share Properties dialogue. Then click **Finish** to complete the creation of the file share resource. Once it has been created, right-click on the resource and select **Bring Online** to ensure that the file share does not fail.

357

10.3 Clustering DFS

The DFS service was originally an add-on to Windows NT 4.0 and was a bit limited at its inception, but has become a significant service within the distributed data access toolkit in recent revisions. DFS is a way of unifying the namespace of distributed file shares throughout an organization.

To an administrator, this has great advantages, for you can store any data on any server in the enterprise and provide your users with one unified namespace. To end users, the advantage is not having to know where every piece of data is located. By connecting to a single namespace, you have access to all company data.

For those of you not familiar with DFS, consider the following example. A network at XYZ Company has four servers, and each server has one file share for each department: operations, sales, human resources, and accounting. All file shares are not located on one server due to a lack of disk space. Without DFS, users must remember that the operations share is on server1, the accounting share is on server2, and so on. This can be difficult for users to manage. It is difficult enough to get most users to understand what a network drive is, much less explain to them that their data is stored on four different servers. Sure, they could go through My Network Places and locate the data, but they would have to find it.

Along comes DFS. With DFS, an administrator can create one DFS root on server1 that would include a folder for each server. That way, users would only have to connect to server1. Once connected (to the DFS root on server1), they would see an accounting folder, an operations folder, a human resources folder, and a sales folder. Access to the data in these folders would still go to all four servers, but the access would be transparent to the user. This simplified namespace allows users to connect to one resource for access to all of the data. Another great advantage to DFS is that administrators can move data without affecting the users. For instance, the administrator at XYZ Company can move the accounting folder from server2 to server5, update the link within DFS, and the users would never notice a difference. They would still connect to server1 to access the accounting folder.

The DFS service is automatically installed with Windows 2000 Server and Windows 2000 Advanced Server and is managed through the Microsoft Management Snap-in DFSGUI.MSC. There is also a command-line utility (*dfscmd.exe*) for managing the namespace through a command line.

Within Windows 2000, you have two options for creating DFS roots. One is domain integrated and the other is standalone. A domain-integrated root is tightly woven together with Active Directory and includes automated synchronization of DFS root replicas across the enterprise. A standalone DFS root will perform the same functions as a domain-integrated DFS root, but unfortunately does not include automatic synchronization. To cluster DFS, you must use a standalone root; the cluster service does not yet support the domain-integrated DFS roots.

To install and configure DFS on a cluster server, open Windows Explorer and locate the shared disk drive you desire to use for the DFS root. Create a directory on that drive. You can name it anything you like, but it is recommended that you use a descriptive name.

Open cluster administrator and right-click the disk group that contains the disk you desire to use for the DFS file share (which should be the same as the drive you used to create your directory). Right-click on the disk group and select **New,** then **Resource** from the menu. In the New Resource dialogue, type a name and description for the DFS file share IP address resource. In Resource type, select **IP Address** from the menu (see Figure 10-15), then select **Next**.

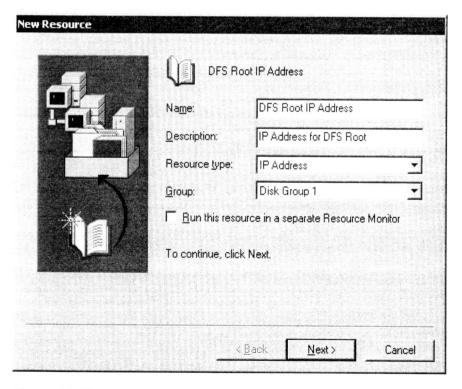

Figure 10-15
Creating the IP address resource.

On the next screen, select any nodes on the right side that you do not wish to host the application in the event of a failure (see Figure 10-16). Click **Remove** to move the nodes from the Possible owners list. This will prevent the resource from failing over to the nodes you removed. Select **Next** to continue.

In the Dependencies dialogue, select the disk group that the DFS file share will reside upon and click **Add** to add it to the Resource dependencies list (see Figure 10-17). The IP address will be dependent upon the disk group, for if the disk is not available, the DFS file share is not available and there is no need for the IP address. Click **Next** to continue.

On the next screen, you must assign an IP address to the IP address resource. This will be the address users access to work with the DFS file share. Type in an address that is not in use by other devices on the network and make sure that **Public Connection** is selected (see Figure 10-18). For this address, make sure you enable NetBIOS. Windows networks utilize NetBIOS for connectivity to file shares, so NetBIOS is required. Click **Finish** to complete the creation of the IP address resource.

Once it has been created, right-click on the resource and select **Bring Online** to ensure that the IP address resource does not fail.

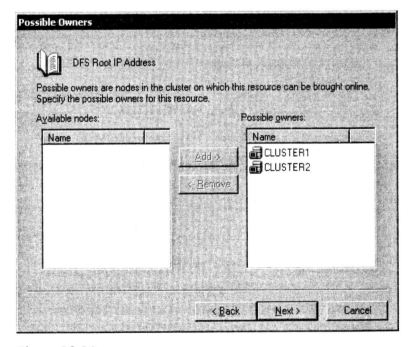

Figure 10-16
Assigning possible ownership.

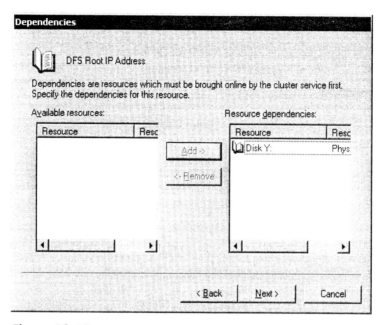

Figure 10-17
Citing dependencies.

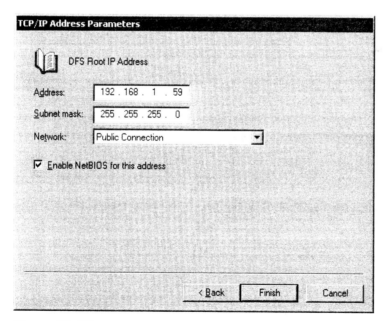

Figure 10-18
Assigning an IP address.

The next step is to create the network name resource you will use for the file share. Right-click on the disk group you are using, click **New**, then **Resource**. Type in a name and a description for the network name resource. Select **Network Name** from the Resource type list (see Figure 10-19) and select **Next** to continue.

On the next screen, select any nodes on the right side that you do not wish to host the application in the event of a failure (see Figure 10-20). Click **Remove** to move the nodes from the Possible owners list. This will prevent the resource from failing over to the nodes you removed. These settings should be consistent with the IP address resource you created earlier. Select **Next** to continue.

In the Dependencies dialogue, select the IP address that you created earlier and click **Add** to add it to the Resource dependencies list (see Figure 10-21). The network name will be dependent upon the IP address, for if the IP address is not available, there will be nothing to bind the name to, and the network name will fail. Click **Next** to continue.

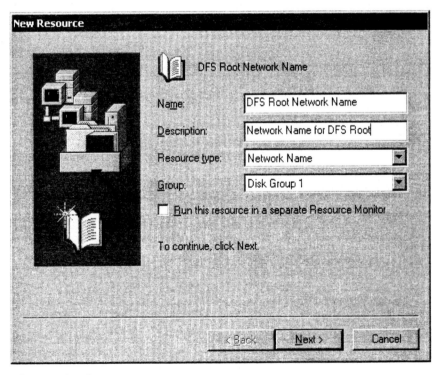

Figure 10-19
Creating the network name resource.

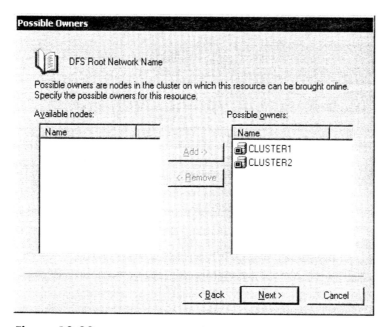

Figure 10-20
Assigning possible ownership.

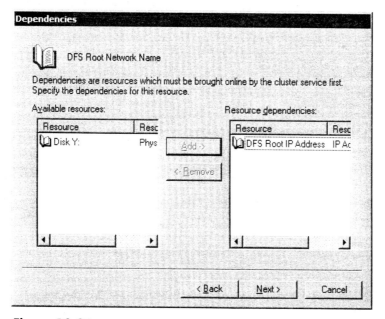

Figure 10-21
Citing dependencies.

In the Network Name Parameters box, type in a name you would like to use for the DFS network name resource (see Figure 10-22). This name should be consistent with NetBIOS naming conventions, for it will be registered within DNS (and possibly WINS) as part of the initiation of the resource. Once complete, click the **Finish** button to complete the creation of the network name resource. Once it has been created, right-click on the resource and select **Bring Online** to ensure that the network name does not fail.

Next, you must create the DFS file share resource. This resource will actually create and control the parameters of the file share. Right-click the appropriate disk group (where you have created the IP address and network name) and select **New**, then **Resource**. In the New Resource dialogue, type the name and description of the file share you want to create. If you are going to create multiple file shares on this cluster server, it is recommended that you use descriptive names. In the Resource type field, select **File Share** (see Figure 10-23). Click **Next** to continue.

On the next screen, select any node on the right side that you do not wish to host the application in the event of a failure (see Figure 10-24). Click **Remove** to move the nodes from the Possible owners list. This will prevent the resource from failing over to the nodes you removed. These settings

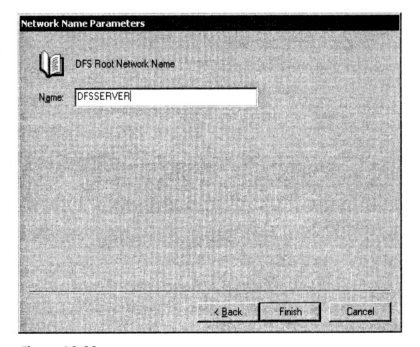

Figure 10-22
Assigning a network name.

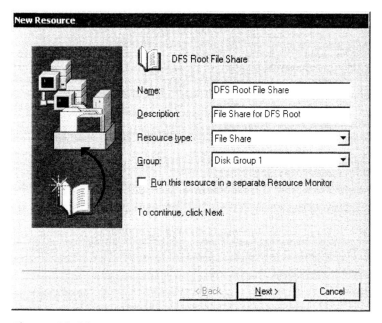

Figure 10-23
Creating the DFS file share resource.

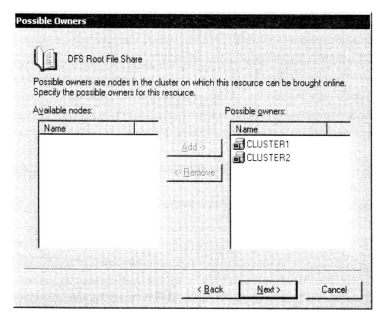

Figure 10-24
Assigning possible owners.

should be consistent with the other resources you created earlier. Select **Next** to continue.

In the Dependencies dialogue, select the network name that you created earlier and click **Add** to add it to the Resource dependencies list (see Figure 10-25). The file share resource will be dependent upon the network name resource, creating a daisy chain of dependencies from the disk group to the file share. Click **Next** to continue.

In the File Share Parameters dialogue, type the name you would like to appear on the network to advertise the DFS file share. Make sure the name does not conflict with any existing file shares on the cluster. Type the path to the directory you created for your DFS file share. This should be a directory in a shared drive (see Figure 10-26). In the User Limit, you can specify the maximum amount of sessions to allow for this resource, or you can select **Maximum allowed**, which will not limit the sessions.

If you click the **Permissions...** button, you can assign the appropriate share permissions as you would with a traditional share. This allows you to secure the share from users that should not have access. Keep in mind that these permissions apply to the share, and not to the directory itself.

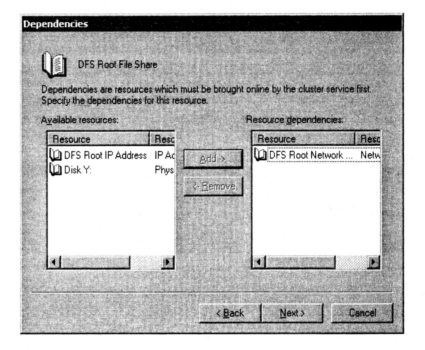

Figure 10-25
Citing dependencies.

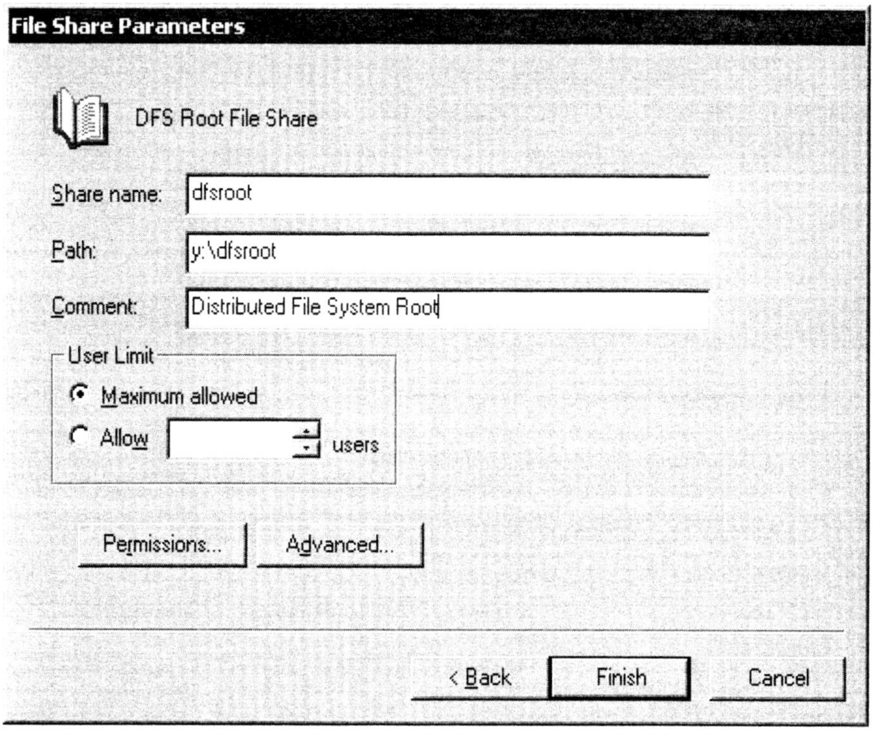

Figure 10-26
Creating the DFS root file share.

Click the **Advanced...** button and select the **DFS Root** option. Click **OK** and then **Finish** to complete the creation of the DFS root. Once complete, right-click on the resource to bring the resource online. As the resource starts, it will write vital DFS information to the registry.

Once the DFS file share is online, open the DFS manager. You can access the DFS manager by clicking **Start**, **Programs**, **Administrative Tools**, then **Distributed File System**. Once the DFS manager is open, verify that the DFS root that you created is present (see Figure 10-27).

Before configuring the DFS root, you have to create the registry entries on the other nodes within the cluster so that failover will work correctly. To do this, go back to cluster administrator, right-click on the DFS file share resource, and select **Take Offline**. Then right-click on the disk group and select **Move**. Select the node you want to move the group to so that all of the resources change ownership. Once that is complete, right-click on the DFS file share resource and select **Bring Online**. This will initiate the DFS root and create the necessary registry entries. Repeat this process for all nodes within your cluster.

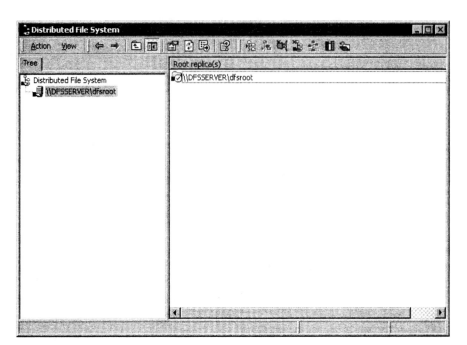

Figure 10-27
Verifying the DFS root.

Once you have configured the DFS root for each node, you can configure your DFS links. This is done through the DFS manager. Details for this operation are beyond the scope of this book. As you manage your DFS cluster, keep in mind the following issues:

- Although you configure DFS through the DFS manager, you must start and stop the service through the cluster administrator or the *cluster.exe* command line.
- If you add nodes to the cluster (or replace nodes), you will have to take the DFS resource offline, move the group to the new server, and bring the resource online again to configure the server to support the DFS root.
- The cluster administrator configuration of the DFS root will override configuration changes made to the DFS root though the DFS manager. You can configure the DFS root through DFS manager, but you cannot delete the DFS root through DFS manager. Deletion and addition of DFS file shares must be done through the cluster administrator.

10.4 Clustering Print Shares

There is no doubt that the ability to print to standalone printers (printers that are not attached to a computer directly) is essential to today's networks. It is true that any standard printer can be attached to a Windows workstation and shared to network users, which is how most small networks survive their printing requirements, but this model begins to suffer when the network grows beyond 5 to 10 printers. Many issues arise because users get confused about which printers are attached to which machines. Naming conventions become a problem because different individuals create the print shares. No—there is no doubt that a networked printer is an asset.

Network printing allows the print server (the computer that hosts the print queue for the printer) to be geographically anywhere within the network. Because it is not directly connected, the server does not have to be close in proximity to the printer that is being shared. Administrators use this to their advantage, centralizing all print queues on a single machine. This allows you to manage all printing operations through one machine. This can have some of the same drawbacks as the previous model, however; for if that one server goes down, so does access to all of the printers.

You can provide fault tolerance and reliability to print sharing through the MSCS. You may think that running a print share on a cluster server is overkill, but there are many organizations that "live and die" based on their ability to print. Plus, the cluster server does not have to be dedicated to this task. You may have an existing cluster server that you wish to use as a host for your print shares.

The installation of a print share on a cluster server is unique, for it requires that you create a print share on each node within the cluster, and then requires that you delete it. This allows the server to load the driver for the printer locally. Once the printer is added to the virtual server, it will ask if you wish to use the existing driver, to which you will respond "Yes." The next section presents the process for installing a shared printer on a cluster server and is broken into three separate sets of instructions. The first section, "Installing the Cluster Resources," configures the necessary resources for the cluster to host the printer. The second section, "Installing the Printer Driver," installs the necessary driver and should be repeated on all nodes within the cluster. The third and final section, "Configuring the Print Server," configures the printer on the cluster server and is completed from any node within the cluster.

10.4.1 Installing the Cluster Resources

The first step to installing a clustered print server is to determine which shared disk will host the spool directory. You will also need to know the make and model of the printer you wish to install, so be sure to jot those down for later reference.

Open Windows Explorer and navigate to the shared drive that you wish to use for the spool directory. Select the drive letter and click **File**, **New**, then **Folder** from the menu. Name the folder *spool* and press **Enter**. This is the directory that will be used for print jobs and printer drivers.

Next, open cluster administrator and locate the disk group associated with the disk you just used to create the spool directory. If a group does not exist for that physical disk resource, create one.

Right-click on the disk group you would like to use and select **New**, then **Resource.** In the New Resource dialogue, type a name and description for the IP address resource you will be using for the virtual print server (see Figure 10-28). Select **IP Address** for the Resource type, and select **Next** to continue.

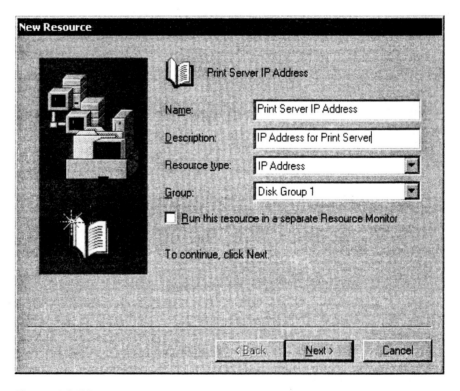

Figure 10-28
Creating the IP address resource.

On the next screen, select any nodes on the right side that you do not wish to host the application in the event of a failure (see Figure 10-29). Click **Remove** to move the nodes from the Possible owners list. This will prevent the resource from failing over to the nodes you removed. Select **Next** to continue.

In the Dependencies dialogue, select the disk group that the print server will reside upon and click **Add** to add it to the Resource dependencies list (see Figure 10-30). The IP address will be dependent upon the disk group, for if the disk is not available, the print server is not available and there is no need for the IP address. Click **Next** to continue.

On the next screen, you must assign an IP address to the IP address resource. This will be the address users access to install the shared printer. Type in an address that is not in use by other devices on the network and make sure that **Public Connection** is selected (see Figure 10-31). For this address, you need to make sure you enable NetBIOS. Windows networks utilize NetBIOS for connectivity to print shares, so NetBIOS is required. Click **Finish** to complete the creation of the IP address resource.

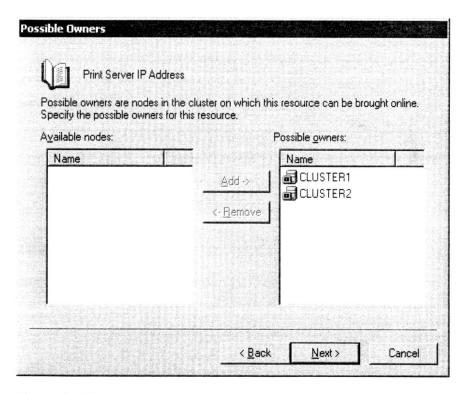

Figure 10-29
Assigning possible ownership.

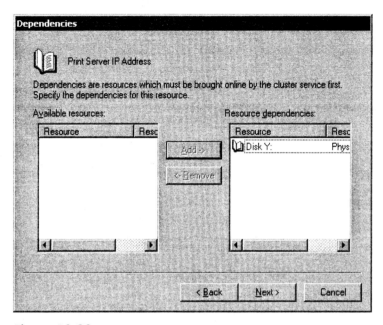

Figure 10-30
Citing dependencies.

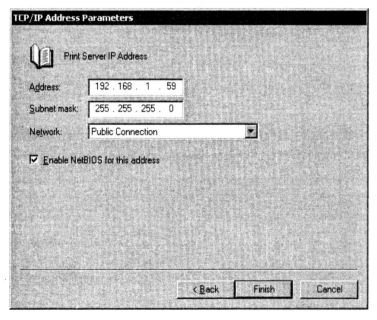

Figure 10-31
Assigning an IP address.

Once it has been created, right-click on the resource and select **Bring Online** to ensure that the IP address resource does not fail.

The next step is to create the network name resource you will use for the print server. Right-click on the disk group you are using and click **New**, then **Resource**. Type in a name and a description for the network name resource. Select **Network Name** from the Resource type list (see Figure 10-32) and select **Next** to continue.

On the next screen, select any nodes on the right side that you do not wish to host the print server in the event of a failure (see Figure 10-33). Click **Remove** to move the nodes from the Possible owners list. This will prevent the resource from failing over to the nodes you removed. These settings should be consistent with the IP address resource you created earlier. Select **Next** to continue.

In the Dependencies dialogue, select the IP address that you created earlier and click **Add** to add it to the Resource dependencies list (see Figure 10-34). The network name will be dependent upon the IP address, for if the IP address is not available, there will be nothing to bind the name to, and the network name will fail. Click **Next** to continue.

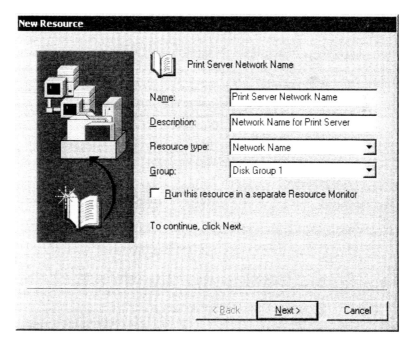

Figure 10-32
Creating the network name resource.

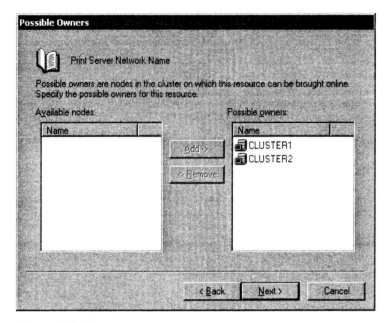

Figure 10-33
Assigning possible ownership.

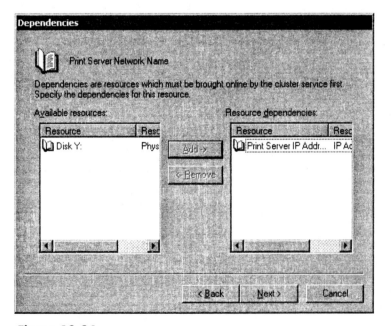

Figure 10-34
Citing dependencies.

In the Network Name Parameters box, type in a name you would like to use for the print server network name resource (see Figure 10-35). This name should be consistent with NetBIOS naming conventions, for it will be registered within DNS (and possibly WINS) as part of the initiation of the resource. Once complete, click the **Finish** button to complete the creation of the network name resource. Once it has been created, right-click on the resource and select **Bring Online** to ensure that the network name does not fail.

Next, right-click the disk group once again and select **New**, then **Resource** from the menu. In the New Resource dialogue, type in a name and description for the print spooler resource (see Figure 10-36). Select **Print Spooler** for the Resource type, then select **Next** to continue.

On the next screen, select any nodes on the right side that you do not wish to host the application in the event of a failure (see Figure 10-37). Click **Remove** to move the nodes from the Possible owners list. This will prevent the resource from failing over to the nodes you removed. Select **Next** to continue.

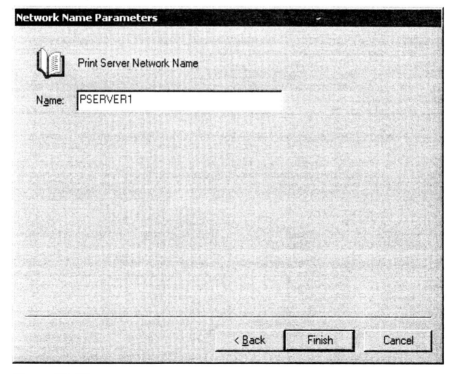

Figure 10-35
Assigning a network name.

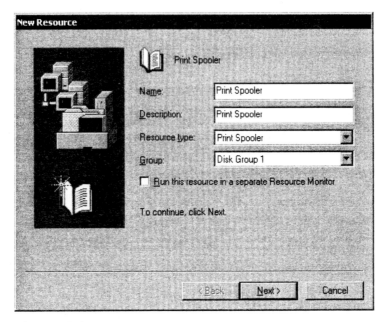

Figure 10-36
Creating the print spooler resource.

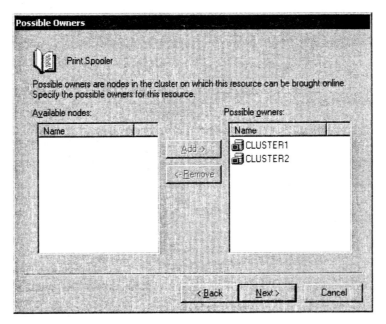

Figure 10-37
Assigning possible ownership.

In the Dependencies dialogue, select the disk group resource and the network name resource, and then click **Add** to add it to the Resource dependencies list (see Figure 10-38). Click **Next** to continue.

On the next screen (see Figure 10-39), type in the full path to the directory that you created on the shared disk for the printer spool files. Click **Finish** when you are done to complete the creation of the print spooler resource. Once it has been created, right-click on the resource and select **Bring Online** to ensure that the print spooler resource does not fail.

Keep in mind that you can have as many printers as you like shared within one disk group, but you can have only one printer spooler. You will not have to create this resource for every printer that you share on the cluster.

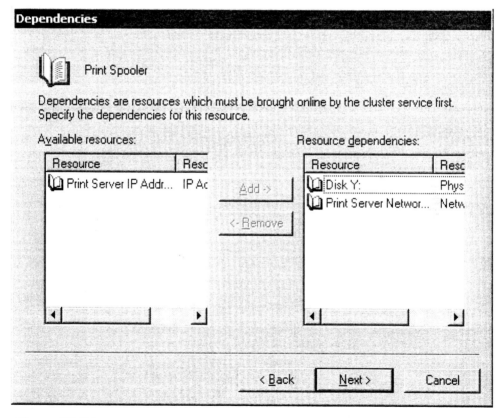

Figure 10-38
Citing dependencies.

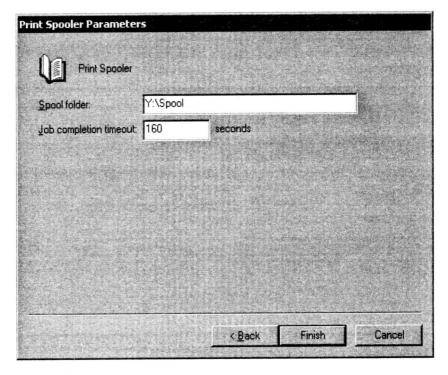

Figure 10-39
Assigning the spool directory.

10.4.2 Installing the Print Driver

The following process will be used to physically install the print driver for your printer on each node within the cluster. This process should be repeated on each node. Once the printer on each node is installed, it will be deleted, so items such as name, port, and share name are trivial.

On the first node, click **Start**, **Settings**, and then **Printers**. Double-click the **Add Printer**. This will start the **Add Printer** wizard (see Figure 10-40). Click **Next** to get started.

On the next screen (see Figure 10-41), select the **Local Printer** option. Because the printer is not physically attached to the cluster node, clear the **Automatically detect and install my Plug and Play printer** check box, and then click **Next**.

As stated earlier, the printer you are creating will be deleted in the final step, so the choice of ports is not really important. Select the LPT1 port and click **Next** to continue (see Figure 10-42).

Figure 10-40
Starting the Add Printer wizard.

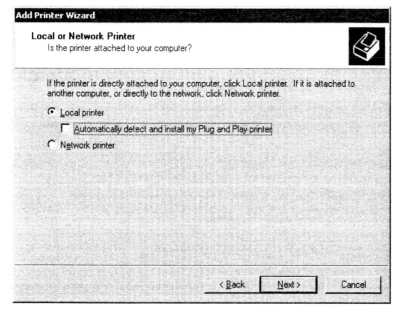

Figure 10-41
Local printer install.

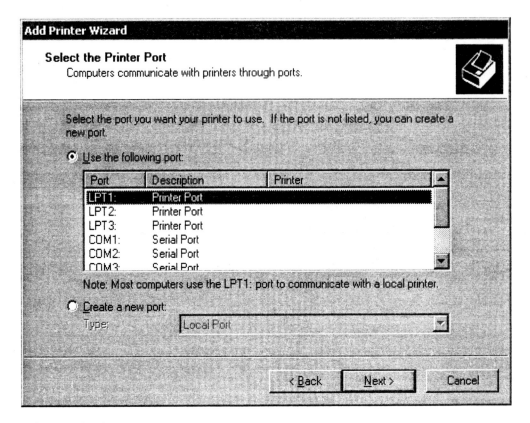

Figure 10-42
Choosing a printer port.

This part is critical. Let's review the object of this process one more time. You are installing a print driver for a fictitious printer so that the cluster node will have the driver for the clustered print share installed locally. It is absolutely essential that you choose the driver of the actual printer you wish to use. To continue, select the make and model of printer that you will be using (see Figure 10-43). If you have a vendor-supplied disk, select the **Have Disk…** button to select the driver. Once complete, press the **Next** button to continue.

On the next screen, type in the name you would like to use for the printer. Again, this printer will be deleted, so the actual name you use does not really matter. Type in any name and select **Next** to continue (see Figure 10-44).

Add Printer Wizard
Add Printer Wizard
The manufacturer and model determine which printer to use.
Select the manufacturer and model of your printer. If your printer came with an installation disk, click Have Disk. If your printer is not listed, consult your printer documentation for a compatible printer.
Manufacturers:
Fujitsu
GCC
Generic
Gestetner
HP
IBM
Printers:
HP LaserJet 4Si/4Si MX PS
HP LaserJet 4V
HP LaserJet 4MV
HP LaserJet 4V/4MV PostScript
HP LaserJet 5
HP LaserJet 5000 Series PCL
Windows Update
Have Disk...
< Back
Next >
Cancel

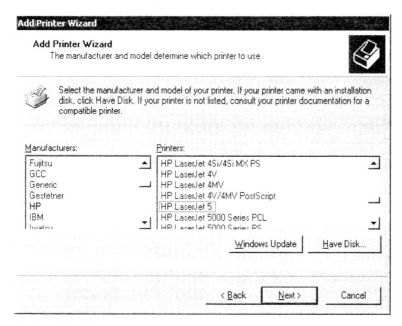

Figure 10-43
Selecting a printer.

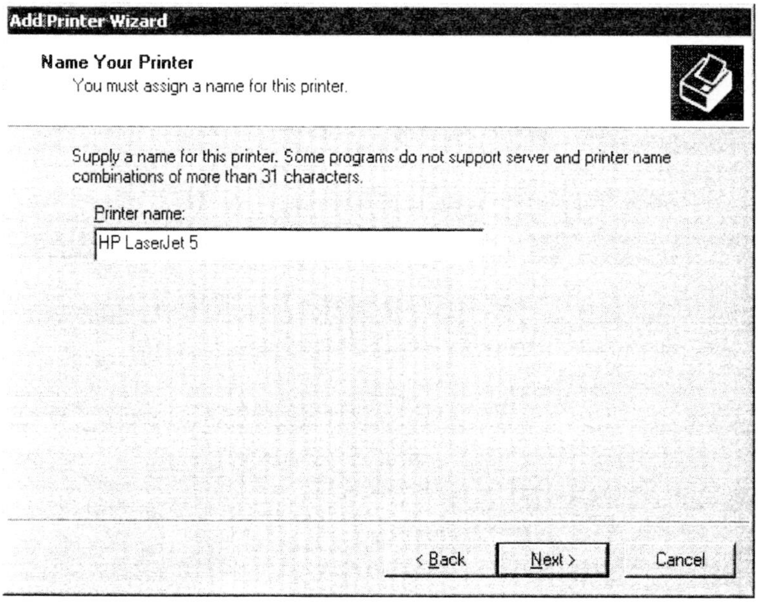

Add Printer Wizard
Name Your Printer
You must assign a name for this printer.
Supply a name for this printer. Some programs do not support server and printer name combinations of more than 31 characters.
Printer name:
HP LaserJet 5
< Back
Next >
Cancel

Figure 10-44
Naming the printer.

If there are workstations on your network that are not Windows 2000-based and you need to provide a driver for these machines, select the **Share as:** option, then click **Next** (see Figure 10-45). Leave the Location and Comment boxes blank, and then click the **Next** button to continue.

The next screen gives you the option of adding location and comment information to the printer (see Figure 10-46). Again, this is trivial because the printer is going to be deleted anyway. Click **Next** to continue.

The next screen (see Figure 10-47) asks if you want to print a test page. Obviously, you cannot print a test page for a printer that does not exist, so choose **No** and click **Next** to continue.

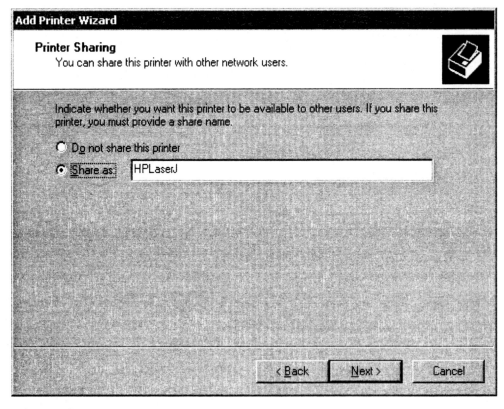

Figure 10-45
Sharing the printer.

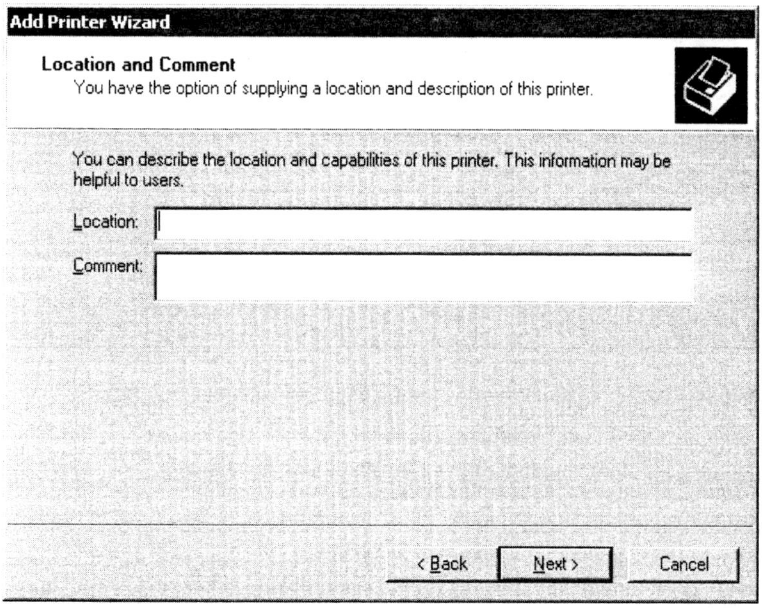

Figure 10-46

Location and comment.

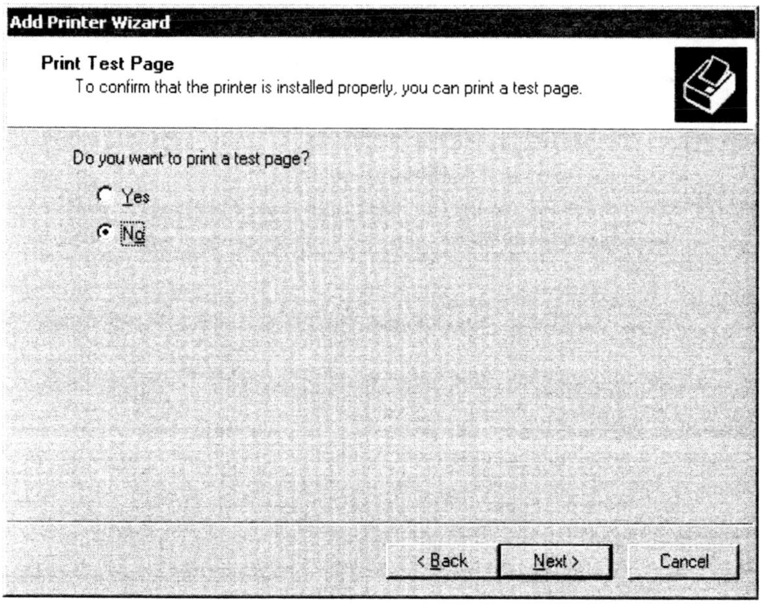

Figure 10-47

Printing a test page.

Figure 10-48
Finishing the Add Printer wizard.

The final screen (see Figure 10-48) confirms that you have completed the Add Printer wizard. Click the **Finish** button to continue. In the Printers folder, you should see the newly created printer. Right-click on the printer and select **Properties**. Click the **Sharing** tab, and then click the **Additional Drivers** button to install additional drivers. Select the non-Windows 2000 drivers you wish to install for this printer, and then close the printer properties.

From the Printers folder, select the newly created printer, right-click, and then click **Delete**. Once you have deleted the printer, repeat the steps presented in this section on every node within the cluster.

10.4.3 Configuring the Print Server

Now that you have installed (and then deleted) the print driver(s) on each node, you are ready to install the virtual print queue for the printer to bring it online.

From any node within the cluster, click **Start**, then **Run**. Type *servername*, where servername is the name of the virtual server you created earlier. This should be the network name you assigned to the disk group that is hosting your print spooler resource. Click **OK** to connect to the virtual server, and then double-click the **Printers** icon. This will open the Printers folder on the virtual server (see Figure 10-49). Double-click the **Add Printer** icon to start the Add Printer wizard. Click **Next** to continue.

The next screen should allow you only one option. If you see any option other than the Remote print server option, then you have connected to the virtual server incorrectly. If this is the case, disconnect from the server and then reconnect, following the previous instructions. If you do not see more than one option (see Figure 10-50), click **Next** to continue.

On the next screen, you must create a printer port for your printer. Your printer should be attached to the network and assigned an IP address (see Figure 10-51). From the drop-down list, you can select the type of print server device you are using, and then click **Next**.

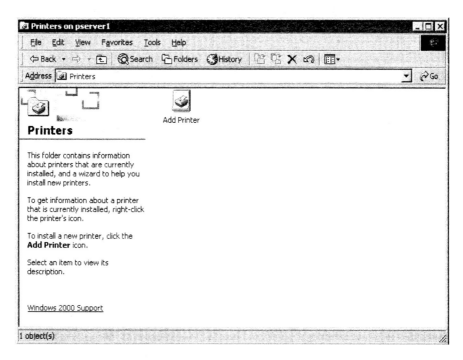

Figure 10-49
Add a printer to the virtual server.

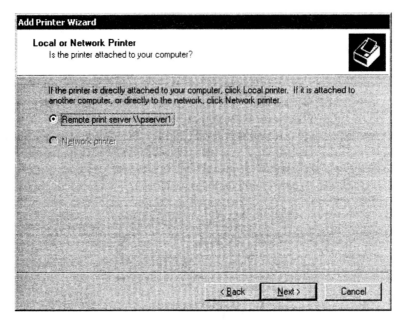

Figure 10-50
Selecting Remote print server option.

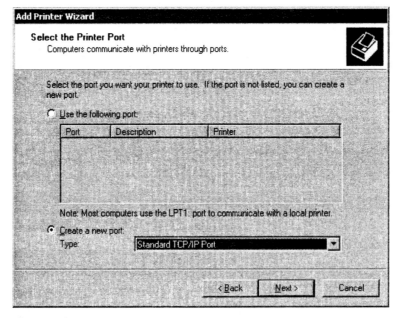

Figure 10-51
Creating a printer port.

The TCP/IP Printer Port wizard will start and remind you that you must have the device that you will be connecting to online and configured for a particular IP address (see Figure 10-52). Click **Next** to continue.

In the Add Port dialogue, type the IP address of the printer that you wish to connect to. The port name will automatically be provided (see Figure 10-53). Click **Next** to continue.

If the wizard does not automatically detect what type of network card you are using for your printer, it will ask you to select a device type (see Figure 10-54). In most cases, **Generic Network Card** will work fine, but if the card you are using is in the list, feel free to select it and then hit the **Next** button to continue.

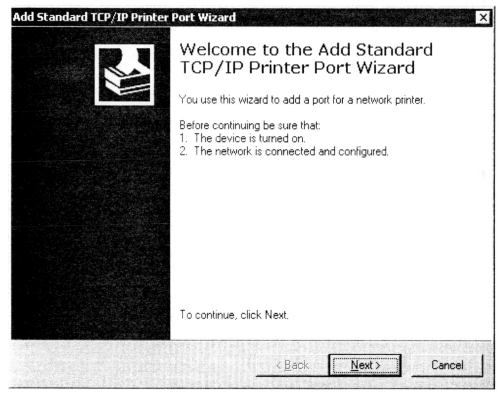

Figure 10-52
TCP/IP Print Port wizard.

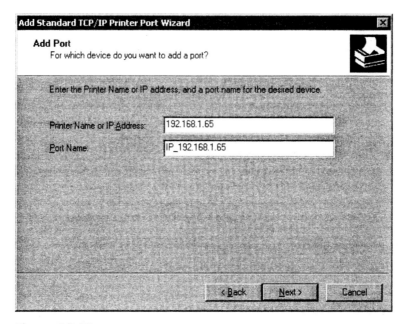

Figure 10-53
Configure TCP/IP printer address.

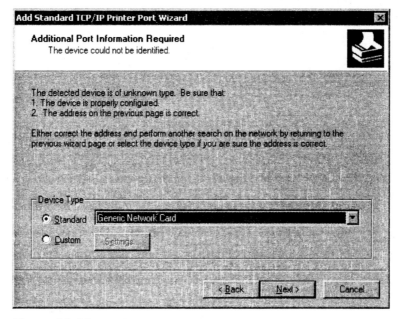

Figure 10-54
Choosing device type.

The Add Port wizard notifies you that you have chosen to create a new port and verifies the IP address and adapter type (see Figure 10-55). Click **Finish** to complete the installation of the port.

The next screen allows you to choose which printer driver you would like to use for the printer. Again, this printer driver should be identical to the driver you installed in the first section. Once you have selected the printer manufacturer on the left and the printer model on the right, click **Next** to continue (see Figure 10-56).

The wizard then asks you if you would like to keep the existing driver or replace the existing driver (see Figure 10-57). The driver already exists because of the previous steps you took to install the drivers on every node. Select **Next** to continue.

On the next screen, type the name you would like to assign to the printer (see Figure 10-58). This name can be practically anything, but it is recommended that you use descriptive names for your printers and workstations. Click **Next** to continue.

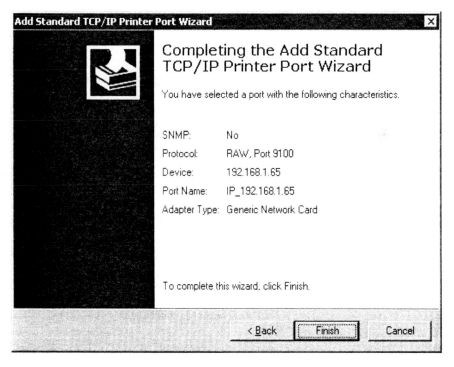

Figure 10-55
Completing the TCP/IP Port wizard.

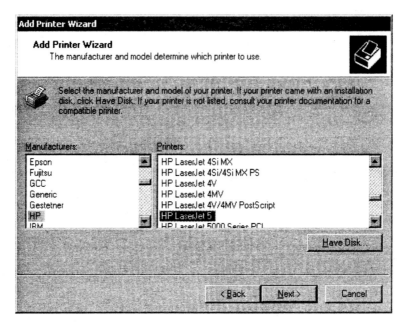

Figure 10-56
Select printer type.

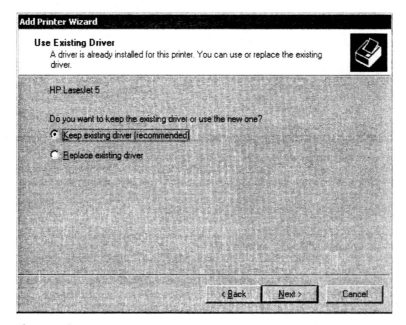

Figure 10-57
Keeping the existing driver.

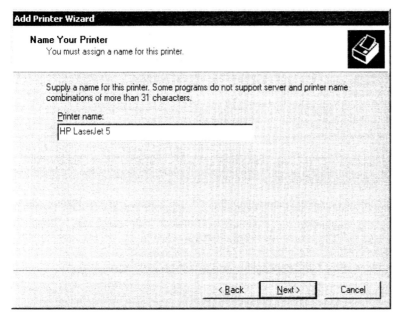

Figure 10-58
Naming the virtual
printer.

The next screen allows you to share the printer on the network. Click the
Share as: option, type in the name of the share you would like to use (see
Figure 10-59), and then click **Next** to continue.

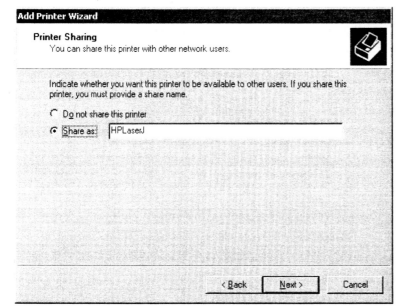

Figure 10-59
Sharing the printer.

Active Directory stores information such as location and comments in fields associated with the printer object. If you would like to associate information with the fields, type the information you would like to assign (see Figure 10-60) and click **Next** to continue.

If you would like to print a test page, feel free to do so. This is a good way to determine if your printer is set up correctly (see Figure 10-61). Click **Yes**, then **Next** to continue and print the test page.

The Add Printer wizard informs you that it has successfully installed the specified print driver to the printer port you selected or created (see Figure 10-62). If all the information is correct, click **Finish** to continue.

Congratulations. You have successfully installed a clustered print server. To test the configuration, connect to the printer from client and print a test page. Be sure to always connect to the *clusterservername**printershare* path rather than to an actual node within the cluster server system.

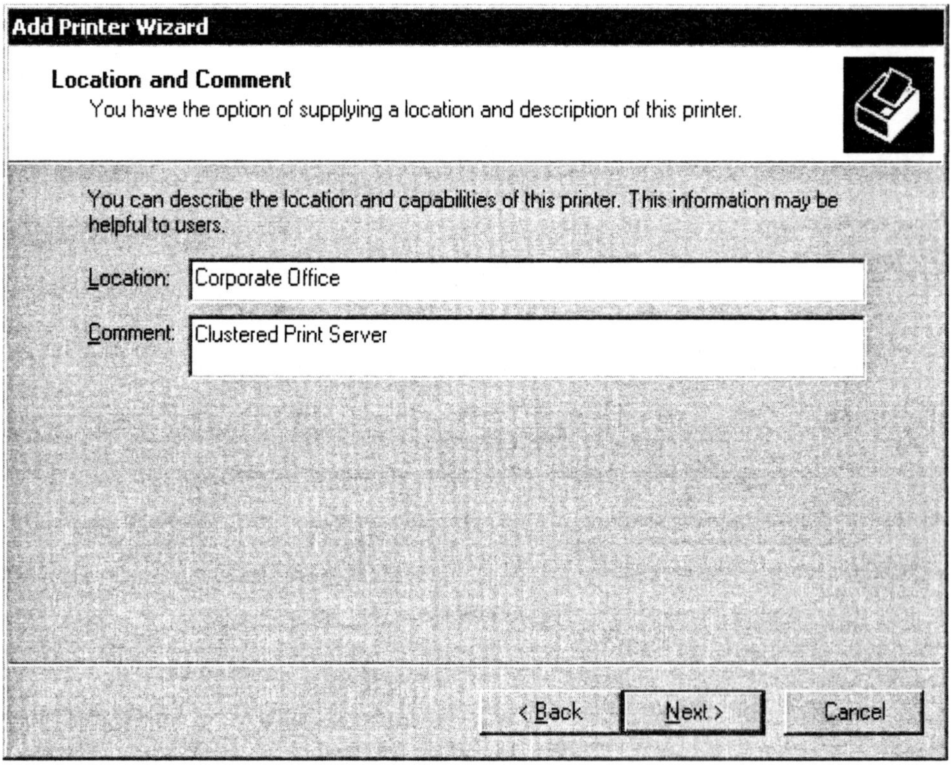

Figure 10-60
Specifying location and comment.

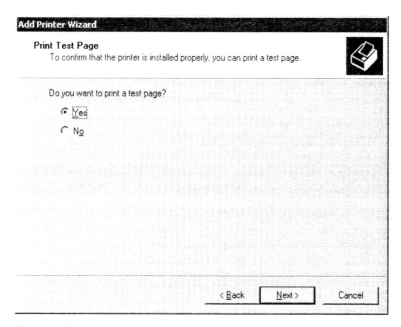

Figure 10-61
Printing test page.

Figure 10-62
Completing the Add Printer wizard.

10.5 Summary

File and print sharing is probably (with the exception of email) the most widely used service on corporate networks. In the past, file and print sharing has been a single-server operation, where one server offered a file or print share. This method was risky, for it did not provide fault tolerance outside of the local machine. A machine failure in this environment caused the service to be inaccessible. This unnecessary downtime causes millions of dollars in loss every year for many fortune 500 organizations.

The combination of Microsoft file and print sharing services and the power and fault tolerance of Microsoft's cluster server solutions offer a robust, fault-tolerant, reliable platform for file and print shares in a corporate environment. File and print shares can now be created on a clustered server, providing more fault tolerance than is possible on a single machine and more flexibility than can be obtained through entire groups of single server-based solutions.

INDEX

A

AC 2000
  AC.EXE, 228
  affinity, 194
  application deployment, 194
  centralized management of cluster nodes,
      193–194
  cluster application management, 219–220
  cluster events, 218–219
  cluster health, 222–223
  cluster statistics, 218
  cluster status, 217–218
  cluster synchronization, 221
  command-line administration, 228
  component load balancing, 194–195, 214–216
  configuring cluster properties, 223–228
  data and configuration synchronization, 193
  FrontPage integration, 194
  installing, 195–213
  local or Web-based administrative tools, 193
  management of, 216–228
  overview, 192
  performance/health monitoring and
      notification, 194
  product features, 193–195

  simplified cluster creation, 193
  three-tiered clusters, 214–216
  Windows 2000 clustering, 39–40
AC 2000 management
  AC.EXE, 228
  cluster application management, 219–220
  cluster events, 218–219
  cluster health, 222–223
  cluster statistics, 218
  cluster status, 217–218
  cluster synchronization, 221
  command-line administration, 228
  configuring cluster properties, 223–228
  overview, 216–217
AC.EXE, 228
Active Directory Users and Computers (Exchange
      Server 2000), 295–296
active/active configuration, 231–232
active/passive configuration, 231
affinity
  AC 2000, 194
  load-balanced clusters, settings for, 172–173
Application Center 2000. See AC 2000
application deployment, 194
applications
  identifying needs of, 48–51
  software requirements, 91

395